W9-ABI-387

Critical Essays on
Rudyard Kipling

Critical Essays on Rudyard Kipling

Harold Orel

G. K. Hall & Co. ● Boston, Massachusetts

Library of Congress Cataloging-in-Publication Data

Critical essays on Rudyard Kipling / [compiled by] Harold Orel.
     p.   cm. — (Critical essays on British literature)
   Includes index.
   ISBN 0-8161-8767-3 (alk. paper)
  1. Kipling, Rudyard, 1865–1936—Criticism and interpretation.
 I. Orel, Harold, 1926– . II. Series.
PR4857.C75 1989
828'.809—dc19   89-30750
                                           CIP

This publication is printed on permanent/durable acid-free paper
MANUFACTURED IN THE UNITED STATES OF AMERICA

CRITICAL ESSAYS ON BRITISH LITERATURE

The Critical Essays on British Literature series provides a variety of approaches to both the classical writers of Britain and Ireland and the best contemporary authors. The formats of the volumes in the series vary with the thematic designs of individual editors and with the number and nature of existing reviews, criticism, and scholarship. In general, the series represents the best in published criticism, augmented, where appropriate, by original essays by recognized authorities. It is hoped that each volume will be unique in developing a new overall perspective on its particular subject.

In his introduction to this volume, Harold Orel provides a succinct yet detailed analysis of the history of critical controversy surrounding Kipling's work, at the same time surveying the entire critical canon. Orel's judgments are fair and balanced, reciting the charges laid against the writer, but also pointing to a long history of favorable commentary from the most respected critics of the late nineteenth and early twentieth centuries. The essays Orel has chosen for this volume demonstrate the complexity of Kipling's contributions and implicitly assert his right to a prominent place in British literature. This collection includes a section on poetry, on Kipling's works about India, and on his later writing, as well as an essay on his posthumously published autobiography and a concluding summary essay by Orel himself.

To Emmet and Dianne Larkin.

CONTENTS

INTRODUCTION

It is unlikely, even in an era highly respectful of very rigorous *explications de texte*, that Rudyard Kipling's creative work will lose its strong appeal either to students of literature or to the general public. At the time of Kipling's death, in 1936, more than fifteen million copies of his books had been sold. The recent expiration of copyrights has led to the proliferation of editions by various publishers who do not publicize their sales records, and practically everything that Kipling included in the thirty-five volumes of the Sussex Edition of 1939 is in print. The astonishingly complex stories written during the second half of Kipling's life seem to attract some of the best minds at work in the universities; the poetry is increasingly often seen as something more than music-hall ballads and banjo rhythms; and more attention is being paid to the "lost Eden" implications of the childhood stories. Cultural historians have almost unanimously rejected the oversimplified views of Kipling as an unthinking champion of imperialism that dominated more than a half-century of controversy. And biographers in the years since World War II have provided us with a far richer, darker, and more unsettling portrait of Kipling's life and mind than any prewar study was able to limn. Three, in particular, have put us all in their debts: Charles Carrington for *Rudyard Kipling / His Life and Work* (London: Macmillan, 1955); Angus Wilson for *The Strange Ride of Rudyard Kipling / His Life and Works* (London: Secker & Warburg, 1977); and Lord Birkenhead for *Rudyard Kipling* (London: Weidenfeld & Nicolson, 1978), posthumously published after a delay of three decades because of the strong objections of Mrs. Elsie Bambridge (Kipling's daughter).

Some essential matters were settled before yeasty generalizations about the development of different stages of Kipling's career could be considered trustworthy. For one thing, scholars needed to be sure which items could be verified. Several efforts at establishing a definitive bibliography were heroically undertaken. I cite E. W. Martindell's *A Bibliography of the Works of Rudyard Kipling (1881–1923)* (London: John Lane the Bodley Head Ltd., 1923); Admiral L. H. Chandler's *Summary of the*

1

Work of Rudyard Kipling (New York: Grolier Club, 1930); Flora L. Livingston's *Bibliography of the Works of Rudyard Kipling* (New York: E. H. Wells and Co., 1927; reprinted 1968), as well as her *Supplement* (1938, reprinted 1968); and James McG. Stewart's *Rudyard Kipling / A Bibliographical Catalogue* (Toronto: Dalhousie University Press and University of Toronto Press, 1959). Additional listings of primary materials may be found in the *Catalogue of the Exhibition by the Grolier Club,* 1929 (New York, 1930), and the *Catalogue of the Ellis Ames Ballard Kipling Collection* (Philadelphia: privately printed, 1935). Ballard noted, on his title page, that not only did he include books, manuscripts, and letters but also "reproductions and rarities." He promised to tell how he got them, why he prized them, and what he failed to get, with inferences and opinions solely his own "and probably wrong." Stewart—whose bibliography, despite some errors and omissions, has become the standard reference—wrote that he had to examine "upwards of four thousand volumes"[1] before he could list or reject them; his problems were complicated by the "enterprise of American publishers," the multiplicity of imprints ("During the period 1890–1902, at least, Kipling was, without doubt, the most popular and widely read of all modern writers"),[2] and the absence of copyright protection in the United States before 1891. As A. W. Yeats conceded, in his editor's preface to Stewart's volume, ". . . later studies may prove [Kipling's] publications to have a more interesting and tortuous history than those of any other contemporary author."[3]

The *Kipling Journal,* published by the Kipling Society continuously since March 1927, contains an enormous amount of information in articles, reminiscences (of varying literary quality), transcripts of speeches, and notes and queries supplied (particularly during its first quarter-century of publication) by men and women who had either known Kipling personally or who had lived in the localities about which Kipling wrote. Its indexes, compiled and published irregularly, are not as detailed as one might wish, but the *Journal* is an indispensable reference despite Kipling's own desire (recorded more than once) to keep his distance from an organization that began its meetings in the last decade of his life.

Readers who wish to read even more of Kipling's writings than Macmillan's Sussex Edition supplies (the AMS Press reprint of 1970 is the text of the Doubleday, Doran "Burwash Edition" of 1941, which in turn is substantially the text of the Sussex Edition) may refer to *The Reader's Guide to Rudyard Kipling's Work,* prepared by Roger Lancelyn Green, Alec Mason, and especially R. E. Harbord between 1961 and 1972 (Canterbury: Gibbs and Sons; later, Bournemouth: Boscombe Printers). This eight-volume edition, in 5,672 pages, not only annotates all of Kipling's books with remarkable and joyous fullness of detail but reprints a large number of sketches, essays, and stories never gathered before.

Additional collections of primary materials, of relatively recent vintage, should be cited: Andrew Rutherford's edition, *Early Verse by Rudyard Kipling 1879–1889 / Unpublished, Uncollected, and Rarely Collected Poems* (Oxford: Clarendon Press, 1986); Thomas Pinney's anthology of Kipling's journalism during his Indian years, published in the *Civil and Military Gazette,* which bears the title *Kipling's India: Uncollected Sketches 1884–88* (London: Macmillan, 1986); and Elliot L. Gilbert's *"O Beloved Kids": Rudyard Kipling's Letters to his Children 1906–15* (London: Weidenfeld and Nicolson, 1983), a welcome gathering of Kipling's letters to his children, Josephine, Elsie, and John. A multivolume edition of the letters, edited by Thomas Pinney, is under way. Pinney is also assembling a one-volume collection of autobiographical writings by Kipling.

The fullest bibliography of secondary materials published to date—now, alas, more than twenty years old, and in need of updating—was compiled and edited, with useful annotations, by Helmut E. Gerber and Edward Lauterbach, in *English Fiction in Transition* 3, nos. 3–5 (1960), and 8, nos. 3–4 (1965). For more recent scholarship and criticism, the reader is bound to find intriguing and varied materials in the annual bibliographies of *The Year's Work in English Studies, PMLA,* and *Victorian Studies.*

Several useful reference works should be cited: F. L. Knowles's *A Kipling Primer* (1900), which carries a fairly early cut-off date; W. Arthur Young's *A Dictionary of the Characters and Scenes in the Stories and Poems of Rudyard Kipling, 1886–1911* (1912), revised by J. H. McGivering and reprinted as *A Kipling Dictionary* (1967); and Thomas Pinney's "Kipling in the Libraries," *English Literature in Transition,* no. 29 (1986). Major collections of Kipling materials, both primary and secondary, may be found in the Baldwin Papers relating to the Kipling family 1875–1945, Manuscripts Section, University of Sussex Library; the Kipling Papers, in the same library, which includes four scrapbooks of press clippings related to Kipling's works that were compiled by Kipling himself; the unpublished letters, large collections of which are in the University of Sussex, Manuscripts Section, the Library of Congress, the Houghton Library at Harvard University, the Berg Collection in the New York Public Library, and the University of Texas; James McG. Stewart's collection at Dalhousie University, Halifax; the libraries of Cornell and Princeton universities; and the India Office Library, which holds the only complete files of the *Civil and Military Gazette* of Lahore and the *Pioneer* of Allahabad in Europe, the United States, or Canada.

Since one aim of my anthology is to avoid duplication or overlap with the selections printed in earlier collections of critical essays on Rudyard Kipling, it is helpful, at this point, to identify and say a few words about the contents of those collections. Elliot L. Gilbert's *Kipling and the Critics* (New York: New York University Press, 1965) begins with the statement, "It would be difficult to think of another artist, dead thirty years, who continues to be at once so popular and so cordially hated as Rudyard Kipling is today,"[4] and continues very soon thereafter with the remark, ". . . he has never enjoyed, and does not enjoy today—except among a very few—any serious critical reputation."[5] Yet these "very few," as the contents of Gilbert's anthology bear witness, include critiques written by some of the most respected names in letters, beginning with praise from Andrew Lang and Henry James, a very early notice by Oscar Wilde, an attack by Robert Buchanan and a parody by Max Beerbohm, and very serious studies by Bonamy Dobrée, Boris Ford, George Orwell, Lionel Trilling, C. S. Lewis, T. S. Eliot, J. M. S. Tompkins, Randall Jarrell, Steven Marcus, and Elliot L. Gilbert. For a reader relatively unfamiliar with the reasons for the controversies clustered over Kipling's reputation, sometimes very hot-tempered indeed, *Kipling and the Critics* is an excellent place to get one's bearings.

Andrew Rutherford's anthology, *Kipling's Mind and Art* (Edinburgh and London: Oliver & Boyd, 1964), reprints essays by Noel Annan, George Orwell, W. L. Renwick, Lionel Trilling, and Edmund Wilson (two of these are in Gilbert's collection), but the specially commissioned articles by George Shepperson, Alan Sandison, Andrew Rutherford, Mark Kinkead-Weekes, J. H. Fenwick, and W. W. Robson are also well worth reading. Rutherford, in his introduction, makes the sensible point that these essays have in common "no single policy (of whitewashing or denigration), but a conviction that in recent decades Kipling has been too readily, too easily dismissed—that even though adverse judgments must be passed on aspects of his work his is a more interesting and complex case than has generally been allowed."[6]

Roger Lancelyn Green, editor of the *Kipling Journal* for several years, edited *Kipling: The Critical Heritage* (London: Routledge & Kegan Paul, 1971). Its sixty-one selections are, for the most part, reviews and periodical articles that trace the history of Kipling's reception from Andrew Lang's first review (1886) to the obituary article that appeared in the *Times Literary Supplement* (1936). Green makes the important point that sales and public interest in Kipling were consistently high from the beginning. Even though Green believes that "Kipling has taken longer than most writers to pass through the valley of the shadow of criticism"[7] (as if indeed he has already emerged "on the further shore"), that statement in the preface must be partially modified by a remark in the introduction: "Rudyard Kipling is the most controversial author in English Literature. Even today his place on Parnassus remains undecided—though a place there he is generally agreed to have, even if some critics would seek it near the summit while others relegate him to the foothills."[8] It may be symptomatic of the uneven quality of the Kipling criticism of the past half-century that Green feels himself obliged to conclude his introduction with severe attacks upon critics who overemphasize "their personal views or special preoccupation,"[9] or who seem to be "too clever by half,"[10] or who employ a simplistic psychological approach or a "frankly clinical psychoanalysis."[11] Green's anthology is a splendid complementary volume to that of Gilbert.

For Chelsea House's Modern Critical Views series, Harold Bloom has collected eight relatively recent essays covering a twenty-five-year period (1961–86) in the volume *Rudyard Kipling* (New York, 1987). The authors represented are Randall Jarrell, Angus Wilson, Irving Howe, Donald Davie, Zohreh T. Sullivan, David Bromwich, Elliot L. Gilbert, and Robert L. Caserio. Bloom, who believes that *Kim* is "Kipling's strongest single work,"[12] argues a case to which all writers on Kipling willingly subscribe, that is, ". . . there is still a largely unknown and profound writer to be uncovered in Kipling."[13]

The emphasis in John Gross's anthology of essays on Kipling, *Rudyard Kipling: The Man, His Work, and His World* (London, Weidenfeld & Nicolson, 1972), is more biographical than critical. Most of the essays are quite short, though some individual essays are very satisfying. Several of the authors knew personally the backgrounds of Kipling stories and have intelligent things to say about the transforming powers of Kipling's imagination.

It is necessary to look again at major strands in Kipling criticism, as represented in these anthologies, before looking more closely at what the writers in my anthology have to say. Charles Carrington has referred to "the legend" that William Ernest Henley stood up and danced on his wooden leg after reading "Danny Deever" in the *Scots Observer* (22 February 1890).[14] Professor David Masson, the "grave commentator on Milton," waved the periodical before the students of his class and cried, "Here's Literature! Here's Literature at last!"[15] These, among the hoariest anecdotes in the histories of literary receptions, suggest, with a startling pungency, how ready many readers of the late Victorian era were for something new, vivid, and deeply stamped by personality. But repeating these stories without a due caution may be riskier than some biographers concede. *Barrack-Room Ballads* was, after all, only part of the "product" that Kipling brought with him to London, and even the earliest of responsible critics found themselves unable to respond with unqualified enthusiasm to the flood of materials that inundated the literary marketplace within two years after Kipling's arrival (including *The Light That Failed*, Kipling's early bid for the kind of fame enjoyed by older and greyer novelists). Andrew Lang, for example, thought of Kipling's literary progenitor as Bret Harte, whose talents were already being considered with serious reservations by critics and reviewers; he noted that Kipling was focusing on "petty characters displayed in all their meannesses" and "the seamy side of Anglo-Indian life."[16] "Probably the sketches are true enough," he wrote, "and pity 'tis 'tis true."[17] For all his recognition of Kipling's strength, Lang was not a true believer, and he spoke of the "invention of the British soldier in India"[18]—the most popular of Kipling's discoveries of a new kind of character—as perhaps the most interesting "fiction" within Kipling's creative work. And Lang was fairly early on the scene with an enumeration of Kipling's faults ("so conspicuous, so much on the surface, that they hardly need to be named"): a false air of hardness, a knowing air, mannerisms (e.g., "But that is another story"), slang, "the too obtrusive knocking of the nail on the head."[19] Lang professed himself not much taken with the art of *The Light That Failed:* "The central interest is not powerful enough; the characters are not so sympathetic, as are the interest and the characters of his short pieces."[20]

Lang's limitations as a reviewer for *Longman's Magazine,* in his widely read column entitled "At the Sign of the Ship," are well known and largely related to his hostility to the direction modern literature was taking. But before we dismiss his reservations about Kipling's art we must remember that Lang was probably the very first English reviewer of Kipling's poetry, and that he wrote several enthusiastic reviews about a young unknown when such praise counted for a great deal in Kipling's mind. Nevertheless, Lang's enthusiasm was very soon tempered by dislike of some of Kipling's habits in storytelling, the stand that Kipling deliberately took toward his characters and his aggressive use of language. Lang's quarrel with the less savory aspects of Kipling's art was not too dissimilar from the changing attitudes of Henry James, who warned Robert Louis Stevenson that Kipling had already "killed one immortal—Rider Haggard" by 1890, and was to be reckoned as Stevenson's "nascent rival";[21] who admired "the infant monster of a Kipling" as a new force on the London scene;[22] who wrote to his brother William that Kipling was "the most complete man of genius (as distinct from fine intelligence) that I have ever known."[23] As the decade waned, so did James's enthusiasm; *The Seven Seas,* despite its manifestation of "absolutely uncanny talent," was "all violent, without a dream of nuance or a hint of 'distinction'; all prose trumpets and castanets and such—with never a touch of the fiddle-string or a note of the nightingale."[24] By 1897 he was writing to Grace Norton that his view of Kipling's prose future had "much shrunken in the light of one's increasingly observing how little life he can make use of. Almost nothing civilized save steam and patriotism . . . Almost nothing of the complicated soul or of the female form or of any other question of *shades. . . .*"[25] James confessed that his hope for Kipling's development as an English Balzac had diminished as Kipling came down "steadily from the simple in subject to the more simple—from the Anglo-Indians to the natives, from the natives to the Tommies, from the Tommies to the quadrupeds, from the quadrupeds to the fish, and from the fish to the engines and screws."[26] And, by the time of the Boer War, James's detestation of Kipling's "loud, brazen patriotic verse" and "the unfortunate Stalky" (which gave Kipling away "aesthetically") had quite overwhelmed his admiration of the "quite diabolically great" talent that Kipling indubitably possessed.[27] Nor did James have much time or sympathy to waste on

Kipling after the Boer War, despite the fact that his friendship for Wolcott Balestier only a decade earlier had brought him into close proximity to the events that culminated in Kipling's marriage to Wolcott's sister.

Oscar Wilde stressed Kipling's absorption with vulgarity: "The mere lack of style in the storyteller gives an odd journalistic realism to what he tells us," he wrote in 1890 after reading *Plain Tales from the Hills*.[28] Like James, he appreciated the genius in Kipling, but added, "Mr. Kipling is a genius who drops his aspirates . . . . He is our first authority on the second-rate."[29] Though Wilde conceded Kipling's right to choose vulgarity as his subject matter, his critical thesis converged on the line being developed by James in his introduction to *Mine Own People* (1891), namely, that Kipling's art lacks only one strain (for James, of course, the most important strain), "The voice, as it were, of the civilised man; in whom I of course also include the civilized woman."

Even Edmund Gosse, who had brought his wife and son to Kipling's wedding and who meant, with great kindness, to advance Kipling's career in a lengthy review of 1891, mentioned that writers like Kipling and Pierre Loti produced on the reader "a peculiar thrill, a voluptuous and agitating sentiment of intellectual uneasiness, with the spontaneous art of which [both writers have] a secret."[30] Gosse confessed himself unable to rely on "the old rhetorical manner of criticism" when confronting the author of *Soldiers Three*.[31] The style excited, disturbed, and attracted him. "I admit all that is to be said in its disfavor. I force myself to see that its occasional cynicism is irritating and strikes a false note. I acknowledge the broken and jagged style, the noisy newspaper bustle of the little peremptory sentences, the cheap irony of the satires on society."[32] He excused "the rattle of the piano at some café concert," of which "there is a good deal too much,"[33] on the grounds that Kipling was still young, still in process of finding himself.

Mixed responses, then, came forth from the very beginning. If Mrs. Oliphant expressed her gratitude for being introduced to an India about which she had entertained only the vaguest of impressions, she could not help remarking on the callowness of Kipling's years as somehow excusing the lapses of taste that so distressed some of her fellow professionals;[34] if William Ernest Henley admired Kipling's use of dialect, he took pains to denigrate Kipling's writing of English ("often inadequate . . . often pert . . . sometimes even common"), to identify "worrying little tricks and mannerisms," to deplore a number of his "maladies most incident to youth";[35] and if Quiller-Couch too used the term "genius" to describe the phenomenon of Kipling (1893), he patronized Kipling—perhaps more than he knew or more than Kipling would have liked—with remarks about Kipling's assailing the reader "with simple and even vulgar metres and dazzling crudities of speech,"[36] and a casual comment to the effect that *"The Barrack Room Ballads* are just doggerel in apotheosis, doggerel lifted out of its sphere by a touch of genius."[37] Kipling was never admired uncritically; never, even in the years of greatest triumph, admitted to the pantheon without strictures on his faults, those "blemishes" which (one might suppose) constituted his greatest strength, or (to change the metaphor) his passport validating his right to shuttle between two worlds.

A sea-change in Establishment attitudes took place around the time of the Boer War. Kipling's political opinions, sometimes shrill but always clear, invited a response. Robert Williams Buchanan's attack (1899), which opened a barrage of attacks, began with the sweeping generalization, "There is a universal scramble for plunder, for excitement, for amusement, for speculation, and, above it all, the flag of a Hooligan Imperialism is raised, with the proclamation that it is the sole mission of Anglo-Saxon England, forgetful of the task of keeping its own drains in order, to expand and extend its boundaries indefinitely, and again in the name of the Christianity it has practically abandoned, to conquer and inherit the earth."[38] Buchanan detested Kipling's concentration on "the baser aspects of our civilization, being chiefly devoted to the affairs of idle military men, savage soldiers, frisky wives and widows, and flippant civilians,"[39] and he denied that Kipling's stories or verse presented a true picture of the Service (or of human nature, for that matter). "Of Mr. Kipling it may be said, so far at least as his verses are concerned, that he has scarcely on any single occasion uttered anything that does not suggest moral baseness, or hover dangerously near it."[40] After an intemperate attack on *Stalky & Co.*, Buchanan proceeded to praise the true imperialism ("the slow and sure spread of what is best and purest in our civilization") as the noble cause that Kipling had betrayed.[41]

This is, to say the least, literary criticism that keeps its eye on practically anything and everything save the literary text itself; but it presaged a new phase in Kipling criticism, and those who spoke up in Kipling's defence—Sir Walter Besant, for example, who wrote in 1900 that much might be excused if we kept in mind that for Kipling, as for Tennyson, war was necessary and could ennoble a people "when the cause is just"[42]— may have chosen the wrong field on which to tilt a lance. There was sourness in Edward Dowden's treatment of Kipling's use of dialect words like "bloomin'";[43] G. K. Chesterton's dismay at Kipling's "precocious old age" that "combines the brutality of youth with the disillusionment of antiquity, which is old age without its charity and youth without its hope";[44] George Moore's detestation of Kipling's excessive use of local color ("He writes with the eye that appreciates all that the eye can see, but of the heart he knows nothing. . . .");[45] Ford Madox Hueffer's barely concealed anger at Kipling's pontificating ("Mr. Kipling set out to attack world problems from the point of view of the Journalists' club smoking-room and with the ambitions of a sort of cross between the German Emperor of caricature and fifth-form public-schoolboy");[46] and H. G. Wells's denunciation of the underlying philosophy of *Stalky & Co.*, "The idea of a *tacit conspiracy between the law and illegal violence. . . .*"[47]

The image of Kipling as a superficial thinker predominated during the first half of the twentieth century and blotted out much of his achievement as an artist. A surprisingly large fraction of the notices devoted to praise dealt with *The Jungle Books,* the *Just So Stories,* and Kipling's treatment of children, as in *Captains Courageous.* T. S. Eliot's admiration of Kipling's verse, as expressed in several widely noticed essays, most strikingly perhaps his introduction to *A Choice of Kipling's Verse* (1941), rendered a minority judgment, and Eliot was roundly censured for having formulated a definition of verse that permitted him to praise Kipling while denying him the laurels of a true poet. Eliot's controversial position allowed Boris Ford, George Orwell, and Lionel Trilling to reconsider (and to endorse) much of the case against Kipling's political opinions. Eliot's complaint, that "Mr. Kipling has not been analysed,"[48] remained largely true for another quarter-century, during which time Kipling's writings were cheerfully slighted or ignored by university dons. Moreover, Eliot's guarded praise ("And yet Mr. Kipling is very nearly a great writer")[49] did not help to focus the attention of serious readers on the merits or the failings of Kipling's poetry, which, taken all in all, remained grievously neglected up till 1965, the year of Andrew Rutherford's address to the British Academy (reprinted here). Indeed, Roger Lancelyn Green's collection of important critical essays on Kipling gives an accurate and dismaying impression that members of the intelligentsia who turned their attention to Kipling (for fleeting moments) refused to grapple with the major issues of conduct, locality, and national obligation so paramount in Kipling's creative work and preferred instead to deal with tangential issues: Kipling's use of technical phraseology in *The Irish Guards,* which to Edmund Blunden seemed to illustrate "mere languidness" and to conflict with a soldier's "memory";[50] Kipling's translations from the *Fifth Book of Horace,* which to Christopher Morley seemed to have evoked singularly obtuse notices from "editorial writers";[51] Kipling's unevenness in *Debits and Credits,* which, so far as Brander Matthews was concerned, exemplified his wideness of range even though Kipling "is not now held in high esteem by the Little Group of Serious Thinkers, who are proud to style themselves 'Young Intellectuals'—altho' they are certainly not as juvenile as they act, and probably not as intellectual as they believe."[52] (Matthews was racking up a score against Kipling's nay-sayers; he offered only a series of aperçus about *Debits and Credits,* then newly published, rather than a serious analysis.)

The way down, however, finally led to the way out, and Kipling's art in the past four decades has received more respectful attention, and elicited a larger number of intelligent responses, than at any comparable period within Kipling's life. Translated into more than thirty languages, Kipling's work has always been a phenomenon of publishing history; he is in a world class, with Shakespeare and Dickens; and more than one hundred books of criticism and evaluation have treated, with varying degrees of discernment, the short stories, novels, and poems printed in some two dozen collected editions and four thousand individual editions. Perhaps it is wisest at this point to identify some notable critical opinions of post-war years and to anticipate the more striking features of the views contained in the essays reprinted in this volume.

C. S. Lewis in 1948 spoke for many readers when he argued that he could not understand "how a man of taste could doubt that Kipling is a very great artist,"[53] at the same time admitting he had never quite taken him to his heart. Reading too much Kipling could lead to a sense of the "unendurable,"[54] though he knew that so sudden a change of feeling could hardly be considered reasonable. The excess of Kipling's art was partly responsible: the style is "all unrelieved vitamins from the first word to the last."[55] But, beyond that, Lewis stressed Kipling's emphasis on work, shared experiences, and the process whereby "the trade-spirit licks some raw cub into shape,"[56] as something like "a doctrine of original sin,"[57] one to which many readers objected. The real problem lay in Kipling's minimizing of the problem of justice. Kipling was devoted to the disciplinary system, though he understood full well its limitations, and he paid allegiance to "the little demigods" of the Inner Rings.[58] Lewis blamed him for not examining their credentials scrupulously: "It is this ubiquitous presence of the Ring, this unwearied knowingness, that renders his work in the long run suffocating and unendurable. And always, ironically, that bleak misgiving—almost that Nothingness—in the background."[59]

If I give generous space to such negative judgments, it is less because I think they will endure and color our final appreciation of Kipling's talent (I am reluctant to use the tired word "genius") than because sufficient time has elapsed to afford the devising of some more objective views toward an empire lost, an arrogance forever rendered obsolete by the press of events, than was possible during Kipling's lifetime. Boris Ford, too, hated the "ideal Subaltern" of Kipling's imagination and concluded an important essay (1948) with the damning judgment that Kipling's "outward tough obstinacy" all too often protected "a soft centre of self-distrust and potential hysteria."[60] He cited *Stalky & Co.* as a characteristic case redeemed partially by its concentration on adolescent psychology, but he was more severe on stories like "The Tie," "The Honours of War," "The Village That Voted the Earth Was Flat," "The Mark of the Beast," and "Mary Postgate," which turn on feelings of revenge. Ford's indictment of Kipling as an incomplete human being who manipulates fiction "from the outside and for preconceived purposes"[61] has had a powerful influence on readers in our time.

It may be that Edmund Wilson, writing only a few years after Kipling's death, published "The Kipling that Nobody Read" (1941) too soon, while still working out the implications of his thesis that the psychic wounds of a writer's childhood directly affect his ability to bend the bow of Philoctetes when he reaches manhood. At any rate, the sensationalism of his essay, which plays up the importance of the opening chapters of *The Light That Failed* and "Baa, Baa, Black Sheep" as an explanation of why "the whole work of Kipling's life" was "shot though with hatred,"[62] has increasingly often been rejected by Kipling critics as vulgarized Freud. Wilson believed that he had discovered the "real Kipling." But there seems to be something peculiarly dated in Wilson's treatment of Kipling's attitude toward the entire Boer War period as a set of ossified opinions, in which "the virtues of Kipling's officers and soldiers consist primarily in knowing their stations";[63] or which claims that the two series of *Puck of Pook's Hill* present a "sugared exploitation of Kipling's Anglo-Spartan code of conduct";[64] or which comes down flatly on the side of Kipling's having learned little or nothing from any event later than the Boer War. This is a static Kipling, and, rather surprisingly, an inartistic one given to cheap tricks and uncritical admiration of an "official class."

Randall Jarrell, in 1961, offers more usable advice on how to read Kipling. Jarrell, like many before his time, believed that "Kipling's account is still unsettled," but he was prescient enough to see that a current hero, Hemingway, would be dislodged within two or three decades, and that we would find ourselves "willing to entertain the possibility that Kipling *was* a writer after all—people just didn't realize the sort of writer he was."[65] Jarrell recorded a wonder-struck observation that Kipling, like Chekhov and Turgenev, had written an enormous number of first-rate stories[66] (fifty or seventy-five of them); though he frankly admitted Kipling's "lack of dispassionate moral understanding," he insisted on the coexistence, in Kipling's best creative work, of intelligence and penetrating insights, of foolishness and blindness. "This is a characteristic of the immortals from which only we mortals are free. They oversay everything. It is only ordinary readers and writers who have ordinary common sense, who are able to feel about things what an ordinarily sensible man should."[67] This is very well said; it helps us to take the measure of Kipling. Jarrell's insistence that one should come to the reading of Kipling's "spontaneous finality" by giving our imagination free rein is healthy because we will appreciate Kipling's "spontaneous finality" all the more, namely, his ability to record speech and events the way they could (and should) take place.

What, then, marks the most recent phase of Kipling criticism? Jarrell's impatience with the old truths about Kipling—the things people know that aren't so—was salutary; it forced reconsideration of the notion that Kipling was a Colonel Blimp, a committed and unthinking imperialist; and it was time anyway to stop talking about the novelty of Kipling's language (1890 was a long time in the past). Refreshing too was Jarrell's admiration of the *mixture* of the best and the worst in Kipling's art because the wary, cranky, and often ungenerous criticism of Kipling's first decade of literary production in England had talked mostly about the more obvious failings of Kipling's technique while paying lip service to the positive qualities.

Steven Marcus, in his introduction to a new edition of *Stalky & Co.* (1962), rendered a characteristically modern service to Kipling's memory: he took one of Kipling's best-known texts, much-maligned, and related it not only to an honorable tradition of romantic idealizing of adolescent boys (Rousseau's *Émile*, the poetry of Blake and Wordsworth, the novels of Dickens, George Eliot, and Mark Twain) but to a complicated morality, a secret idealism, a faith in "primitive, ancient, classical, masculine" concepts once known as the heroic virtues.[68] That reading of *Stalky & Co.* may not palliate our dislike of torture or bullies, or reconcile us to the "open and mutual antagonism between the boys and masters"[69] that everyone takes for granted as the natural order in a Victorian public school; but Marcus is right to remind us that the code of speech in this collection of stories "resonates and is confluent with the life for which [the boys] are being trained"[70] and with the strict and complex code of the life of an officer and gentlemen, that is, the learning process whereby the boys grow into their destined roles as players in the Great Game, as rulers of a vast colonial Empire. Marcus's reading informs us of the correspondence between the boys' code of speech and Kipling's own writing style (which so impressed writers like Ernest Hemingway and Isaac Babel).

Welcome, too, has been the deepening sense in recent criticism that Kipling's ideas are misread if we believe that Kipling was convinced of the unshakable rightness of his moral position. George Shepperson, for example, found himself unable in 1964 to settle for easy generalizations about Kipling's attitude toward mixed breeds and the whole touchy subject of miscegenation. He was puzzled by anomalies in *The Light That Failed* (e.g., the woman model, of mixed blood, who became for Dick Heldar an inspiration for his depiction of both sea-devils and sea-angels);[71] by the "mistrust and sometimes despair" with which Kipling regarded "the civilising mission of the white man";[72] by the unwillingness (inability?) of Kipling to define imperialism with the self-confidence of, say, John Buchan in *A Lodge in the Wilderness*, published in 1906.[73] Alan Sandison stresses the vulnerability of the Anglo-Indians who are doomed to "ludicrous failure" and adds, "Even the great British Raj and all its achievements dwindle into insignificance in the face of India's inexorable powers of assimilation."[74] Sandison's emphasis on what he sees as Kipling's dramatization of "inadequate western morality"[75] is salutary; Kipling's contemporaries rarely considered the matter. And Noel Annan is breaking new ground when he betrays impatience with H. G. Wells's overfamiliar notion that Kipling was a social Darwinist. Annan believes that Kipling has worked out "a highly articulated functional analysis of society in which none but socialized individuals exist," a conservative theory of human existence and political life, and an awareness of spiritual facts "such as repentance, forgiveness, love, and supernatural (or inexplicable) forces which can mitigate the harshness of existence, however little Kipling is willing to allow his readers to forget the harshness."[76] Kipling, in this reading, turns out to be "almost the sole analogue in England at the turn of the century to Durkheim and Weber and the German and Italian thinkers (whom H. Stuart Hughes treats in his book *Consciousness and Society*) who were in revolt against mid–nineteenth-century constructs of the individual and society."[77]

I am not suggesting that we must agree with most of these new interpretations, but rather expressing my gratitude that they make Kipling into a far more interesting Prospero working his magic on an enchanted island that he owns completely. We have been waiting, almost without being aware of it, for this long-overdue revaluation. Above all, we are now prepared to see Kipling as an artist. I am struck by how often the old centers of controversy (the "Gardener," "Mary Postgate," the stories of revenge and of practical jokes), while still attracting attention, seem less important today than dozens of other creative works that barely received consideration as parts of the canon in the first half of this century. I have in mind Roger Lancelyn Green's *Kipling and the Children* (London: Elek Books, 1965), a sophisticated and completely convincing treatment of the value of a substantial segment of Kipling's work, as well as Robert F. Moss's useful study, on a small scale, *Rudyard Kipling and the Fiction of Adolescence* (New York: St. Martin's Press, 1982). J. H. Fenwick's "Soldiers Three," in Andrew Rutherford's anthology, reconsiders the soldier stories as "closely integrated, fully achieved works of art." This judgment takes us a long way beyond the praise of the "authenticity" of "The Three Musketeers," "The Taking of Lungtungpen," "The Daughters of the Regiment," "The Madness of Private Ortheris," and thirteen others, by soldiers and officers who reported that what Kipling had seen in India, they too had seen and could confirm. Elliot L. Gilbert's *The Good Kipling / Studies in the Short Story* (Athens, Ohio: Ohio University Press, 1970) moves rapidly beyond the mere identification of Kipling's controversial aspects ("Not at All My Favorite Author") and prominent aspects of his worldview ("The Law of Nature, the Law of Art") to an extended consideration of matters that all too often are taken for granted, though they shouldn't be ("The Art of the Simple") and close readings of puzzling stories such as "Mrs. Bathurst" ("The Art of the Complex").

J. M. S. Tompkins, in *The Art of Rudyard Kipling* (London: Methuen & Co., 1959), has put us all in her debt, despite a number of modest remarks in her preface that she had worked consistently within the tales and other works by Kipling with scant consideration of biographical and other secondary sources; that she had not dealt "at length with any aspects of Kipling's work which require to be approached through the political conditions out of which they arose";[78] and that, as a consequence, she had not attempted either "a comprehensive survey of Kipling's work or a formal assessment of his achievement."[79] Professor Tompkins's fifth chapter, a study of the importance of revenge in Kipling's creative work, is a model of patient and sympathetic analysis of a subject that has deeply disturbed generations of Kipling's readers. She is also excellent in handling the oft-repeated generalization that Kipling did not change. Everywhere she concerns herself with a Kipling who delighted in "pattern and intricacy of all kinds,"[80] who resembled in striking ways the best Elizabethan writers, and whose full meaning (in his later years) must be derived from image, symbol, and hint, for full appreciation of which "The reader must also be an investigator."[81] She recognizes his failures. Even if everyone agreed as to which they are (and those who nominate stories as "the worst" are often opposed by those who nominate the very same stories as "the best"),[82] "There is enough left."[83] I know of no modern critic who would contradict her final judgment: "The worst faults, as the strongest evidences of original genius, are in the first half of his work. His later tales deserve more impartial study than they have received."[84]

Some words, finally, about my gathering of these essays and the rationale behind their organization are in order. I have endeavored to select writings that represent a fair cross section of critical interests and approaches during the past twenty-five years and that (in the case of extracts from longer works) make good sense when reprinted independently of their original contexts. I want to emphasize Kipling's work as a poet, which helped to establish his first claim to fame, and notoriety, in London when the last decade of Victoria's reign began. Two addresses, given originally before members of the British Academy, provide clearly different responses to a substantial body of work—as substantial as that of Thomas Hardy, and indeed of most Victorian poets. Andrew Rutherford does not deny the crudity of technique and attitude in many of the poems, but he insists on Kipling's "normally high standards of poetic craftsmanship," and he argues that Kipling's politics are, surprisingly often, transmuted into poetic art. Jacqueline S. Bratton, responding some years later to Rutherford's address, chooses to stake her defense on a treatment of Kipling's "magical methods" and "magical motives," and on such matters (long slighted) as Kipling's use of incantation, repetition, and words of power and ritual, in both short stories and poems.

Maurice Hungiville, like Rutherford and Bratton, sees Kipling as a special case. In his reception study, he properly calls attention to the extraliterary forces that were important to both Kipling critics and to Kipling cultists, and that helped to explain both the early astonishing popularity and the subsequent indifference. It surely is no accident, as Hungiville points out, that professional poets (Eliot, Bridges, Auden) have been largely responsible for making Kipling's poetry seem fresh and worthwhile again.

Four essays on Kipling's relation to India follow. First, James Harrison's essay on the Edenic pattern in *The Jungle Books* is a detailed treatment of the correspondence between Kipling's law of the jungle and a religious creed: "For religion, to Kipling, was always more a matter of consensus than of truth or falsehood, of social fact than of supernatural faith, of what exists because people believe in it than of what people believe in because it exists." Harrison's conviction that Kipling's jungle is postlapsarian, but not without hope that Mowgli can re-enter his paradise at will, is bracing, particularly when we recall how easily (and often) one truism has been repeated: that Kipling's Eden is permanently lost at the end of "The Spring Running."[85]

Second, Peter Havholm has some important things to say about the words "simple" and "complex" in his treatment of Kipling's use of fantasy. The subject matter draws a useful distinction between *The Light That Failed*, a novel unsuccessful because of its overly reductive view of human nature, and the short stories that begin with the first *Jungle Book* and continue well past the writing of "They," stories that employ simple matter to suggest the complexities of childhood and that provide numerous "glimpses of joy." His use of a term coined by Tolkien, *eucacatastrophe*, is a model of how to employ jargon in a way that genuinely enlightens the reader unfamiliar with a specialized meaning.

Third, Leonard Shengold has written a very long essay of psychoanalysis, based on both biographical materials and the evidence contained within Kipling's creative work. I have space only to reproduce the summary and conclusions as an excerpt from Dr. Shengold's essay, and I recommend to those who find his views stimulating a perusal of the whole work. "Soul murder" is also a specialized term, and the weight of evidence contained in the fuller essay helps to establish its validity. Yet even this fragment contains a great deal of interest, and it is based on a sounder conceptual framework than Edmund Wilson employed in the writing of "The Kipling That Nobody Read."

The last essay in this section is a cheerfully unorthodox reading of *Kim* by David H. Stewart. Readers who have not come across it before will find the number of original insights generous indeed, ranging from the helpful distinction between colloquial language and journalism to the enumeration of four distinct languages in *Kim*, as well as an analysis of a number of other features enhancing the aural appeal of the novel. The conclusion, that Anglo-Indian English is as different as American English from the language of the homeland, is not a platitude, but a truth that all readers of Kipling do well to consider.

Five essays constitute the heart of a section called "The Mature Craftsman." They include the gracefully written eleventh chapter of J. I. M. Stewart's *Rudyard Kipling*, which maintains, with a convincing amplitude of detail, that Kipling, again and again, "plucks something affirmative from the abyss"; John Bayley's demonstration that Kipling, in more short stories than we realized, performs conjuring tricks to convince us of the authenticity in the look of the thing; Peter Hinchcliffe's heroic effort to reconcile the "discontinuities and paradoxes" in Kipling's work by treating *Puck of Pook's Hill* and *Rewards and Fairies* as (surprisingly) the main line of his development rather than "dead ends"; Peter E. Firchow's painstaking and subtle treatment of "Mary Postgate," a critical crux in Kipling's canon if ever there was one; and Lisa A. F. Lewis's examination of the connections between the individual units of *Debits and Credits* (a task that needs to be performed for a number of other collections of Kipling's short stories).

Harry Ricketts examines *Something of Myself,* Kipling's posthumously published memoir that may be as intriguing for its omissions as for what it actually says. We are grateful to have any kind of a memoir at all, of course, but we need, and want, more, and Ricketts suggests important considerations that every reader of *Something of Myself* will find thought provoking.

The last essay, my own, is broader, perhaps, than its title indicates. I discuss the reasons why Kipling's reputation, more than a half-century after his death, is bound to rise. We are not done with Kipling the jingo or Kipling the banjo-player, and perhaps we never will be; but we will hear more, a lot more, about Kipling the artist, who was, I believe, the greatest short story writer in the English language, a poet whose talents were severely underestimated, a superb chronicler of human activities and emotions, a spokesman for important segments of the reading public, and one of the most astonishing personalities in the entire history of English literature.

HAROLD OREL

University of Kansas

Notes

1. James McG. Stewart, *Rudyard Kipling / A Bibliographical Catalogue* (Toronto: Dalhousie University Press and University of Toronto Press, 1959), xii.

2. Ibid.

3. Ibid., vi.

4. Elliot L. Gilbert, *Kipling and the Critics* (New York: New York University Press, 1965), v.

5. Ibid., vi.

6. Andrew Rutherford, *Kipling's Mind and Art* (Edinburgh and London: Oliver and Boyd, 1964), x.

7. Roger Lancelyn Green, *Kipling / The Critical Heritage* (London: Routledge and Kegan Paul, 1971), xvii.

8. Ibid., 1.

9. Ibid., 31.

10. Ibid.

11. Ibid., 32.

12. Harold Bloom, *Rudyard Kipling* (New York: Chelsea House, 1987), vii.

13. Ibid.

14. Charles Carrington, *Rudyard Kipling* (London: Macmillan and Co., 1955), 154.

15. Ibid.

16. Andrew Lang, "Mr. Kipling's Stories," *Essays in Little* (1891); reprinted in Gilbert, *Kipling and the Critics*, 3.

17. Ibid.

18. Ibid., 4.

19. Ibid., 6.

20. Ibid.

21. Henry James, letter to Robert Louis Stevenson, 21 March 1890; reprinted in Green, *Critical Heritage*, 67.

22. James to Stevenson, 12 January 1891; reprinted in Green, *Critical Heritage*, 68.

23. James to his brother William, 6 February 1892; reprinted in Green, *Critical Heritage*, 68.

24. James to Jonathan Sturges, 5 November 1896; reprinted in Green, *Critical Heritage*, 69.

25. James to Grace Norton, 25 December 1897; reprinted in Green, *Critical Heritage*, 69.

26. Ibid.

27. James to Charles Eliot Norton, 28 November 1899; reprinted in Green, *Critical Heritage*, 69.

28. Oscar Wilde, "The True Function and Value of Criticism," *The Nineteenth Century*, September 1891; reprinted in Gilbert, *Kipling and the Critics*, 7.

29. Ibid.

30. Edmund Gosse, "Rudyard Kipling," *Century Magazine* (October 1891); reprinted in Green, *Critical Heritage*, 106.

31. Ibid., 106–7.

32. Ibid., 107.

33. Ibid.

34. Mrs. Oliphant, [anonymous] review of *Life's Handicap*, *Blackwood's Magazine* (November 1891); reprinted in Green, *Critical Heritage*, 136.

35. William Ernest Henley, [anonymous] review of *Soldiers Three, Plain Tales from the Hills*, and *Departmental Ditties*, *Scots Observer*, 2 May 1890; reprinted in Green, *Critical Heritage*, 55–56.

36. Sir Arthur T. Quiller-Couch, "Reviews and Reminders. II. On Some Living English Poets," *English Illustrated Magazine* (September 1893); reprinted in Green, *Critical Heritage*, 176.

37. Ibid.

38. Robert Williams Buchanan, "The Voice of the Hooligan," *Contemporary Review* (December 1899); reprinted in Green, *Critical Heritage*, 235–36.

39. Ibid., 237.

40. Ibid., 243.

41. Ibid., 248.

42. Sir Walter Besant, "Is It the Voice of the Hooligan?" *Contemporary Review* (January 1900); reprinted in Green, *Critical Heritage*, 258.

43. Edward Dowden, "The Poetry of Mr. Kipling," *New Liberal Review* (February 1901): 267.

44. G. K. Chesterton, review of *Just So Stories, Bookman* (London) (November 1902); reprinted in Green, *Critical Heritage*, 273.

45. George Moore, "Kipling and Loti," *Pall Mall Gazette* (July 1904); reprinted in Green, *Critical Heritage*, 289.

46. Ford Madox Hueffer, *The Critical Attitude* (1911); reprinted in Green, *Critical Heritage*, 304.

47. H. G. Wells, *The Outline of History* (1920); reprinted in Green, *Critical Heritage*, 307.

48. T. S. Eliot, review of *The Years Between, Anthenaeum*, 9 May 1919; reprinted in Green, *Critical Heritage*, 322.

49. Ibid., 326.

50. Edmund Blunden, review of *The Irish Guards in the Great War, Nation and Athenaeum*, 28 April 1923; reprinted in Green, *Critical Heritage*, 332.

51. Christopher Morley, review of "Horace, Book Five" and *Debits and Credits, Saturday Review of Literature*, 2 October 1926; reprinted in Green, *Critical Heritage*, 333.

52. Brander Matthews, review of *Debits and Credits, Literary Digest* (November 1926); reprinted in Green, *Critical Heritage*, 337–38.

53. C. S. Lewis, "They Asked for a Paper," a lecture (1948) printed in *Kipling Journal* (September and December 1958); reprinted in Gilbert, *Kipling and the Critics*, 99.

54. Ibid., 100.

55. Ibid., 101.

56. Ibid., 105.

57. Ibid., 106.

58. Ibid., 116.

59. Ibid., 117.

60. Boris Ford, "A Case for Kipling?" *Scrutiny* 11, no. 1 (1948); reprinted in Gilbert, *Kipling and the Critics*, 72.

61. Ibid., 71.

62. Edmund Wilson, "The Kipling That Nobody Read," *Atlantic Monthly* 167 (1941); reprinted in Rutherford, *Kipling's Mind and Art*, 21.

63. Ibid., 44.

64. Ibid., 54.

65. Randall Jarrell, "On Preparing to Read Kipling," introduction to *The Best Short Stories of Rudyard Kipling* (New York: Hanover House, 1961); reprinted in Bloom, *Rudyard Kipling*, 11.

66. Ibid., 19.

67. Ibid., 21.

68. Steven Marcus, introduction to *Stalky & Co.* (New York, 1962); reprinted in Gilbert, *Kipling and the Critics*, 159.

69. Ibid., 157.

70. Ibid., 160.

71. George Shepperson, "The World of Rudyard Kipling," in Rutherford, *Kipling's Mind and Art*, 130–31.

72. Ibid., 132.

73. Ibid., 140.

74. Alan Sandison, "Kipling: The Artist and the Empire," in Rutherford, *Kipling's Mind and Art*, 156.

75. Ibid., 157.

76. Noel Annan, "Kipling's Place in the History of Ideas," in Rutherford, *Kipling's Mind and Art,*" 120.

77. Ibid.

78. J. M. S. Tompkins, *The Art of Rudyard Kipling* (London: Methuen and Co., 1959), x.

79. Ibid., ix.

80. Ibid., 258.

81. Ibid.

82. Green, *Kipling / The Critical Heritage,* 8.

83. Tompkins, *The Art of Rudyard Kipling,* 259.

84. Ibid.

85. I recommend Constance Scheerer's "The Lost Paradise of Rudyard Kipling," *The Dalhousie Review* (Spring 1981), as a fine complementary study.

Kipling's Poetry

Some Aspects of Kipling's Verse　　　Andrew Rutherford[*]

Kipling's subtlest artistry, his deepest psychological insights, his most sensitive intuitions, are to be found not in his verse but in the best of his prose fiction; and the claims to be made for his poetry are therefore more modest than for works like "The Man who would be King," "Without Benefit of Clergy," "On Greenhow Hill," the Puck and Mowgli stories, *Kim*, "The Wish House," and "The Gardener." Yet he can now be seen in retrospect as one of the best minor poets of the late nineteenth and early twentieth centuries, and it is regrettable—though understandable —that his reputation should have been so long obscured by the fogs of political and literary controversy.

In some ways, of course, he asked for it. Deliberately polemical and partisan, many of his poems have naturally evoked polemical and partisan responses. Deliberately unfashionable, consciously out of step with modern poetic movements, sometimes defiantly lowbrow, his art has—not surprisingly—been regarded often with disgusted or amused contempt. Hostile critics, on the other hand, have shown over the years a capacity for prejudice and special pleading equal to Kipling's own. Those who maintain that his poems smell of blood and tobacco (like Dick Heldar's paintings), or that "his mind was a very crude instrument . . . always devoid of finer feeling and emotional discipline,"[1] have taken little account of works as various as "The Way Through the Woods," "Gethsemane," "The Storm Cone," and "The Appeal." The view that he is essentially the bard of Anglo-Saxon racialism must be qualified by verses like those on "Buddha at Kamakura," which typify his anthropological but warmly human interest in mankind in all its variety, and his ability to project himself imaginatively into the minds of men of other races and cultures. Those who see him as the quintessential jingo, bawling England's praises, should read as a corrective poems like "The Islanders," "The Dykes," and "The City of Brass," in which he denounces his country for her ineffi-

[*]From the *Proceedings of the British Academy* 51 (1965): 375–402. Reprinted by permission of the British Academy. This essay was read 8 December 1965 as a Chatterton Lecture on an English Poet.

ciency and decadence: few patriots have had a sharper awareness of the discrepancy between their ideals and the reality. The belief that he was first and last a militarist, glorifying brutality and battle, is hard to reconcile with "The Settler," which stresses the waste and futility of war, the need for reconciliation and atonement, or with "The Mother's Son," that sad record of a psychological casualty of the trenches, or with his grimly stoical acceptance (in "For All We Have and Are") of the outbreak of war in 1914:

> Our world has passed away,
> In wantonness o'erthrown.
> There is nothing left today
> But steel and fire and stone! . . .
>
> Comfort, content, delight,
> The ages' slow-bought gain,
> They shrivelled in a night.
> Only ourselves remain
> To face the naked days
> In silent fortitude,
> Through perils and dismays
> Renewed and re-renewed.

It is a mood (need I say?) far removed from the facile exultation commonly associated with war poetry of that period.

Such examples could easily be multiplied, but although they have their value in modifying an inadequate popular stereotype, they are unlikely to convince the unconverted of Kipling's standing as a poet. For one thing, it might be argued, such a defence concerns itself too exclusively with his philosophy or "attitudes" and too little with his art, too much with the content and too little with the quality of his writings; while the unsympathetic reader may also feel that here (as in other apologias) a new, acceptable pseudo-Kipling is being fabricated from carefully selected elements, while much objectionable material is ignored or deliberately suppressed. There might be some truth in this suspicion, since the critic who has winnowed bad from good to his own satisfaction is tempted to describe his author in terms of the positive achievements, not the lapses; but the best of Kipling is not necessarily representative of the whole. "Recessional," for example, strikes a solemnly impressive note of warning against national hubris, pleading for humble and contrite hearts amid the pride and pomp of Victoria's Diamond Jubilee, but having drafted the famous stanzas Kipling confided to his friend Rider Haggard that

> . . . my objection to that hymn is that it may be quoted as an excuse for lying down abjectly at all times and seasons and taking what any other country may think fit to give us. What I wanted to say was: "Don't

gas but be ready to give people snuff"—and I only covered the first part of the notion.[2]

"Don't gas but be ready to give people snuff": the sentiments are not in themselves disreputable, but the aggressive common sense and perky complacent slang contrast disconcertingly with the high meditative mode adopted in the hymn. Nor is this simply a contrast between the author and the man, for the aspect of Kipling's mind which we glimpse here issues not infrequently in execrable verses (like "Et Dona Ferentes," that embarrassing celebration of the dangerous politeness of the English). This does not, of course, detract from the merits of "Recessional" itself—I have never understood the anti-Kiplingite assumption that we may discount a good poem (or story) because the author has also written bad ones. But the contrast does suggest the danger of substituting an ideal "or essential" Kipling for the real one: there are quantitative as well as qualitative judgements to be made here, and the honest critic must acknowledge that nearly all the charges commonly brought against Kipling *can* be documented from his poems. The error lies in accepting that indictment as the whole truth.

In discussing Kipling's verse we are, however, faced with a preliminary difficulty of some magnitude. His poems are now most easily available in the self-styled "Definitive Edition," based on his own revision of the last "Inclusive Edition" published in his lifetime, yet this is in some ways a most unsatisfactory volume.[3] The "Songs from Books" have suffered from their first collection by the enforced separation from their narrative contexts. Take "Rimini," for example, sub-titled "Marching Song of a Roman Legion of the Later Empire":

> When I left Rome for Lalage's sake,
>   By the Legions' Road to Rimini,
> She vowed her heart was mine to take
> With me and my shield to Rimini—
>   (Till the Eagles flew from Rimini—)
> And I've tramped Britain and I've tramped Gaul,
> And the Pontic shore where the snow-flakes fall
> As white as the neck of Lalage—
> (As cold as the heart of Lalage!)
> And I've lost Britain, and I've lost Gaul,
> And I've lost Rome and, worst of all,
> I've lost Lalage!

This gave me pleasure when I read it as a boy, and it gives me pleasure still—of a simple, unsophisticated kind. An obvious criticism might refer to the discrepancy between sentiment and rhythm, for in marching and work songs metrics have an extra literary function to fulfil; but if we turn to the story "On the Great Wall") from which these verses are taken, we find that discrepancy clearly acknowledged:

> And I've lost Britain and I've lost Gaul
> (the voice seemed very cheerful about it). . . .

And no excessive claims are made for the song as poetry, its ephemeral character being stressed by the singer himself:

> "It's one of the tunes that are always being born somewhere in the Empire. They run like a pestilence for six months or a year, till another one pleases the Legions, and then they march to that."

Thus the necessary "placing" is done unequivocally in the course of the narrative itself, whereas it is merely hinted at by the sub-title in the collected verse.[4] In this volume, furthermore, we lose our sense of the connexion between poem and narrative. Parnesius had told, in "A Centurion of the Thirtieth," of Maximus's ambition to become Emperor of Britain, Gaul, and Rome: the light-hearted soldiers' song about losing all three anticipates Maximus's failure, and "the Pontic shore where the snow-flakes fall" foreshadows bleakly his death "by the sea" at the hands of Theodosius. Thus the song, simple in itself (and dramatically appropriate to the singer), forms part of the complex thematic patterning of this series of tales. Similarly, the poems which separate the various narrative sections help to create new dimensions of meaning, while themselves acquiring additional weight from the context in which they appear. Here, pre-eminently, we have a case of "[Kipling's] verse and prose [being] inseparable," so that, in Eliot's words, "we must . . . judge him, not separately as a poet and as a writer of prose fiction, but as the inventor of a mixed form."[5] Frequently, however, the relation between poems and narrative is less organic. The epigraphs in the early volumes are best taken with the stories for which they were written, and on which they provide explicit or implicit commentaries; but the later stories can usually be detached from the intervening poems without loss—often indeed they gain from the separation, though the poems may suffer, tending as they sometimes do to present with crude simplicity what is rendered by the prose in subtle obliquities of narrative technique.

Such problems are not confined, however, to the "Songs from Books." They also arise in the case of poems detached from their verse contexts. Although many of the poems were first published individually in newspapers and magazines, they are best read in the little volumes in which they were then collected (and it was to this arrangement that Kipling returned in the great Sussex Edition of his works, which has the best claim to be regarded as definitive). Thus the notorious "Loot" as an anthology piece provokes a different reaction from "Loot" as part of the series of *Barrack-Room Ballads*—experiments in a kind of poetic sociology, involving the deliberate and virtuosic use of an inadequate vocabulary and defective *persona*. In such cases, it might be suggested, the series rather than the individual poem seems the appropriate unit for critical study. Now the posthumous "Definitive Edition," like the earlier Inclusive Editions, preserves only to a limited extent the arrangement of poems in the original collections. The entire contents of *Departmental Ditties* are transferred without any alteration, but the other volumes are subjected to a good deal of rearrangement, often (as Mr. Hilton Brown has noted) of a puzzling and arbitrary kind. It is logical enough to follow the original "Barrack-Room Ballads" with those printed in *The Seven Seas*, and to pass directly from these to "Service Songs" from *The Five Nations*. But it is hard to see why these poems should be placed so late in the collection, or why they should come *after* "Epitaphs of the War" and two other poems dated 1918. Why, again, should "Gethsemane 1914–18" be sandwiched incongruously between a poem about absconding financiers, written in 1902, and "The Song of the Banjo," dated 1894? Incongruities almost as blatant can sometimes be explained, if not altogether justified: when the "Dirge of Dead Sisters (For the Nurses who died in the South African War)" is followed by "The Vampire," Kipling presumably means to acknowledge Woman in her most beneficent and most malignant aspects, and a similar intention seems to underlie the grouping of the anti-feminist "Female of the Species" with "A Recantation." Sometimes, again, the juxtapositions are positively felicitous: Mr. Shanks has drawn attention to the grim propriety of Kipling's placing "The Lesson" (on what England ought to learn from the Boer War) alongside "Mesopotamia 1917" (which shows how completely that lesson had remained unlearnt). And more generally, one can often see in the arrangement of the poems an impulse to bring together pieces with the same theme or similar preoccupations, so as to group them by subjects rather than by dates, and to show significantly recurring elements in the pattern of national experience.

In spite of these organizing principles, however, one's first and final impression is of the chaotic nature of this volume. Firstly, because the policy of grouping like with like is not carried out consistently. Secondly, because the transitions from one group to the next are sudden, unmarked, and disconcerting. We may, like Mr. Shanks, appreciate Kipling's following "Recessional" with "For All We Have and Are," but it is startling to find that the next poem is "The Three-Decker," written twenty years before as an amusing allegorical description of the old three-volume novel. Kipling has passed here from political themes to a series of poems on art and the artist, but the reader is given no warning of the change. Thirdly, and most serious of all, within most of the "runs" of poems, and throughout the volume as a whole, there is a perverse, almost wanton disruption of chronology. This is regrettable, not so much because it makes it difficult to trace Kipling's development as an artist—in point of fact little "development" took place in his poetical techniques—but because it obscures the original groupings and inter-relationships of his verses, and their connexion with contemporary circumstances. As their titles indicate, each of the original volumes had a central theme, different aspects of which were treated in different poems; and although there was in each a large element of miscellaneous poems (or "other verses"), they had each a kind of unity which came from their being products of a particular phase of Kipling's life, and a particular phase of history or public affairs. His poetry has its roots not in an inner life, spiritual or psychological, but in his responses to the world around him, and it has to be read with an awareness of that temporal context. (His own partial recognition of this can be seen in his assigning dates to so many poems in the chronological jumble of the Inclusive Edition.) To stress their essential relation to such chronological contexts is not to reduce Kipling's poems to the status of period-pieces—though that may be part of their interest and appeal: it is rather to insist that, as Professor Trilling has said, "the literary work is ineluctably an historical fact, and, what is more important . . . its historicity is a fact in our aesthetic experience."[6]

The very extent of Kipling's popularity marks the gulf between his world and ours, for he was one of the last English poets to command a mass audience. Nor need we assume (as guardians of our own minority culture) that this quantitative success could be achieved only at the cost of qualitative failure. This might sometimes be the case, but the basic difference between Kipling's poetry and the coterie art of the nineties or later decades is one of kind rather than quality. He was dealing largely with what Professor Dobrée has described as "public themes"—themes which correspond to the common needs and interests of humanity and which therefore evoke a general, but not necessarily a debased or imprecise response. Like the traditional poet as Dr. Hough describes him, he "addresses his readers in the confidence that he will be understood; that his rhetoric and his mode of address will be familiar to them from their previous reading of poetry; and he appeals to an order of feeling that he assumes to be common to himself and them, simply as human beings, or as members of a particular civilisation."[7] The enthusiasm with which Kipling's verses were received—an enthusiasm to be gauged not merely by the pronouncements of reviewers, but by his enormous sales in Britain and America—shows that in his case these assumptions were well justified—that the values and emotions expressed in his art are not to be explained away in terms of his personal inadequacies, prejudices, or neuroses, but were widely acceptable throughout the English-speaking world. He helped to give them greater currency, of course, for like Dryden (to whom Eliot so usefully compares him) he was at once and unashamedly artist and propagandist. Hence a double motive inspired much of his verse, since he wanted to communicate with (and influence) as wide an audience as possible, while maintaining the highest standards of literary craftsmanship, as he understood them.

Sometimes, admittedly, this balance was upset, Kipling himself would have denied that he ever sacrificed artistic quality to "direct appeal": "... never play down to your public," he wrote in his old age, "—not because some of them do not deserve it, but because it is bad for your hand."[8] Yet the not infrequent badness of his own hand—the unevenness of his verse—suggests that his judgement was unreliable; and although he may never have consciously played down to his public, its demands did little to reinforce or refine the urgings of his own artistic conscience. From his parents, certainly, he got encouragement, criticism, and helpful advice, and he tells us in his autobiography that "those two made for me the only public for whom ... I had any regard whatever till their deaths, in my forty-fifth year."[9] Their influence, however, was less constant (though still considerable) once he had left India, and the comments of critics and reviewers were no substitute, since he despised their whole tribe except for a very few respected friends like Henley, Saintsbury, and Charles Eliot Norton. Nevertheless, there was a wider public whose opinion he did value—initially the members of the Club at Lahore, to whom he had to justify his work on each day's paper; then, further afield, the "men in the Army and the Civil Service and the Railway" who wrote to him suggesting that the rhymes he had published in the *Civil and Military Gazette* might be made into a book, and telling him how "some of them had been sung to the banjoes round campfires, and some had run as far down coast as Rangoon and Moulmein, and up to Mandalay."[10] Appreciation of this kind, from the critically unsophisticated Sons of Martha, always delighted Kipling with its testimony to his poetry's authenticity and general appeal, but it may have been potentially corrupting for him as an artist. His rather special relationship with such audiences is epitomized in Arnold Bennett's journal entry for 22 October 1898. "This is my idea of fame," writes Bennett:

> At an entertainment on board H.M.S. *Majestic*, Rudyard Kipling, one of the guests, read "Soldier and Sailor Too," and was encored. He then read "The Flag of England." At the conclusion a body of subalterns swept him off the stage, and chaired him round the quarter-deck, while "For he's a jolly good fellow" was played by the massed bands of the Fleet and sung by 200 officers assembled.[11]

The verses Kipling chose to recite on this occasion were so well suited to his audience's tastes and prejudices, that he may seem (both as entertainer and as poet) to have been giving them simply what they wanted—to have been offering them an acceptable confirmatory image of themselves and their ideals. Such an hypothesis need involve no charge of insincerity, since Kipling's values were so largely theirs, but it is this very community of values that constitutes the danger: an aesthetically undemanding public's readiness to accept his views might sometimes make him careless of the artistry with which these views were formulated, and reluctant to scrutinize the views themselves. Thus some of his worst poems—"Et Dona Ferentes," "The Puzzler," "The Female of the

Species"—seem attributable not merely to elements of insensitive stupidity in his own nature, but to a too easily reached understanding with insensitive and stupid readers.

Such failures must, however, be kept in perspective: with their crudity of technique as well as attitude, their style based on a lowest common denominator of communication between poet and public, they are aberrations (though of a recurrent type) from Kipling's normally high standards of poetic craftsmanship. Yet these standards are themselves significantly different from those applicable to his prose. "Verse, naturally, came first" when he began to write, and he always tended to think of it as the simpler medium. When the Merchant in the Preface to the Outward Bound Edition bids us remember that "many of the cloths are double and treble-figured, giving a new pattern in a shift of light," he is referring to prose textures: Kipling never seems to have aimed at this kind of complexity in verse, the main object and power of which, he told Haggard, were "to put things in a form in which people would not only read but *remember* them."[12] At the outset of his career he had indeed realized that "it was necessary that every word should tell, carry, weigh, taste and, if need were, smell":

> Thus [he tells us], . . . I made my own experiments in the weights, colours, perfumes, and attributes of words in relation to other words, either as read aloud so that they may hold the ear, or, scattered over the page, draw the eye. There is no line of my verse or prose which has not been mouthed till the tongue has made all smooth, and memory, after many recitals, has mechanically skipped the grosser superfluities.[13]

Although such earnestness commands respect there is a certain naivete, a theoretical inadequacy, about this artistic credo which may be connected with Kipling's indifference or hostility to the main literary movements of his lifetime. When Yeats, his exact contemporary, dismisses him as one who, at the turn of the century, had never heard of the defeat of "Victorianism" or who did not believe in it, the judgement strikes us as grossly unfair.[14] Kipling may have had something of the "moral discursiveness" of Tennyson, the "political eloquence of Swinburne," and "the psychological curiosity of Browning," but it is not self-evident to us (as it was then to Yeats) that such "impurities" are in fact poetic defects; and he does less than justice to Kipling as an innovator—far more notable and revolutionary than Yeats himself—in the poetry of the Nineties. "The Lake Isle of Innisfree" and "The Road to Mandalay" are both exercises in nostalgia, but there can be no doubt which is more original and poetically vital. The comparison with Yeats, however, highlights immediately the limitations of Kipling's originality, which seems somehow to have lacked the potentiality of growth. In his later prose fiction he came to develop a complex, closely organized, elliptical and symbolic mode of writing, which ranks him as a major innovator in the art of the short story, but there is no comparable development in his poetry. "The Dead King," an unpleasantly fulsome tribute to Edward VII, is written in a consciously experimental metre—which achieves only an effect of awkward over-elaboration. Kipling's gift was, clearly, for simpler, more traditional verse-forms. There are, on the other hand, some classically inspired experiments of considerable interest: his imitations of Horace's Odes, which enabled him to treat public themes and private emotion with a combination of eloquence and restraint; or his "Epitaphs of the War" ("naked cribs of the Greek Anthology," he is said to have called them) in which pity and indignation (or pity and admiration) issue at best in spare concentrated epigrams like the couplet on "The Coward":

> I could not look on Death, which being known,
> Men led me to him, blindfold and alone.

Or the quatrain on a "Convoy Escort," which epitomizes a whole Service ethic of duty and self-sacrifice:

> I was a shepherd to fools
>   Causelessly bold or afraid.
> They would not abide by my rules.
>   Yet they escaped. For I stayed.

For the most part, however, he was content to use, even in the nineteen-twenties and thirties, styles and conventions which he had evolved in the eighteen-nineties: "his tools remain the same," as Mr. Stewart says, "and his medium scarcely enriches or subtilizes itself."[15] "The Bonfires," published in November 1933, is a poem of immediate contemporary relevance, protesting as it does against the empty pretentiousness and wishful thinking of current politics—not least with regard to appeasing Hitler's new Germany. Yet the style would not have been surprising thirty years before, and the very self-consciousness of the ballade form distracts attention from the dangers alluded to. One can see how Kipling came to be disregarded by many not merely because he was politically unacceptable, but because he seemed a literary anachronism.

None the less, he had throughout his career a remarkable capacity for converting his own weakness to strengths. The psychological insecurity, the need to feel that he belonged and was accepted, the urge to assert his membership of an in-group, which made him, in C. S. Lewis's phrase, "the slave of the Inner Ring," were the very qualities which enabled him to treat so successfully that "immense area of human life" concerned with men's work and their sense of professional brotherhood.[16] His admiration for the Service Classes sometimes resulted in the merging of his finer individual awareness with "the commonest collective emotions" of such limited communities as an Anglo-Indian Club, a barrack-room, or an officers' mess; but it also enabled him to present poetically a whole phase of British imperial experience in terms of the consciousness and ideals of the men most directly involved. If his worship of efficiency went too often with a disregard for the ends to which efficiency was being applied, it saved him from identifying himself completely with the Establishment (as Buchan did), and provided the basis for his exposures—among the best before Sassoon's—of military incompetence. While the simplicity of poetic taste which led to his Philistine disregard for new developments in poetry also made possible his bold use of popular and traditional art-forms, in works that can still astonish by their originality and power.

Their apparent simplicity, moreover, is itself deceptive, since each of his poetic modes emerges from, and gives expression to, a whole complex of social, political, and moral values.

He began unambitiously, with *vers de société* in established Anglo-Indian fashions. Such poems "arrived merrily," he tells us, "being born out of the life about me,"[17] and "merrily" is the keyword: *Departmental Ditties* is what the title suggests—a collection of essentially light-hearted verses on governmental processes. Yet the "Prelude" he wrote for the first English edition is a passionate declaration of solidarity with the Anglo-India guyed in most of the subsequent verses. Looking back to British life as he had known it in the East, Kipling saw it now in terms of hardships and dangers willingly endured, of duty steadfastly done, and the poem is an apology for what may seem his own disloyalty in presenting that life as one of frivolity and mild corruption. But the apology itself is potentially misleading:

> I have written the tale of our life
>   For a sheltered people's mirth,
> In jesting guise—but ye are wise,
>   And ye know what the jest is worth.

In publishing these poems in London he may have been offering the tale of their life for a sheltered people's mirth, but it had already been written in jesting guise for the Anglo-Indians themselves—who knew what the jest was worth in the sense of knowing not that it was false (as this poem might imply) but that it was at least half-true. His original readers relished the jokes precisely because they were the jokes of their own service. "Old is the song that I sing," runs the epigraph to the first narrative in the collection—

> Old as my unpaid bills—
> Old as the chicken that *kitmutgars* bring
> Men at dâk-bungalows—old as the Hills.

Neither "kitmutgars" nor "dâk-bungalows" was glossed in the early editions, any more than such terms as *dasturi, thana, byles, koïl, siris,* and *satbhai* in other poems, or slang expressions like "the gay thirteen-two" or "three days casual on the bust," or references to Simla institutions like Benmore, Annandale, and Peliti's. These were things his readers *knew,* just as ancient chickens at dâk-bungalows were facts of their experience, and they would relish the way in which the hills of cliché, capitalized, became those in which appointments have been wangled from time immemorial. Kipling's "artless songs" are for the most part mere diversions, but a society reveals itself in its diversions; and as the world of the *Ditties* recedes from us in time, they acquire something of the adventitious charm of faded sepia photographs in old albums. The hazards of disease and death which Kipling describes in *Something of Myself* were met by Anglo-India with its own brand of stoicism, sometimes Christian, sometimes flippantly ironic, and the latter mood is well rendered in verses like "The Undertaker's Horse" or "A Ballad of Burial":

> If down here I chance to die
>   Solemnly I beg you take
> All that is left of "I"
>   To the Hills for old sake's sake.
> Pack me very thoroughly
>   In the ice that used to slake
> Pegs I drank when I was dry—
>   This observe for old sake's sake.

Light to the point of triviality, such verses none the less succeed in catching a mood which has helped many men endure, and by articulating it for his society's own amusement Kipling reveals that society to outsiders and to posterity. The speaking voice makes no pretension to distinction or subtlety, but we are conscious as we read of a weight of experience, not individual but communal. Like all good society verse, however frivolous, the *Ditties* imply a code of manners and values accepted by the members of the group which provides at once the subject-matter and the reading public. Writing from within that group, Kipling views its faults and failures half satirically, half-indulgently, noting its "official sinning" and unofficial adulteries with ironic detachment—though his indignation on Jack Barrett's behalf shows that there are limits to his comic tolerance. And indeed the humour of *Departmental Ditties* depends on the contrast, unstated but assumed throughout, between the frivolous world portrayed in many poems and the everyday world of the Indian services, dedicated to efficiency, duty, and toil. (It is the fear that English readers may not grasp this contrast that lies behind the last stanza of the "Prelude.") For this everyday world Kipling felt an whole-hearted admiration, and at the thought of criticism from outsiders he drops his mask of cynicism and leaps to Anglo-India's defence with "Pagett, M.P."—the classic expression of the man-on-the-spot's irritation at ill-informed parliamentary interference.

One or two poems ("Arithmetic on the Frontier," "The Grave of the Hundred Head") anticipate what is to be a major interest of subsequent collections—life as it is lived not in Simla or the districts but on the imperial frontiers. This is a natural consequence of Kipling's dynamic conception of Empire as a continual struggle of Order against Chaos:

> Keep ye the Law—be swift in all obedience—
> Clear the land of evil, drive the road and bridge the ford.
>> Make ye sure to each his own
>> That he reap where he hath sown;
> By the peace among Our peoples let men know we serve the Lord.

The ideal is far from ignoble: it is a high, heroic endeavour to which Kipling summons his chosen people. But the activist ethic depends for its appeal on the sense of difficulties to be overcome, and one suspects that once the land *has* been cleared of evil, the roads and bridges built, peace and order established, things may seem rather dull.[18] Only at times, for Kipling found something heroic in any work well done under arduous conditions, but crises and emergencies—floods, famines, or riots, for example—which test men's true quality measured in terms of ultimate breaking strain appealed to his imagination more than any smooth-running routine. It was natural, therefore, that he should be attracted to tales of Burma or the North-West Frontier—areas where the Carlylean conflict of Order and Anarchy was at its most spectacular and adventurous. Late Victorian yearners for romance—men like Stevenson and Andrew Lang—had sought it usually in the past: the place of Dumas in their theorizing is significant. Kipling, on the other hand, found romance in reality—in the everyday, apparently humdrum work of administrators and engineers; but he also demonstrated the reality of romance by showing that heroic adventures were not anachronisms but facts of contemporary life. "The Lament of the Border Cattle Thief" (in *Barrack-Room Ballads*) draws attention by its title to the similarities between Frontier conditions and those of the old Scottish Border, and the poetic mode, appropriately, is that of the traditional ballad. Kipling uses this dramatically to enter with imaginative sympathy into the robber's anarchic fierceness; so that the poem satisfies simultaneously his anthropological curiosity, his interest in violence, and his belief in the rule of Law—for the very success with which the anarchic fierceness is rendered justifies by implication Britain's policing of the area. His direct imitations of old ballads rarely rise above the level of pastiche; but poems like "The Ballad of East and West" or "The Rhyme of the Three Sealers," where he has found a manner of his own, can stand comparison with traditional pieces like "Kinmont Willie" or "The Battle of Otterburn." Only an instinctive literary snobbishness prevents most readers from admitting this. They may feel uneasily that the older ballads are the natural product of a turbulent age, whereas Kipling's are examples of conscious literary atavism; but he was writing of a world where such episodes as he described did actually take place, and he might have retorted that it was not he himself, but the reluctant reader, who was seeking to evade reality.

It may be argued, however, that a modern balladist, unlike his traditional counterpart, should have values transcending those of the participants in the action he describes. The question hardly arises in "The Ballad of East and West," where the warrior's code invoked is nobly chivalric and Kipling's endorsement of it causes no embarrassment, chiming as it does with the reader's own emotional response. In "The Ballad of Boh Da Thone," on the other hand, Captain O'Neil's unregenerate past in the Burmese War is contrasted with his peaceful married life to the latter's disadvantage, and there is a distasteful element of delight in violence for its own sake in Kipling's lively description of a dacoit attack:

> Then belching blunderbuss answered back
> The Snider's snarl and the carbine's crack,
>
> And the blithe revolver began to sing
> To the blade that twanged on the locking-ring,
>
> And the brown flesh blued where the bayonet kissed,
> As the steel shot back with a wrench and a twist . . .
>
> Oh, gayest of scrimmages man may see
> Is a well-worked rush on the G.B.T.

"The steel came out with a wrench and a twist" is a line from Kipling's schoolboy poem on "The Battle of Assaye": its recurrence here suggests that this is an area where his concern for authenticity mingles with relish (and the implications of "blithe," "sing," and "kissed" need no commentary). Indeed his enjoyment of the whole episode is frankly acknowledged in the last couplet quoted, which was cut from the later collected editions. It cannot merely be dismissed as an armchair warrior's emotion, for it corresponds—as those with some experience of frontier soldiering will recognize—to an enjoyment which both dacoits and escort would undoubtedly have found in the excitement of the skirmish. But we may legitimately expect a poet to bring finer perceptions, a more sensitive morality, to bear on his material.

This, however, was no part of Kipling's intention. Finer perceptions and more sensitive moralities seemed to him at this stage in his career to be attributes of the Sons of Mary—among whom he included literary critics—attributes cultivated in the security and comfort guaranteed them by the Sons of Martha. A Jamesian sensibility like Eustace Cleever's (in "A Conference of the Powers") was in his view a hot-house plant of civilization, which could flourish only when insulated from the realities of life as he knew it to be—from the realities that sustain and protect civilization itself:

"To me," said Cleever softly, "The whole idea of warfare seems so foreign and unnatural, so essentially vulgar, if I may say so, that I can hardly appreciate your sensations."

To force readers—even readers as refined as Cleever—into an awareness of soldiers' "sensations" was one of Kipling's primary aims, most notably in the dramatic lyrics or monologues of *Barrack-Room Ballads*. And the primitivism apparent in his choice of subject matter and persona is based ultimately on his conviction that the activities and consciousness of coarser but more useful "people who do things" provide richer material for art than do the delicate perceptions of the highbrow. In these *Ballads* he was dealing with a society lower than his own in intelligence, education, and sensitivity—a society of which he was not part, though he had observed it sympathetically. For this purpose he adapts the technique of *Departmental Ditties* by writing ostensibly as a member of the group for other members, thus revealing it to the world at large. This involves the adoption of the fictional persona of a private soldier, based not on the individualized and all-too-articulate Mulvaney (whose Irish rhetoric was a continual temptation to Kipling to overdo things), but on the average Tommy "whose vocabulary," he was well aware "contained less than six hundred words, and the Adjective."[19] The adjective, with other obscenities or blasphemies, was unprintable in Kipling's day, so that he had to use weaker expletives like "blooming," "beggar," and "sugared"; but it was a convention readily understood by large sections of his audience who could (if they wished) make the appropriate substitutions. Otherwise his aim is a stylized authenticity, based on Cockney mixed with soldiers' slang and technicalities which go unexplained, forcing the reader into a kind of intuitive comprehension. Kipling was sometimes accused of surreptitiously extending the soldier's vocabulary by smuggling in poeticisms of his own, but it was not an objection made by soldiers themselves—probably because he found his models in art-forms with which they were themselves familiar—the songs he had heard sung in canteens, round campfires on manœuvres, or, above all, in the London music-halls.[20] "The smoke, the roar, and the good-fellowship of relaxed humanity at Gatti's" (just opposite his lodgings in Villiers Street) formed the milieu in which these ballads were conceived. As Professor Carrington observes, they are essentially "songs for the 'Halls' in which the 'patter' dominates the musical setting," for in spite of their subsequent success as drawing-room ballads, they were not originally meant to be sung: although Kipling usually had tunes in mind as he wrote, these were highly idiosyncratic aids to composition, not part of the finished product.[21] But the poems do imply a speaker and an audience, and gain by being read aloud, for it is thus that we can best appreciate their colloquial vigour and the simple but intoxicating rhythms which are a major source of the pleasure Kipling's verse provides. (The fashionable equation of simple, strongly marked rhythms with artistic crudity is surely as misleading as the assumption that to explicate complexities in Kipling's prose technique is necessarily to demonstrate emotional or philosophic subtlety.)

These ballads constitute a documentary account, remarkably frank and inclusive except where sexual matters are concerned, of the soldier's life in peace and war; and since this is presented through the soldier's own eyes, we are made to participate imaginatively not merely in his activities but in his modes of thought and feeling. The dangers inherent in this method, and indeed in the whole cult of the primitive, are exemplified by "Loot"—a poem which has therefore received more than its due of critical attention. Although it is clearly a documentary item, it is also a deliberate outrage to bourgeois morality, and there is a zest, a gusto in the verses which have suggested to many critics that Kipling's own emotions are involved. The identification of poet and speaker is never complete, since the linguistic indexes of class are a continual reminder of the poem's *dramatic* status. Yet it can be argued that (since no morally normative standards are implied) this distinction merely enables Kipling and the reader to indulge vicariously impulses which they would be ashamed to acknowledge openly in their own persons.[22] We may admire the frankness which allows Kipling to include such a poem in his collection, instead of presenting a more idealized picture of the strong man Thomas Atkins and his imperial doings, but his own ready acceptance of such doings reveals the potentially debasing as well as liberating factors in his choice of medium and persona.

Critics have erred, however, in taking "Loot" as typical of the series as a whole. Primitivism may result in a cult of brutality, but it can also provide new perspectives on strange and familiar aspects of experience. The expansionist enthusiasm of the Nineties was given new piquancy and power when transposed into the idiom of the Barrack-Room Balladist:

> Walk wide o' the Widow at Windsor,
>   For 'alf o' Creation she owns:
> We 'ave bought 'er the same with the sword an' the flame,
>   An' we've salted it down with our bones.
>   (Poor beggars!—it's blue with our bones!)
> Hands off o' the sons o' the Widow
>   Hands off o' the goods in 'er shop,
> For the Kings must come down an' the Emperors frown
>   When the Widow at Windsor says "Stop!"
>   (Poor beggars!—we're sent to say "Stop!")

The assumptions here are identical with those of "The English Flag": there is the same pride in imperial achievement and the same awareness of the human cost (to the Empire-builders), but this poem is more firmly rooted in the psychological realism of the ordinary soldiers' wry distaste for their own part in the process, though there is no repudiation of the process itself—rather a reaffirmation of faith in it, all the stronger for the incipient challenge overcome. Kipling's spokesman for the barracks can also direct attention to what Wordsworth called "the great and simple affections of our nature," the opposite extreme from "Loot" being found in a poem like "Ford o' Kabul River." ("Never," as Le Gallienne said of another ballad in the series, "is the miracle of art more fully brought home to us than when such coarse material is thus touched to finer issues."[23])

> Kabul town's by Kabul river—
>   Blow the bugle, draw the sword—
> There I lef' my mate for ever,
>   Wet an' drippin' by the ford.
> Ford, ford, ford o' Kabul river,
>   Ford o' Kabul river in the dark!
> There's the river up and brimmin', an'
>   there's 'arf a squadron swimmin'
> Cross the ford o' Kabul river in the dark.

This verse-pattern is sustained throughout, the first four lines of each stanza lamenting the loss of a comrade, the last four (or chorus) recreating with a change of tense and metre events as they happened, the two time-scales merging only in the desolation of the final stanza. The recurrent line "Blow the bugle, draw the sword" forms a refrain ironically qualified by the context in each case, so that its martial fervour seems a mere futility. (In the collected verse the line reads "Blow the trumpet . . .'—a change made in the interests of accuracy, since it is clearly a cavalry regiment that is involved; but there is a loss of the potent alliteration of the original, and it is pleasing to find that Kipling restored the earlier reading in the Sussex Edition.) The poem is simple but dignified in its grief, for the measured rhythmical control (with pervasive hints of muffled drumbeats and slow marching) guarantees its emotional integrity throughout. Wholly free from sentimentality, avoiding too the factitious consolations of conventional elegy, it finally disposes of the view that Kipling's choice of a popular medium and "low" persona must result in crude emotion or crude art. (Indeed the advantages of his proletarian, Other Ranks style can be gauged by contrasting "Ford o' Kabul River" with the pretentious mythologizing, the inflated rhetoric, of his elegiac dedication of *Barrack-Room Ballads* to his own dead friend Wolcott Balestier.)

One is tempted to linger over the varied and virtuosic use Kipling made of this poetic idiom—to consider the ways in which he presents delightedly the waywardness of unregenerate humanity together with an assertion of the supreme values of Law, Order, Duty and Restraint, Obedience, Discipline. Or one might turn to his adaptation of the same technique in his Barrack-Room Ballads of the Boer War, to render a new phase in military experience, to reveal the weaknesses of the "red little, dead little Army" he had thought so admirable, and to criticize the society which had made that Army in its own image. The Kipling who, as proprietor of Bateman's, idealized the hierarchic social structure of rural England, was capable of presenting its defects, its restrictiveness (scenic and social), through the disillusioned eyes of a returned Irregular:

> 'Ow can I ever take on
> With awful old England again,
> An' 'ouses both sides of the street,
> An' edges two sides of the lane,
> An' the parson an' gentry between,
> An' touchin' my 'at when we meet—
> Me that 'ave been what I've been?

Rich as this vein is, however, Kipling himself found it inadequate for many of his purposes. In *Kim* he goes furthest in acknowledging the limitations of the private's mode of vision, but all through his career he was conscious of issues, especially political issues, which demanded solemn, dignified, and lofty treatment, in a higher style than the Barrack-Room Balladist could provide without incongruity. It is the treatment rather than the issues which I want to consider briefly in the remainder of this lecture. Poems like "The Song of the Women" in *Departmental Ditties*, "The English Flag" in *Barrack-Room Ballads*, "A Song of the English," in *The Seven Seas*, "The Burial" and "Recessional" in *The Five Nations*, "The Covenant" and "The Houses" in *The Years Between*, exemplify the problems involved, and often, it must be admitted, Kipling fails to solve them. There *is* a good deal of bombast in his political verse, especially when he is writing in what Le Gallienne called his "Methodistical-jingoistic manner," in which Jehovah of the Thunders, Lord God of Battles or of Hosts, is invoked rather too frequently—and too confidently—in the cause of British Imperialism. Often too, as Mr. Stewart has suggested, we are conscious of a surfeit of kinship imagery—the Mother country welcoming her colonial sons and daughters, the daughter nations holding lofty converse with the mother, brothers proclaiming kinship with their brothers in other lands. Yet the Five Free Nations, linked rather than divided by the Seven Seas, are not merely celebrated in windy rhetoric: they are also presented in vivid, sharply realized vignettes of scenery and human life—in "The Flowers," for example, or "The Native Born" (in spite of its embarrassing chorus), or "The Song of the Wise Children." Often too the old magic still works, the rhetoric and rhythms stir our emotions, we respond strongly, deeply, not unworthily, to some of the best verse-propaganda in the language. We must surely pay tribute, no matter what our own political allegiances may be, to the impassioned invective of "Cleared" or "Mesopotamia 1917," the flamboyant patriotism of "The English Flag," the fervour and prophetic wisdom of "The Islanders," the

superb secular hymnology of "The White Man's Burden," the solemn denunciation of German frightfulness in "The Outlaws 1914."

Kipling, however, is more versatile than even this list would suggest.
He can also captivate us by his epigrammatic formulation of unfashionable views:

> And . . . after this is accomplished, . . . the brave new world begins
> When all men are paid for existing and no man must pay for his sins. . . .

Or he may divert us and discredit his opponents by deft caricature of attitudes
which he despises, like those of the Progressive in "Natural Theology":

> Money spent on an Army or Fleet
>   Is homicidal lunacy. . . .
> My son has been killed in the Mons retreat.
>   Why is the Lord afflicting me?
> Why are murder, pillage and arson
>   And rape allowed by the Deity?
> I will write to the *Times,* deriding our parson,
>   Because my God has afflicted me.

Another recurrent formula is his use of emblematic incidents to convey
harsh political wisdom. "The Pirates in England," for example, one of the
poems written for C. R. L. Fletcher's school history book, tells how as
power passes from Imperial Rome in her decadence, the order she has
sustained in Britain disappears in anarchy. The Wall, Kipling's symbol for
the barrier between civilization and savagery, is crossed by the Picts,
agents of a new terrible disorder:

> They killed the trader, they sacked the shops,
>   They ruined temple and town—
> They swept like wolves through the standing crops
>   Crying that Rome was down.
>
> They wiped out all that they could find
>   Of beauty and strength and worth,
> But they could not wipe out the Viking's Wind
>   That brings the ships from the North.
>
> They could not wipe out the North-East gales,
>   Nor what those gales set free—
> The pirate ships with their close-reefed sails,
>   Leaping from sea to sea.
>
> They had forgotten the shield-hung hull
>   Seen nearer and more plain,
> Dipping into the troughs like a gull,
>   And gull-like rising again—

> The painted eyes that glare and frown
>   In the high snake-headed stem,
> Searching the beach while her sail comes down,
>   They had forgotten them!

The orgy of destructive anarchy brings its own nemesis, which comes not by chance, but as a natural, necessary consequence: the winds and the pirates whom they bring are so closely associated here that they are felt to be of the same order of inevitability: both are seen as part of the very nature of things. This sense of inevitability is intensified by the poem's rhythmical structure. Although made up of stanzas formally and syntactically self-contained, it constitutes (like so many of Kipling's poems) a single unbroken rhetorical movement, what Professor Léaud calls a poetic "monad," and to quote it in part or to interrupt it with commentary is to destroy its very life. The brief narrative is so vividly imagined and so informed by passionate conviction that we overlook its historical inaccuracy; for by this reshaping and telescoping of events Kipling quintessentializes what for him (as for Carlyle) was a fundamental truth of history—that any order, falling into decay, will be overwhelmed and replaced by anarchy, which brings in turn its own terrible antidote since the Gods of the Copybook Headings cannot ultimately be denied.

Closely related to this mode but distinct from it is the poem based structurally on an expanded metaphor. An early example is disastrously mishandled. "The Galley-Slave" appeared in the first English edition of *Departmental Ditties*, and like the "Prelude" to that collection it voiced Kipling's deeper feelings about the Indian Empire he had treated with such flippancy in many of the ditties themselves. He now sought to express, through the symbolic figure of the galley-slave, the paradoxical love and loyalty a man may feel for the service in which he has toiled, suffered, and grown old. To ignore the metaphorical structure of the poem is therefore to miss its whole point, though this is not to say that it is successful—rather to suggest the terms in which its weaknesses should be defined:

> Yet they talk of times and seasons and of woe the years bring forth,
> Of our galley swamped and shattered in the rollers of the North;
> When the niggers break the hatches and the decks are gay with gore,
> And a craven-hearted pilot crams her crashing on the shore.

> She will need no half-mast signal, minute-gun, or rocket-flare,
> When the cry for help goes seaward, she will find her servants there.
>   Battered chain-gangs of the orlop, grizzled drafts of years gone by,
>   To the bench that broke their manhood, they shall lash themselves and die.

The literal description clearly operates as allegory: the galley is British India; "the rollers of the North" refers to the Russian menace; "the niggers [breaking] the hatches" to a native insurrection; the "craven-hearted pilot" to a gutless Government or Viceroy; while the energy of the verb-phrases—"swamped and shattered," "crams her crashing on the shore"—revitalizes the worn old metaphor of the ship of state. In "gay with gore," on the other hand, Kipling yields too easily to the lure of alliteration, and the phrase (together with the exuberant rhythm) suggests not anything as sinister as a lust for blood, but a kind of schoolboy relish for the disaster quite at variance with the mood he is seeking to establish. Then the image of the niggers breaking the hatches is an extraordinary one to come from the pen of an imperialist. One can hardly assume that Kipling is being uncharacteristically cynical (on the literal level about slave-trading, on the allegorical, about the relationship of governors and governed), or that this is a momentary recognition of a half-truth about Empire, which he would normally repudiate. It seems to be mere careless writing, and the discrepancy between vehicle and tenor in his metaphor becomes still more marked in the next stanza. The basic idea—that men who have served India will return to her in her hour of need—is unexceptionable, but the notion of ex-*slaves* coming to the rescue offends our sense of probability, while we cannot help being conscious of the sheer impossibility of their knowing about the galley's plight. (Kipling would have been better advised to forgo the rhetorical flourish of the first line, and to allow the galley its distress signals.) This lack of correspondence between the two levels of meaning occurs elsewhere in the poem: "the mutter of the dying never spoiled the lover's kiss" may have been true of Simla and the Plains, but it is ludicrously inapplicable to conditions in a galley; "the bench that broke their manhood" is applicable to the galley but not to service in India. The Empire may be said to have taken her servants' manhood, but hardly to have broken it, and the element of distorting over-statement in the phrase appears again in the references to brands, galls, welts, and scars: even allowing for the dangers and discomforts of life in India, these seem exaggerated, inappropriate symbols for the marks it leaves on men. There is no need, however, to mutter darkly about Kipling's neurotic hunger for cruelty, for the lack of imaginative realization makes these images as innocuous as the shootings in a boy's adventure story. When he wrote of galley-slaves with full imaginative awareness, the effect is very different: in "The Song of the Galley-Slaves" (from "The Finest Story in the World") the harsh vivid detail, the irregular yet monotonous rhythms, and the reiterated cry of protest which forms the refrain, all help to make the rowers' lot disturbingly present to our imaginations. "The Galley-Slave," by contrast, is hardly about galley-slaves at all, and one's criticism must be directed at the impropriety of Kipling's choice of basic metaphor, and the ineptitude with which it is exploited.

In spite of this failure, however, Kipling's mind worked habitually in metaphoric modes. (It is not really surprising to find that he admired the "high and disposed allegory" of Phineas Fletcher's *Purple Island*.) One of the most telling rhetorical devices in "The Islanders" is his use of polemical puns, based on a perception of latent metaphor, to intensify the irony of his questions about enemy invasion:

> Arid, aloof, incurious, unthinking, unthanking, gelt,
> Will ye loose your schools to flout them till their brow-beat columns melt?
> Will ye pray them, or preach them, or print them, or ballot them
> > back from your shore?
> Will your workmen issue a mandate to bid them strike no more?

While in poems like "The Dykes" (which is more strictly comparable with "The Galley-Slave") he succeeds in elaborating a descriptive narrative vividly compelling in itself, but embodying throughout an insistent and precise allegorical significance. Still better is the artistry of "Rimmon," where he abandons the fatal facility of the fourteener ("a craft that will almost sail herself," he calls it in one revealing aside) for a ballad stanza which imposes stricter formal limits. These help to concentrate his indignation at the Old Guard's reluctance to embark on major army reforms after the Boer War—his disgust at their reassertion of the peace-time *status quo*:

> Duly with knees that feign to quake—
> > Bent head and shaded brow—
> Yet once again, for my father's sake,
> > In Rimmon's house I bow.
>
> The curtains part, the trumpet blares,
> > And the eunuchs howl aloud;
> And the gilt, swag-bellied idol glares
> > Insolent over the crowd.
>
> *'This is Rimmon. Lord of the Earth—*
> > *Fear him and bow the knee!'*
> And I watch my comrades hide their mirth
> > That rode to the wars with me.
>
> For we remember the sun and the sand
> > And the rocks whereon we trod,
> Ere we came to a scorched and a scornful land
> > That did not know our God;

> As we remember the sacrifice,
>   Dead men an hundred laid;
> Slain while they served His mysteries,
>   And that He would not aid. . . .

Kipling's Biblical analogies, often misused, are justified in this case by their precision, for the poem's ironic force resides not merely in the diminishing comparisons which he goes on to develop, but in the detailed correspondences between the Old Testament-based narrative and contemporary reality; while there is a peculiar piquancy about the lines where he allows the two levels to merge (in the description, for example, of the uncleanly image girded about the loins "with scarlet and gold"—these being the colours of peace-time ceremonial).

A final example of high seriousness successfully achieved, of political ideas poetically rendered, is provided by "The Settler," which was first published in *The Times* on 27 February 1903, with an epigraph from a speech delivered by Joseph Chamberlain in Cape Town a few days before:

> I leave this shore more convinced than ever that the forces—the natural forces—that are drawing you together are more potent than those evil influences which would tend to separate you. . . . Above all, South Africa needs the best capacities of all its children.

The poem echoes and re-emphasizes Chamberlain's views on the need for reconciliation between Boer and Briton, yet this detracts in no way from Kipling's fully personal apprehension of war's sterile destructiveness, as opposed to the fruitful labours of peace:

> Here, where my fresh-turned furrows run,
>   And the deep soil glistens red,
> I will repair the wrong that was done
>   To the living and the dead.
> Here, where the senseless bullet fell,
>   And the barren shrapnel burst,
> I will plant a tree, I will dig a well,
>   Against the heat and the thirst.

Here, as in the soldier ballads, he speaks through an assumed persona, but one less particularized in terms of social status, one less restricted in vocabulary and insight. In this stanza the Peace–War, Life–Death antitheses issue in vivid metaphoric terms: the earth "glistens red" in literal truth as the ploughshare turns up the wet rich soil, but the words also remind us that it has been soaked with blood; and this interplay between the two levels of meaning is continued in lines where elements of practical farming ("I will plant a tree, I will dig a well") are also profoundly symbolic actions. Pervasive too is the contrast between the recent conflict of race against race and the "holy wars" now to be undertaken against natural forces destructive of fertility: the transformation the poem pleads for is epitomized in the fine conception of turning to irrigation purposes the river-lines once so fiercely defended by the Boers, and the water-holes at which British detachments had sought to ambush wandering commandos. The idea which Kipling goes on to propound, of South Africa as a granary of Empire, cannot move us as it did his original readers, but the corn-imagery is potent in its more permanent associations with the natural cycle of life, growth, fertility, rebirth:

> Earth, where we rode to slay or be slain,
>   Our love shall redeem unto life;
> We will gather and lead to her lips again
>   The waters of ancient strife,
> From the far and the fiercely guarded streams
>   And the pools where we lay in wait,
> Till the corn cover our evil dreams
>   And the young corn our hate. . . .
>
> Here, in the waves and the troughs of the plains,
>   Where the healing stillness lies,
> And the vast, benignant sky restrains
>   And the long days make wise—
> Bless to our use the rain and the sun
>   And the blind seed in its bed,
> That we may repair the wrong that was done
>   To the living and the dead!

Needless to say, South Africa's subsequent history casts an ironic shadow over this poem. Few now can see that unhappy country as "a large and sunlit land where no wrong bites to the bone," and Kipling himself noted bitterly in later years that after the war the Boers had been put "in a position to uphold and expand their primitive lust for racial domination." He could not have been expected to foresee that the partnership of white races which he advocated in 1903 would be finally achieved under Boer hegemony, in the interests of just such a policy. Like so many of his poems, "The Settler" is the product of a single historical moment and partakes of that moment's limitations. Yet written as it was at the end of a savage racial war, it shows a generosity to the defeated enemy and an understanding of the nature of war itself, which compel a respect not always accorded to Kipling—a respect fully warranted by his combination here of humane wisdom and poetic power.

It is a useful reminder that political and moral insights, like artistic excellence, are the prerogative of no one system of ideas; that the poetry of imperialism is not, therefore, a contradiction in terms; and that Kipling, in spite of lapses into prejudice, doggerel, or bombast, provides some of the most remarkable examples in the last hundred years of the transmutation of politics into enduring art.

Notes

1. Boris Ford, "A Case for Kipling?" *Scrutiny*, xi (1942), 24, 32.

2. Morton Cohen ed., *Rudyard Kipling to Rider Haggard*, London, 1965, pp. 33–34.

3. T. S. Eliot's well-known anthology, *A Choice of Kipling's Verse*, follows the arrangement of poems in the "Definitive Edition," and partakes therefore of its defects.

4. While it is true that marching songs need a succession of verses as well as a good chorus, the metrical banality of the three long stanzas which he added in the collected edition blurs our pleasure in the verse-pattern of the original. Kipling's deliberate expansion of chapter headings and other verse fragments was seldom felicitous.

5. *On Poetry and Poets*, London, 1957, p. 228.

6. *The Liberal Imagination*, London, 1951, p. 184.

7. *Image and Experience*, London, 1960, p. 40. Cf. Bonamy Dobrée, *The Broken Cistern*, London, 1954, pp. 1–7, 144–6.

8. *Something of Myself* (Uniform Edn.), London, 1937, pp. 150, 218.

9. Ibid., p. 89.

10. "My First Book," *The Works of Rudyard Kipling*, Sussex Edn., London, 1938, xxx. 6.

11. *The Journals of Arnold Bennett*, ed. Newman Flower, London, 1932, i. 81.

12. Morton Cohen, op cit., p. 102.

13. *Something of Myself*, pp. 205–6, 72–73.

14. *The Oxford Book of Modern Verse*, Oxford, 1936, pp. ix–xii.

15. *Eight Modern Writers*, Oxford, 1963, p. 293.

16. *They Asked for a Paper*, London, 1962, pp. 90–92.

17. *Works*, Sussex Edn., xxx. 4.

18. Cf. "Georgie Porgie," *Life's Handicap:* "When the Government said that the Queen's Law must carry up to Bhamo and the Chinese border the order was given, and some men whose desire was to be ever a little in advance of the rush of Respectability flocked forward with the troops.... The Supreme Government stepped in as soon as might be, with codes and regulations, and all but reduced New Burma to the dead Indian level; but there was a short time during which strong men were necessary and ploughed a field for themselves."

19. "In the Matter of a Private," *Soldiers Three and Other Stories.*

20. Critics who have wondered whether the verses would in fact appeal to "ordinary soldiers" seem never to have tested their hypotheses in barrack-rooms or sergeants' messes. A contemporary statement, by a more than usually articulate Medical Corps orderly, appeared in the *Cape Times* in January 1898. The poetry may be execrable, but the sentiments are unambiguous:

"... you're *our* partic'lar author, you're our patron an' our friend,
You're the poet of the cuss-word an' the swear,
You're the poet of the people, where the red-mapped lands extend,
You're the poet of the jungle an' the lair,
　　An' compare
To the ever-speaking voice of everywhere. ..."
　　　　(Margaret Lane, *Edgar Wallace*, London, 1938, p. 98).

21. *Something of Myself*, pp. 79–81; Charles Carrington, *Rudyard Kipling: His Life and Work*, London, 1955, pp. 352 et seq.

22. A similar pattern can be observed in "The Grave of the Hundred Head," where in-

stead of a proletarian narrator a native protagonist, the savagely loyal subadar, serves to disarm moral criticism, enabling readers to relish (anthropologically, as it were) a revenge massacre which they could hardly have condoned if it had been ordered by a British officer.

23. *Rudyard Kipling: A Criticism*, London, 1900, p. 32.

Kipling's Magic Art   Jacqueline S. Bratton[*]

In "The Song of the Banjo" Kipling gives that instrument a voice, and it speaks of

> ... tunes that mean so much to you alone—
> Common tunes that make you choke and blow your nose—
> Vulgar tunes that bring the laugh that brings the groan—
> I can rip your very heartstrings out with those.[1]

The poet admired the banjo, and respected its power. It spoke, he claimed, with the wisdom of the centuries; and much of his own poetry is set to its tunes. They are an embarrassment to his critics. The first Chatterton lecturer on Kipling, Professor Andrew Rutherford, bravely avowed his boyish pleasure in some of the "simple, unsophisticated" poems; less confident critics have approached Kipling with elaborate caution, for fear of the banjo tunes: only "the good Kipling" is respectable reading for the critically mature.[2] But it is not stories like "Mary Postgate" that contain, it seems to me, the kernel of Kipling's art; rather it is the vulgar ditties, laden, like the potent cheap tunes which are interwoven with our lives, with quite illegitimate emotional power. If one is to understand his art and his aims, it must be through an understanding of the uncritical, emotional responses which he deliberately sought to call up.

Just as the banjo tunes are charged with emotions which belong to the situations they recall, rather than to their independent power, so many of Kipling's verses are inextricably embedded in frameworks of circumstance which add to their significance. Each framework is personal, and "means so much to you alone"; but it is also public, and forms a bond with those to whom, we discover, it is also significant. The voice of the Radio Uncle who read the *Just So Stories* to me has a special place in the hearts of thousands of others of my generation. It is not simply that many of Kipling's pieces belong to that adolescent world where we are always reading things for the first time, and so linking them emotionally with whatever mountain, hill, or stream was first illuminated for us by their visionary gleam; rather that the verses appeal on a primitive poetic level, at

[*]From the *Proceedings of the British Academy* 64 (1978):209–232. Reprinted by permission of the British Academy. The essay was read 18 October 1978 as a Chatterton Lecture on an English Poet.

which each poem's delivery, its circumstances, purposes, and concomitant rituals are as important as its content. Kipling deliberately sought in much of his poetry to evoke this aspect of the enjoyment of verse—its connection, as he felt, with other aspects of life. Poetically used words were his tools for intensifying and dignifying the emotional experience of everyday life, and leaving each of his readers to return to his own life with a new idea of its importance and its shape.

This is, as T. S. Eliot pointed out, a magical conception of the use of art.[3] Eliot cited R. G. Collingwood's definition: "A magical art is an art which is representative and therefore evocative of emotion, and evokes of set purpose some emotions rather than others to discharge them into the affairs of practical life." Collingwood further defined the effect of magic as "the exact opposite of a catharsis" intended to "develop and conserve morale" because the "emotions aroused by magical acts are not discharged by those acts."[4] He gave Kipling's art as an instance, and added further generic examples: all military music, hymnody, and those poems in which the subject-matter is propaganda and is held to be more important than the manner of writing. T. S. Eliot did not feel that this notion of art was sufficient to cover all aspects of Kipling's work; and some of the corollaries which Collingwood offers as consequent upon the definition do not relate to Kipling's methods and achievements. Collingwood was of the opinion that magic could only become "true art" in the hands of an artificer by whom the artistic and the magical motives, the interest in perfecting the creation itself, and in its emotional effectiveness for a particular task, were not felt to be distinct, and that this state of mind has been impossible since the Middle Ages. But to present Kipling, the craft-obsessive mason and maker of tribal lays, as a post-medieval magical writer to whom the "goodness or badness" of a poem "has little, if any, connexion with its efficacy in its own proper work" is to miss the point of his magic. I would like to examine, therefore, the magical methods, as well as the magical motives, of Kipling's verses, and attempt to explore his verse and his ideas about it by means of the notion of the magical power of words.

Kipling himself did not say much about the springs of art; what ideas he did articulate have been felt to be inadequate to the analysis of his stories, especially the later, denser examples; but they chime well with a magical view of his verse. In *Something of Myself*[5] he speaks throughout of his sense that his artistic life was controlled from outside; he begins by "ascribing all good fortune to Allah the Dispenser of Events" and later attributes all good work to "the peremptory motions of my Daemon," which caused him to produce stories so nearly vicariously, as it were, that when he looked at them and at his success, he felt "'Lord ha' mercy on me, this is none of I.'" In the course of some few stories and poems he elaborates upon this idea: the best-known example is "Wireless,"[6] the story in which a consumptive chemist's assistant, of most homely and modern aspect, becomes, when drugged, a receiver through some accidental cosmic sympathy for certain lines of Keats which are drifting about the ether struggling to get themselves expressed. Through the juxtaposition with experiments with wireless Kipling implies that poetry is like radio, "the Power—our unknown Power—kicking and fighting to be let loose . . . There she goes—kick—kick—kick into space." The magic, it seems, rests in the words themselves, and has in this case very little to do with the poet and his personality or motives. It is a version of the inspirational theory of poetry, as Kipling's choice of a Romantic poet indicates and the narrator's pronouncement later in the story underlines: he says (in the slightly pontificating tone that many of Kipling's literary narrators adopt) that we must "Remember that in all the millions permitted there are no more than five—five little lines—of which one can say: "'These are the pure Magic. These are the clear Vision.'" They are, you will recall, the fragment of Keats the chemist is struggling to get right:

> Charm'd magic casements, opening on the foam
> Of perilous seas, in faery lands forlorn

and a snatch of "Kubla Khan":

> A savage place! as holy and enchanted
> As e'er beneath a waning moon was haunted
> By woman wailing for her demon-lover.

They are quintessential Romantic lines, appealing to the supernatural as a source of creativity.

In verses about the creative process Kipling offers a variation on Romance as the root and object of poetry. It becomes "the Boy-god" who inspires engineers driving steam-trains as he inspired cavemen tipping arrow heads and sailors trimming sails, all of them looking back the while and mourning his passing; it is the identity of purpose that unites a cockney singer with 'Omer smiting his blooming lyre and which conversely set apart Ung the artist and his father from their clients who cannot see the pictures waiting to be made.[7] It is a man's appeal to some force outside himself, to vision, history, and idealism. One notices that the extension of the idea immediately takes in not only other arts, but also activities which are not artistic in their nature—Kipling perceives a continuum of human activities which all have their own versions of the combination of inspiration and craftsmanship. Everything from civil administration to cooking is a magical gift, and its possessor is dignified and justified by his painstaking practice of it. The writer, then, is gifted with words; they are the Magic; his is the obligation to work it.

Collingwood specifies in his definition of the magical artist that it is important for his artifact to be representational: since it is created not for its intrinsic beauty, but for the emotional effect it will have, the only vital requirement for success is that its meaning and purpose should be clearly articulated.[8] At first blush this seems to fit much of Kipling's verse. It is often said that his poems are simpler than his stories, and have fewer levels of meaning; that they can be taken in at first reading and offer no further reverberations or complexities. This, indeed, was the basis of that critical view of his work which dismissed the verse as good bad poetry or not poetry at all but mere balladeering.[9] But it is not what Kipling understood by the magical power of verse. He did indeed intend to write for those who would use his verses "to develop and conserve morale," to raise their emotions to be discharged in action; but he sought, therefore, for ways of using words not simply, to deliver a message to the greatest number of active persons, but covertly, obliquely, magically, as a charm, to put spells on them. They listened to the story he told, and responded not to its superficial meaning alone, but to its tone. The effect of words lay for him in their irrational potency; and in shaping the obvious and simple phrase, understood by all, to the tune that would work on the hearer of an irrational level.

Kipling's way of working on verse confirms the primacy in the imaginative process of the inarticulate pattern: he would take up a tune, picking it out of the air or asking another person for a suggestion, and work the works out of himself to its cadences, which he would alter as he worked to suit his purpose. The selection of the patterning tune would be at random not, I think, because it was irrelevant, as some critics have implied,[10] but because it was the *donnée*, the Daemon-given element—the most important element of all. To see the connections between the original poem and Kipling's one must consider their irrational levels. Sometimes Kipling plays off the tonal and the articulated statements in ironic counterpoint; but more often, more characteristically, the words become incantations whose force is generated chiefly by their stress, their repetition, and tonal values they acquire. In *Captains Courageous* there is a scene in which the uses of song are made plain.[11] The boy Harvey, who is being educated by his contact with the simple working life, listens to a fo'c'sle sing-song. After a ballad with "an old-fashioned creaky tune" and a beautiful chorus which "made Harvey almost weep, though he could not tell why," the black Scottish cook sings, and the effect is "much worse . . . he struck into a tune that was like something very bad but sure to happen whatever you did. After a little he sang, in an unknown tongue . . . the tune crooned and moaned on, like lee surf in a blind fog, until it ended with a wail." It is, he says, the song of Fin M'Coul. They are overwhelmed. Then the ship's boy sings, and is reproved for approaching in his song taboo words, the last verse being "a Jonah." Suddenly the black Celt is moved to prophecy and second sight. A complex of magical notions surrounds the singing of sailors' songs; they are potent words, influencing the success of the trip as well as the spirits of the crew, and equally potent when only their tune is understood.

The appropriateness of this apparently very primitive version of the poetic use of words to Kipling's chosen audiences need not be laboured. Moved by his Daemon and by his convictions to address poetry to those ignorant of its sophisticated languages, to children, for example, and to soldiers, he was obliged to rely heavily upon the understanding which can be derived from comprehending only the tone of voice in which the language is spoken. In exploring the magical qualities of Kipling's verse I shall accordingly begin with the verses in which this restriction is most powerful, his poems for or about "the people," the soldier songs with their reliance upon popular forms, and his writing for children or adolescents, where he resorts to a use of words inspired by childish story-telling and play. The techniques developed in these special writings were carried over into the "mixed form" of stories and poems which marks the apex of his achievement, and they became tools for subtle and complex purposes.

There are several stories which hinge upon the irrational power of words used by popular singers or by children. "The Village that Voted the Earth was Flat"[12] is based upon the premise that a song, conceived and delivered in the music hall, could affect all England profoundly and one village permanently. The punishment of universal derision is visited upon the cruel and greedy village through the power of illusion: in a fake crusade they are persuaded to vote that the earth is flat; and then it is driven home by the song that is made about them. This ditty, deliberately banal, and deteriorating into guttural belches and delirious howls, is composed in Kipling's own manner, by modelling upon an existing song, "'Nuts in May' with variations"; but its power is compulsive, even frightening. It is launched in music hall and cinema, and then "the thing roared and pulverised and swept beyond eyesight all by itself—all by itself" until it finally prostrates the House of Commons:

> Then, without distinction of Party, fear of constituents, desire for office, or hope of emolument, the House sang at the tops and at the bottoms of their voices, swaying their stale bodies and epileptically beating with their swelled feet. They sang "The Village that voted the *Earth* was flat": first, because they wanted to, and secondly—which is the terror of that song—because they could not stop.

There is an instance of words chanted and sung to precipitate action amongst another, perhaps less rational group, Stalky and Co's schoolmates, in "The United Idolaters."[13] They delight in words: "As the Studies brought back brackets and pictures for their walls, so did they bring back odds and ends of speech—theatre, opera, and music-hall gags—from the great holiday world." These fragments act as jokes, and also talismanically, the possession and use of jargon being, for Kipling especially, a sign of the potent inner ring. In this story a craze for *Uncle Remus* sweeps the school, and nonsense chants pass from boy to boy. Eventually the stirring effect of the words issues in action, rival quasi-religious allegiances grow up, some supporting Brer Terrapin and others the Tar Baby, and "House by House, when the news spread, dropped its doings, and followed the Mysteries—not with song . . . Some say . . . that the introits of the respective creeds ('Ingle—go—jang'—'Ti—yi—Tungalee!') carried in themselves the seeds of dissent." Battle ensues, and as a result of the destructive orgy, exhilarating and cathartic to the boys, a practical purgation follows: a misfit temporary master, who does not understand the Coll., is forced to leave.

Kipling's version of effective poetry for the people, rather than for literary critics, has many sources. The most obvious is the London music hall. Kipling's acquaintance with the halls, in so far as it influenced his writing, seems to have been brief but intense. In the autumn of 1889 he moved to lodgings in Villiers Street, and plunged into the life of the metropolis. Already a sought-after new writer, he held himself aloof from literary circles, and deliberately sought to know England at the level of the streets. In *Something of Myself* he recorded the three-month involvement with the music hall opposite his lodgings, Gatti's-under-the-Arches, where he "listened to the observed and compelling songs of the Lion and Mammoth Comiques, and the shriller strains—but equally 'observed' —of the Bessies and Bellas." The experience of "the smoke, the roar, and the good-fellowship of relaxed humanity at Gatti's 'set' the scheme for a certain sort of song."[14] The songs were the *Barrack-room Ballads*, based on his observation of soldiers in India and of the Guardsmen who frequented Gatti's, and filtered through the attitudes of the "elderly but upright bar-maid" he took with him to the hall. In "My Great and Only,"[15] which is more contemporary evidence of these events, since it was one of the sketches he sent back to his Indian newspaper from his English visit, he expatiated more fully on his exploration of "the diversions of heathendom" as exemplified by the London music hall. In his sketch he claimed to have written a music-hall song, and to have had it performed with great success by a Comique singer. There are various unlikely or discrepant details in both these accounts. He does not say, for instance, how a barmaid came to have free time to accompany him regularly to evening performances in the music hall; and while he apparently gives convincing detail of his meeting the singer, through advertisements for songs in the theatrical press, it is not explained how the man came to be performing, at that moment, at Gatti's. If the writing and performance of Kipling's music-hall song is a fiction, however, it is only the more interesting; for the story is in that case a fantasy of success in a kind, one may presume, that he coveted for himself, at a period when literary recognition was coming to him very freely already.

Kipling clearly knew much about the hall. Many details of "My Great and Only" fit exactly with the events of Gatti's in these months. It seems very likely that there was, as he claims, a singer with whom he became friendly. They were friendly people, and susceptible to admiration and cigars. It may have been Leo Dryden, who was the singer who delivered the song that in the sketch Kipling says was a rival to his own composition. It was called "Shopmates," a parody of a tragic ballad called "Shipmates," and itself, according to Kipling, "a priceless ballad" of "grim tragedy, lighted with lurid humour." It is more likely that his acquaintance was James Fawn, who appeared at Gatti's on the same bill as Dryden for the week beginning 11 November and stayed after him until the Christmas change of bill on 23 December. Fawn was a versatile comic singer, who began with convivial and character songs—the less "swell" end of the Comique range—and moved on in later years to be an old-fashioned red-nose comic. In these months he was involved in a successful court action to protect his most famous song, "Ask a P'liceman," from performance by another singer in a pantomime. This may have suggested Kipling's ironic remark that he was taught about property rights in songs by the singer he befriended, who stole his from him. The current topic of debate in music-hall circles was the issue of "protected" material, as Kipling mentions in the sketch; he also says there that his song borrowed the chorus of a "protected" piece, which seems to make it less likely that his song was performed freely, as he suggests.

In "My Great and Only" snatches of Kipling's song are given, and another verse from it is introduced, as being sung by Ortheris, at the end of the story "Love o' Women,"[16] where it serves as a last facet in the framing of a grisly incident. It is clearly the forerunner of the *Barrack-room Ballads;* but it is not so clear that Fawn would have sung it. Its resemblance to his songs is more apparent than real. The differences emerge when it is set beside the song which I take to be its inspiration, which Fawn did sing in the autumn of 1889. This was called "The Soldier," and was written by E. W. Rogers and published by R. Maynard in 1890. Rogers was a successful song writer, who worked for Marie Lloyd and George Robey as well as Fawn, producing among other things "The Lambeth Walk." Kipling knew "The Soldier"; he quoted, or rather rewrote, the most significant verse of it in relation to his own piece in "The Army of a Dream," a story published in 1904.[17] "The Soldier" has six verses, and a chorus which varies, as that of Kipling's music-hall song does, with each repetition. Roger's song, however, follows the usual pattern of the music hall character study and takes up a new, unrelated aspect of its subject for each verse. This practice had a practical use, in that a song going badly could be cut or stopped at any point. Kipling had noticed the structure; he says that his song consisted of a chorus plus "four elementary truths." It is clear, though, from the portions given, that its story was one indivisible whole. While the song Fawn sang presented in turn various soldiers from a militiaman to General Gordon, Kipling's tells the story of a guardsman's rejection by an undercook, and his subsequent wooing of a housemaid. It has a punchline ('An' . . . she can't foot the bill') which really only makes sense in relation

to the convention about soldiers' sponging on women which is enunci-
ated in the other song:

> Who is it mashes the country nurse? The soldier!
> Who is it borrows the lady's purse? The soldier!
> Getting it toddles towards the bar
> Orders a drink and a big cigar,
> Hands it back quietly, and says ta! ta! the soldier!

This is the stanza improved upon in "The Army of a Dream."

> 'Oo is it mashes the country nurse?
> The Guardsman!
> 'Oo is it takes the lydy's purse?
> The Guardsman!
> Calls for drink, and a mild cigar,
> Batters a sovereign down on the bar,
> Collars the change and says "Ta-ta!"
> The Guardsman!

The description of the gallery at Gatti's, when he thought they
"would never let go of the long-drawn howl on 'Soldier'" could easily
refer to their response to Fawn singing Roger's song. The piece is a typical music-hall character sketch; it is superficially completely explicit,
simple, and repetitious, while the complexity of the audience's response
to the character presented is accommodated by juxtaposition. The listeners are invited in each verse in turn to recognize a different aspect of the
soldier: his laughable conceit in his ludicrous uniform, his humanity in
enjoying a good tune and a good drink, his culpable unscrupulousness
with women; finally a contrast is made between the despicable fake soldier, the militiaman, and the real one, whom "we must admire." Crosscurrents are added by the mentioning of well-known names, Kassassin,
Roberts. Kipling rejects this broad sweep of reference. His soldier resembles a broadside ballad hero, the protagonist of a drama of pride and passion on a humble level. The refrain he borrowed, "And that's what the girl
told the soldier," suggests the series of innuendoes it no doubt originally
accompanied; but the pattern of the chorus he adds to it owes more to
older popular tradition, and accommodates a much more compressed,
economical, and powerful use of words than in the real song Fawn sang:

> Oh, think o' my song when you're gowin' it strong,
> And your boots are too little to 'old yer,
> And don't try for things that are out of your reach,
> And that's what the Girl told the Soldier,
> Soldier! Soldier!
> *That's what the girl told the soldier.*

The whole piece, pulled together by the repetition of descriptive lines in
the first and last verses which no music-hall writer could have pro-

duced—"At the back o' the Knightsbridge Barricks / When the fog's a-gatherin' dim"—has an art which far outstrips E. W. Rogers.

What Kipling really admired, I feel, was not the songs, though he repeatedly said they were "works of art,"[18] but their presentation, and their audiences' response. Their effect upon the people was magical; its potential at a time when poetry seemed to be shrinking in upon itself and appealing to fewer and fewer readers, was unlimited. At the end of "My Great and Only" he invoked the "mighty intellect" who would one day "rise up from Bermondsey, Battersea, or Bow ... coarse, but clear-sighted, hard but infinitely and tenderly humorous, speaking the People's tongue ... and telling them in swinging, urging, ringing verse what it is that their inarticulate lips would express." Here, and again in "The Village that Voted the Earth was Flat," he described the triumphant reception of the potent song. As the Comique began, the poet clutched his pot of beer, and hoped for the presence of heavy-booted guardsmen. At the first verse he fancied he "could catch a responsive hoof-beat in the gallery ... Then came the chorus and the borrowed refrain. It took—it went home with a crisp click." They joined in the chorus, with a howl, and were "hooked ... With each verse the chorus grew louder"; and at the final repetition, "as a wave gathers to the curl-over, singer and sung-to filled their chests and hove the chorus, through the quivering roof—horns and basses drowned and lost in the flood—to the beach-like boom of beating feet." The potent animality of the images is very noticeable.

The song in "The Village that Voted the Earth was Flat" is sung by a woman clearly modelled on Nellie Farren, whom Kipling saw in burlesque at the Gaiety, and admired for her boyish charm, but also, it seems clear, for the devotion which she inspired in the gallery boys:[19]

> She swept into that song with the full orchestra. It devastated the habitable earth for the next six months. Imagine, then, what its rage and pulse must have been at the incandescent hour of its birth! She only gave the chorus once. At the end of the second verse, "Are you *with* me, boys?" she cried, and the house tore it clean away from her ... It was delirium. Then she picked up the Gubby dancers and led them in a clattering improvised lockstep thrice round the stage till her last kick sent her diamond-hilted shoe catherine-wheeling to the electrolier. I saw the forest of hands raised to catch it, heard the roaring and stamping pass through hurricanes to full typhoon; heard the song, pinned down by the faithful double-basses as the bull-dog pins down the bellowing bull, overbear even those; till at last the curtain fell ... Still the song, through all those whitewashed walls, shook the reinforced concrete of the Trefoil as steam pile-drivers shake the flanks of a dock.

Notice the insistence upon sub-human, but immensely powerful, expression. The power with words to move masses of people to physical demonstration was the art Kipling wished to learn from the music hall.

A further important aspect of that magic is also contained in these scenes. The worker of the spell is the performer; the writer feels his power in private, safe even from the awareness of his existence amongst those whom he moves. 'Dal, the woman singer, is vulnerable, being as overwhelmed in emotion as her audience, and can only whisper her gratitude huskily; but Kipling, safe in the knowledge that "They do not call for authors on these occasions" felt that whatever joy might be sent him, the success of his music-hall song gave him perfect felicity, an utter happiness which fame greater than Shakespeare's could not surpass. As the lines of the song mutated in the instant oral tradition of the drunken music-hall audience under his window that night, he murmured to himself, "'I have found my Destiny.'" If none of it really happened, such an invention is even more striking than the recording of feeling supercharged by the heat of the moment. The desire for self-effacement has often been observed in Kipling's poems: it is, of course, the whole burden of his epitaph; and it issued first in conjunction with the desire to express and call out strong emotion, in the character-song formula of the *Barrack-room Ballads*. The occasion on which he actually attained the sort of overwhelming success which he describes so ecstatically here was to come later, with "The Absent-Minded Beggar." He certainly enjoyed the popularity which the song (and pockets full of tobacco) gave him with the troops in South Africa, but he hardly felt the piece was his own. He gave its profits to the fund for the troops, and for some time he left it out of his collected verse; the remark that he would shoot the man who wrote it, if it were not suicide, is often taken to mean that he was ashamed of its "elements of direct appeal," its open sentimentality, and backhanded aggressiveness.[20] I think it more likely that it is a rather coy reference to his disowning of the song, coupled with the ambivalence he always shows towards great popular success. There is a tantalizing mystery for him in the compulsive tune which thrusts itself on the attention long after conscious critical faculties have rejected it in wearied revulsion. In "The Absent-Minded Beggar" he created that self-activating artifact, and in reality, as in the fantasy of "My Great and Only," "Builded better than he knew." His disclaimer has the same force as the last line of the earlier piece, which dismisses his success: "and the same, they say, is a Vulgarity!"

The *Barrack-room Ballads*, however, have more about them than that. In them the music-hall strain is tonally dominant; but like all his ballads, they draw formal and verbal elements from many other kinds of popular poetry. Poets of the people, in 1889, wrote not only for the halls, but also for the newspapers and magazines and the drawing-room; for the schoolchild and reciter, as well as for the variety artist. Kipling felt their verse too partook of the magical, in that it affected large audiences of unliterary persons, and evoked emotion closely concerned with action, issuing in practical results within the communities for which it was written. In *Captains Courageous* the fishing community, gathered together for its memorial day, is moved by a recitation by an "actress from Philadelphia," whose "wonderful voice took hold of the people by their heartstrings"[21] despite the inferiority of the port of Brixham as she describes it to their own town. The Victorian popular poets drew upon sources of which Kipling too was aware, and to which he could turn directly, in older popular verse: upon folk-song and oral ballads, broad-sides and chapbooks, hymns, and the post-Romantic tradition of narrative verse on patriotic, historical, and nationalistic subjects which was fathered by Scott and Macaulay. A ballad like "Danny Deever" welds together Rossetti's "Sister Helen" and an obscene army song; "The Widow's Party" takes the highly serious ballad of "Edward, Edward," familiar still from the Romantic versions of Percy and Scott, and treats it as a writer for the broadsides or the early music hall would, undercutting it by rendering it in comic cockney. "Snarleyow," under a name from Marryat, couples a stanza shaped like that of a comic ballad by W. S. Gilbert, "Etiquette," for example, with a music-hall chorus of downbeat cynicism, to tell a story George Sims would have made tear-jerking and Kipling makes tragic. The elements of all nineteenth-century ballad making can be traced in the collection, with additions from sources which supply rhythm, without any words at all, like the tramp of feet on a route march or the rather different beat of parade-ground drill. In rendering the character song of Tommy Atkins, inspired by the Indian Army, James Fawn, and the gallery at Gatti's, Kipling brought batteries of verbal magic from many sources to bear upon the model and the audience, and his spell was hugely successful.

The first of the *Barrack-room Ballads* were published by W. E. Henley, in the magazine he wielded as a weapon in his struggle with Aestheticism. Soldierly poems were very much to his purpose. He also edited such poems into "a book of verse for boys," *Lyra Heroica*, in 1892. He thought it the first such collection, but it was anticipated by several popular poets and editors of books of recitations, including Frederick Langbridge who, in the autumn of 1889 as Kipling studied humanity in the streets of London, was editing *Ballads of the Brave: poems of chivalry, enterprise, and constancy*, to be "a good Boys-Poetry-Book." He was in turn inspired by William Cox Bennett, who had aspired to the creation of a history of England in verse, for the inspiration of the working classes and the young, in 1868. These are clearly magical uses of poetry, following Collingwood's definition, intended to inspire emotions to be discharged into the business of life. Kipling was the inheritor of these ambitions, and indeed partook more fully than he would have liked to think of the drive to convert and educate which came down to the late Victorian Empire-builders from their Evangelical parents. Accordingly he felt that children, like uneducated adults, were fit audience for his spell-binding; and just as his music-hall-inspired poems for the soldier drew upon all aspects of nineteenth-century popular poetry, so he brought the resources of a craft much wider than that of the average versifier of history to bear upon the educative task. In 1911 Kipling co-operated with C. R. L. Fletcher in producing a history book with inter-spersed verses; but his best historical / educative poems accompany his own fictional writing for children. In the Mowgli stories, *Kim*, and most clearly in *Puck of Pook's Hill* and *Rewards and Fairies*, one may see the full scope of his mixed form of story and songs, where the verses contribute at levels beyond or below or alongside the rational, augmenting, or modify-ing the pattern of the narrative with magical reinforcements.

In his earlier writing for children the education aimed at was moral, and only in a very general sense historical. He sought, through the stories and verse of *The Jungle Books*,[22] to evoke the child's sense of the possibil-ity of belonging to a society with a character, aims, and organization tran-scending but also protectively encompassing the individual. The Law is set out, and illustrated; dissent of various kinds is voiced, and accommo-dated or suppressed; and emotional acceptance, the internalizing of the sanctions enforcing social control, is encouraged, all through the use of verses beside or within the narratives.

The basic attraction of the Mowgli stories is the transformation of do-mestic realities—mother and father and brothers, and uncles and other adult teachers—by the exotic settings of Mowgli's jungle, which makes both the exotic accessible and safer, and the everyday more exciting and important. The pleasurable juxtaposition begins on the first page: the chapter heading to "Mowgli's Brothers" is a quite alien and exciting sec-tion of something called "Night-song in the Jungle." The verse is high and mysterious, about "the hour of pride and power"; the first sentence of the story is domestic, half-comic, about scratching and yawning and spread-ing out the paws "to get rid of the sleepy feeling in their tips." Wolves are humanized and made familiar; their jungle law, the moral ordering of the universe which accommodates both wolves and little boys, when they obey it, has been mentioned and is to be demonstrated.

The use of incantation and repetition, and of words of power and rit-ual, is pervasive in the stories; Mowgli repeatedly saves himself by the Master-Words of the Jungle, repeated in all the right languages. The Law Baloo teaches is couched in eminently chantable verse, which he, and his pupils real as well as fictional, deliver in "a sort of sing-song," and learn from it their part. Conversely in the story of "Kaa's Hunting" the Bandar-log have their song, expressing the philosophy which leads to their horri-bly ignoble death, and demonstrates their social worthlessness. But the impulse of Mowgli to selfish and careless play, which he must learn is wrong, is shared by the child reader. At the end of the tale, after punish-ment and forgiveness, the story is flipped upwards, indeed almost under-cut, by the addition of the text of the monkeys' song, which delights by its verbal energy, irony, and invention: "Here we sit in a branchy row . . . Then join our leaping lines that scumfish through the pines . . ." It is offered to be enjoyed, and now that we have learned by the story to see through its at-tractions, we can also enjoy our superiority to its enticements.

There is a related effect in "Rikki-Tikki-Tavi," where the vanity and empty-headedness of the taylor-bird are mocked and criticized throughout the story, as he wastes time making a series of premature or unhelpful songs instead of assisting in the fight against the cobras. At the end, though, his chant in honour of Rikki-Tikki-Tavi is given:

> Who hath delivered us, who?
> Tell me his nest and his name.
> Rikki, the valiant, the true,
> Tikki, with eyeballs of flame,
> Rik-tikki-tikki, the ivory-fangèd,
> the hunter with eyeballs of flame.

This combines a joke for the adult reader of the story, in that it is a parody of Swinburne, a good example of the excited poet foolishly singing for the victories of others, with a comic-heroic praising of the mongoose which is very satisfying to the child listener or reader as a contrast to the modesty he shows himself at the end of the tale.

A rather different use of the division between layers of the story which the juxtaposition of narrative and verse can give is the climactic use of "Mowgli's Song," at the end of "Tiger! Tiger!" The tale has demonstrated Mowgli's, the individual's, essential separateness: having learnt the Law of the Jungle, which admits him to the society of the disciplined and truly adult, he has made the painful discovery that others do not keep the Law, and so no ideal community exists; he has gained only his selfhood, and the society of a few equal individuals. Adherence to the Law under this disillusion is the hardest moral lesson to learn, especially where duty is taught entirely, as it is here, in terms of society, without relating it to a superhuman power which offers future justification. Mowgli passes the test, and triumphs over his enemies, and departs laconically at the end of the story into the grown-up world which he has entered through his ordeal. The reader, however, is presumed not to have arrived yet at this transition; and so after the tale, his emotions of angry triumph, and pain and grief for Mowgli's sufferings, are given expression in a verse. "Mowgli's song" is the song of the younger self, the reader; in strange, unrhymed verse "that came up into his throat all by itself" it voices the reader's protest, and asks the unanswerable question as to why the world is so hard, and ends with "My heart is heavy with the things that I do not understand."

The combination of song and story in this way is not pursued in the following books: *Captains Courageous* uses songs integrated with the narrative, as do some stories in *The Day's Work:* "The Brushwood Boy," for example, has a music-hall song sung by the troops and a sort of children's song to the piano used to reveal the possessors of a common dreamworld to each other, suggesting again a magical idea of the sources and powers of poetry. In *Kim* deliberately riddling use is made of snatches of verse for chapter headings: it is not so much that their relevance to the story is obscure, rather that they set the incidents or emotions of the chapters they head into quite other contexts, and deliberately jolt the attention of the reader away from the immediacy of the tale. They stress the fictional nature of the story: it is capable of expression, they suggest, in other terms, the incidents are not uniquely real but related to art and archetypes often expressed differently. They appear to be snatches from longer poems. These were then later completed, but it was important at their first use that they were not recognizable, so that they seize the attention and suggest the existence of other tales unread. Poetry is felt, as in "Wireless," to have a life of its own, only occasionally and intermittently accessible to the reader, through the poet, and for him equally impossible to command, dependent upon the revelations of his Daemon. Their effort upon the story is like that of an epic simile; they relate the aspect of the story which they isolate to other worlds, enlarging and at the same time distancing the narrative, controlling focus and perspective. Their expression in rhythms and vocabulary so remote from those of the story is deliberately unsettling.

In the *Just So Stories*[23] the intercutting of different modes is even stranger; it arose out of the circumstances of oral narration, and is uncomfortable for the reader who has only the printed page. There is a pervasive sense of the private language and the shared joke. This is felt most obviously in the contrasting styles of the stories, which are in a heavily stylized, poetic language, and of the commentary accompanying the pictures, which attempts to reproduce the factual simplicities and unexpected twists of conversation with small children. Responses to questions Kipling's own children asked are incorporated, and attempts are made to extend the shared jokes to other children. In this book the verses, which were completed after the stories, are broadly of two kinds. Some, like the mouth-filling sing-song of Old Man Kangaroo, are poems for children to chant, using words for their amusing qualities of sound. Others take up the implicit relationship between the adult and the child to whom he tells the fantastical tales and bring their domestic life into focus. An example is "When the cabin portholes are dark and green," the vignette from the life of a travelling family which appears at the end of the story of "How the Whale Got its Throat." This domestication of the story by the verse can have a moralizing effect, as in "The Camel's Hump," where the fun of chanting and the relation of the story to the world of the nursery combine to drive home the moral point:

> Kiddies and grown-ups too-oo-oo,
> If we haven't enough to do-oo-oo,
> We get the hump—
> Cameelious hump—
> The hump that is black and blue!

Kipling's affection for his daughter which prompted the book is most openly expressed in the verses; in the intimate and tender poems which he attaches to the stories of Taffimai he combines the expression of his personal feeling with a humour and ingenuity which also please the child reader.[24] These poems move decisively towards the kind of writing for children that he was to develop in the Puck stories. They have the primitive poetic satisfaction of delightful rhymes: "racial talks and such" / "gay shell torques and such," "Broadstonebrook" / "come and look." They extend the world already introduced in their stories, and without the explicitness of narrative they make available a complex of feeling that attaches to that world for Kipling. His sense of the transience of childhood is connected in the poems to the loss of past times, and the child, unable to conceive of either idea herself, is put in touch with both through simple images of the natural world and by the connection which is made to the particular, mortal, but endlessly recurring love of father and daughter.

> There runs a road by Merrow Down—
> A grassy track to-day it is—
> An hour out of Guildford town,
> Above the river Wey it is.
>
> Here, when they heard the horse-bells ring,
> The ancient Britons dressed and rode
> To watch the dark Phoenicians bring
> Their goods along the Western Road . . .
>
> But long and long before that time
> (When bison used to roam on it)
> Did Taffy and her Daddy climb
> That down, and had their home on it . . .
>
> Of all the tribe of Tegumai
> Who cut that figure, none remain,—
> On Merrow Down the cuckoos cry—
> The silence and the sun remain.
>
> But as the faithful years return
> And hearts unwounded sing again,
> Comes Taffy dancing through the fern
> To lead the Surrey spring again.

In these verses one also feels Kipling's ability to convey the sense of history as something real, of which the child reader or listener is a part;[25] but the flowering of this is in *Puck of Pook's Hill*[26] and *Rewards and Fairies*.[27] The former was unequivocally meant for tales told to children, with his own, now old enough to be introduced to less fabulous histories, as its first audience. In *Something of Myself*[28] he wrote of *Rewards and Fairies* as stories which "had to be read by children, before people realised that they were meant for grown-ups" and it is in that volume that he takes the next step in his use of poems, working "the material in three or four over-laid tints and textures," which took the mixed form away from the writing for children which had inspired it to become the major medium of his mature work. The crosscurrents between the poems and the various levels of the stories came to serve as a means of holding together the parts of his audience, and satisfying them at different levels of comprehension, intellectual and emotional. The poems for children had always had this function in some ways. In *Puck of Pook's Hill* he worked to spread the significance of the stories through the various effects of narrative and verse, and so bring home the awareness that history affects everybody's life, and that the child is involved in, and may begin to approach emotionally, processes beyond comprehension on a rational level. With linked verses and tales Kipling impresses the linkedness of all things.

The techniques already developed in writing for children are taken further. The shift of point of view, so that the verse voices the attitude of someone who has been seen only incidentally in the story, is carried over from *The Jungle Books* into the "Pict Song" which concludes the story of "The Winged Hats." It is used with a new seriousness. The awareness that political and imperial struggles, with which the story involves us, are felt quite differently by the subject peoples in the background and underfoot is an important insight, dramatized and made available by the verses. Other juxtapositions have an effect more like the chapter headings in *Kim,* in that the poems, surprising the reader by their difference of tone from the stories they accompany, make him aware of the same set of ideas or circumstances existing in different contexts. An example is the "Smuggler's Song" which concludes "Hal o' the Draft," which not only shifts the focus of our sympathy from Hal and the king's agent to the smugglers they have outwitted, but also makes us perceive the smuggling as outliving the richly Elizabethan setting of the story, and occurring in Georgian times. Hal's recognition of the ballad Dan sings, and his interest in new objects in modern England that he can make use of in his own art, have already made clear a vital continuity of human interests and occupations. It gives life to the history that Dan can't be bothered with when it comes as a lesson.

The humanizing of the lessons of history makes them, of course, less clear cut, and so on other occasions the stories are summed up and their import made more explicit in the verses. At the end of the series of Saxon and Norman stories in *Puck of Pook's Hill* the runes of prophecy on Weland's sword, which have been seen to be fulfilled, are given as a magical verse, and the reader perceives the continuity of the events thus epitomized. The verses are used to simplify or make concrete the message of the story more often in *Rewards and Fairies,* where they are used by Kipling in his effort to make complex stories of adult activities comprehensible to the child reader. "If" is placed as a summary of the qualities needed and exemplified in the political manoeuvres discussed in the American tales, in the midst of which it appears; after "Simple Simon," the layered and elliptical tale of the dedication of Francis Drake, refracted through Cattiwow's struggle to shift the log and Simon's devotion to his friend and his untimely iron ships, the essentials of Drake's character and its making are summed up in a very simple form in "Frankie's Trade," an appropriate sea shanty. The story of St. Wilfrid and his priest and the conversion of the heathen Meon, which handles ideas about faith and allegiance and diplomatic relationships, is simplified but also deepened and affirmed in the verses at the beginning and end. "Eddi's Service" shows Eddi the priest in a more Christian and saintly light than he appears in the story; and "Song of the Red War-boat" voices the heathen's devotion to his leader which is overborne and perhaps subsumed by the Christian's service to his God.

There is a very wide range of form and tone in these poems, reflecting the variety of their functions. Ballads and shanties are appropriate to the settings of some stories, and they are suitable to the purposes of incantation and epitome; in other places the need is for a poem which will elevate or dignify, supplying ritual weight rather than working rhythms to stories which break down "history" into tales of individual lives for the sake of the child's response. In these tales the lesson to be learnt is important in general terms, and its relation to a system of belief and behaviour to which they too owe allegiance needs to be solemnly understood. This is the governing motive of the books: Kipling's belief in history and the importance of place, continuity, and tradition, in moulding people to their destiny and duty. It is expressed in the songs of Puck and Sir Richard, and "A Tree Song," all voicing love for England; in Thorkild's song of love for his native shore; in the dialect verses praising Sussex called "A Three Part Song," and in "A British-Roman Song," rising to the climactic "Children's Song" at the end of *Puck of Pook's Hill,* when Dan and Una and the readers are supposed to find their own voices to add to the songs of praise. Love of country thus approached through history necessarily involves, as in the work of Sir Walter Scott, a sense of mortality, of the loss of past times and the transience of one's own; and "Cities and Thrones and Powers," perhaps the best poem of the earlier volume, captures the poignancy which is so important in the intensity of the emotions involved:

> Cities and Thrones and Powers
> Stand in Time's eye,
> Almost as long as flowers,
> Which daily die:
> But, as new buds put forth
> To glad new men,
> Out of the spent and unconsidered Earth,
> The Cities rise again.

This is placed at the beginning of the long story of Rome's doomed Empire, and is laden with rhythmic suggestion of that fall. But the story begins by shifting the mood abruptly and ironically to a matter-of-fact and homely level: "Dan had come to grief over his Latin." This is a tonal effect developed from the juxtaposition of domestic and exotic in the *Just so Stories;* here it serves both to bring home the relevance of the tale to the reader, and to relieve him of some of the awe and solemnity of the subjects handled by giving a familiar point of reference. A similar effect opens "A Doctor of Medicine," a grim story about the plague with Culpepper as its ironically treated hero; there the opening is a hymn about astrology, set, I think, to the tune of "Immortal, Invisible, God only wise," which depends bathetically to the opening of the tale: "They were playing hide-and-seek with bicycle lamps after tea."

The reverse of this effect is seen when Kipling uses a much more complex poetic form than that of the hymn to add intensity of feeling unavailable to the child reader on an explicit narrative level. The story of the "Marklake Witches," for instance, has overtones which Dan and Una do not grasp. The reader is admitted to some of them with the author's help over the fictional children's heads, but there are levels which only adults familiar with matters of prejudice and ignorance will infer. All the weight of sadness in the tale is, though, conveyed in "The Way Through the Woods," in a poetic image of limitation and loss available to all readers through the sound of the poem:

> They shut the way through the woods
> Seventy years ago.
> Weather and rain have undone it again,
> But now you would never know
> There was once a road through the woods
> Before they planted the trees.
> It is underneath coppice and heath,
> And the thin anemones.
> Only the keeper sees
> That, where the ring-dove broods,
> And the badgers roll at ease,
> There was once a road through the woods.

The shifts between the high and the homely are much more complex than in the earlier books, especially when the group of poems and stories is a long one. *Puck of Pook's Hill* begins with such a series. We have the mysterious "Harp Song of the Danish Women," and then the story descends to the cockleshell boat the children sail in the stream. Their vessel is dignified by their imaginations, until the tale moves, by the teasing contrast made between their scraps of modern science and his medieval hardihood, to Sir Richard's real voyage. It ends in further jokes. Then Thorkild's sea shanty strikes a heroic note, but the ensuing story plunges into corrupt power politics; the whole is resolved by the gnomic runes on

Weland's sword. By the time Kipling had followed this method through to the end of the second book, his loading of the stories with allegories and allusions had rendered the connections quite obscure on a conscious level to any but an inquiring critical eye. "The Tree of Justice" contrives to connect a ballad about poachers and fairies, Old Hobden, the children's dormouse, the keeper's gallows, the mad King Harold and the bitter jester Rahere, thieving gipsies, and an enigmatic carol about the cycles of the world. It is quite possible, however, that the child who had followed and learned by Kipling's method through the two volumes might respond to the final song on a level of intuitive appreciation as acute as any.

For my final point is that Kipling believed in the power of art, and especially of poetry, to influence the imagination beyond the level of consciousness, with a magical, irrational, effect, which he pursues. Throughout these stories literature is used as a link with the past, as one of the most powerful bonds between people, an epitome of tradition and a potent weapon for it. The stories make this explicit, while the poems seek to wield the book itself in that way, to cast its spell upon the reader. An extended example is the first Roman tale, "A Centurion of the Thirtieth." It begins with the potent "Cities and Thrones and Powers," and shifts for its locating, homely note to learning Latin. This is a meaningless chore to Dan at the beginning of the tale; but the *Lays of Ancient Rome* are stimulating, and the game Una plays from them leads to her contact with the ancient Roman Parnesius. He, ironically, has never been taught the history of his own people. He has, however, a living faith, which he expresses in his hymn to Mithras, in Latin which to the children has "deep, splendid-sounding words" (in the story of St. Wilfrid, too, they respond to the tunes of Latin chant, deeply stirred by the *Dies Irae*). The story closes with "A British-Roman Song" in an English metre derived from a classical one, and the next tale, leading straight on, opens with a new Lay of Ancient Rome, a jaunty marching song for the legions whose theme in fact foreshadows the doom of the Empire. Thus the songs within the stories are potent in themselves, incantations and evocations, and learning is done through emotional responses to them, leading to the understanding of them on other levels.

This, then, is what poetry was for Kipling. He used and explored its irrational, magical powers, hoping to intensify and enlighten by directing the most primitive of our responses to words. His ballads, chants, and incantations are not falsely naïve, not a rejection of complexity and subtlety in poetry; rather they are the strong essences of a literary craft most subtle in its methods. To approach the deeper springs of motive and character he used verse, as Dan and Una innocently use the words of *A Midsummer Night's Dream*, conjuring up Puck, who leads them through songs and stories to the possession of their heritage. Kipling's poems conjure up people, who lead his readers to understand others and themselves, and the emotional language that we have in common.

Notes

1. "Song of the Banjo," 1894, quoted from *The Definitive Edition of Rudyard Kipling's Verse* (London, 1940), p. 98.

2. See Andrew Rutherford, "Some Aspects of Kipling's Verse," *The Proceedings of the British Academy,* li (London, 1965), 378; and the discussion of critical attitudes in Elliot L. Gilbert, *The Good Kipling* (Ohio, 1971), pp. 3–13.

3. T. S. Eliot, *A Choice of Kipling's Verse* (London, 1941), Introduction, p. 20, n. 2.

4. R. G. Collingwood, *The Principles of Art* (Oxford, 1938), pp. 66–9.

5. London, 1937, pp. 1, 113, 78.

6. *Traffics and Discoveries,* 1904, Sussex Edition, vol. vii, pp. 215–43.

7. "The King," 1894, *Definitive Edition,* pp. 376–7; "When 'Omer Smote 'Is Bloomin' Lyre," *Definitive Edition,* p. 351; "The Story of Ung," *Definitive Edition,* pp. 345–8.

8. Collingwood, op. cit., pp. 68–9.

9. See, for instance, George Orwell's essay "Rudyard Kipling," 1942, *Collected Essays* ed. S. Orwell and I. Angus, 4 vols. (London, 1968), vol. ii, pp. 184–97, 194, and T. S. Eliot's use of the term "ballad-maker," op. cit., p. 6.

10. See Charles Carrington, *Rudyard Kipling, His Life and Work* (London, 1955), p. 356.

11. *Captains Courageous,* 1897, *Sussex Edition,* vol. xx, 67–74.

12. *A Diversity of Creatures,* 1917, *Sussex Edition,* vol. ix, 163–214.

13. *Debits and Credits,* 1926, but in the *Sussex Edition* included in *Stalky and Co.,* vol. xvii, 193–216.

14. Op. cit., p. 80–1.

15. *The Civil and Military Gazette* (Lahore, Jan. 1890), reprinted in *Abaft the Funnel* (New York, 1909), *Sussex Edition,* vol. xxix, 259–67.

16. *Many Inventions,* 1893, *Sussex Edition,* vol. v, 359–92.

17. *Traffics and Discoveries,* 1904, *Sussex Edition,* vol. vii, 245–305.

18. See his correspondence about the music halls, and especially the song "Ka-foozle-um," published in J. B. Booth, *The Days We Knew* (London, 1943), pp. 29–35. The extant printed version of "Ka-foozle-um" is by S. Oxon, printed in 1865, and is a jocular tale of the wooing of a Turkish maiden by a Jew of whom her father disapproves and whom he eventually murders; its humour is reminiscent of W. S. Gilbert. The tune seems to have been popular with the writers of burlesques. Lewis S. Winstock, in his article "Rudyard Kipling and Army Music," *Kipling Journal,* June 1971, pp. 5–12, mentions that it has now become an obscene song, "The Harlot of Jerusalem," and speculates as to what versions Kipling knew; the apparent nonsense word "ka-foozle-um" seems to have had overtones of brotheldom as early as 1825, when scene seven of *The Life of an Actor,* performed at the Adelphi, took place "Outside of Mrs. Cafooslem's Boarding House."

19. See the account of her following in W. Macqueen-Pope, *Nights of Gladness* (London, 1956), pp. 143–4. They ran as a bodyguard every night by her carriage, and welcomed her back from tours with huge banners emblazoned "The Boys Welcome Their Nellie." The impresario Bat in this story seems to owe something to the Gaiety manager George Edwardes. In a bad poem addressed "To Lyde of the Music Halls" ("A Recantation," *Definitive Edition,* pp. 369–70) about Marie Lloyd, invoking her by the extraordinary title of "Singer to Children!" he again stressed the power and consequent obligations of the popular singer:

> Yet they who use the Word assigned,
> To hearten and make whole,
> Not less than Gods have served mankind,
> Though vultures rend their soul.

20. See *Something of Myself*, pp. 150–1.

21. Op. cit., p. 193.

22. 1894 and 1895; *Sussex Edition*, vol. xii.

23. 1902; *Sussex Edition*, vol. xiii.

24. We have the testimony of several readers, including Rosemary Sutcliff ("Rudyard Kipling," Three Bodley Head Monographs (London, 1968), pp. 95–6) that children are aware of the depth of love expressed in the Taffimai stories.

25. See Rosemary Sutcliff, "Kipling for Children," *Kipling Journal*, Dec. 1965, pp. 25–8: "history is something to do with oneself."

26. 1906; *Sussex Edition*, vol. xiv.

27. 1910; *Sussex Edition*, vol. xv.

28. *Something of Myself*, p. 190.

Epithets and Epitaphs: Rudyard Kipling's Reputation as a Poet   Maurice Hungiville*

In 1919 T. S. Eliot referred to Rudyard Kipling as a "neglected celebrity" and regretted that the minds of contemporary critics were not "sufficiently curious, sufficiently brave" to examine Kipling's poetry.[1] The fact that the examination of Kipling's poetry required inordinate amounts of curiosity and bravery was due to the violent forces which had transformed Kipling's reputation as a poet into a bitter battleground of conflicting political and artistic ideologies.

By 1900 Kipling's readers had divided themselves into two irrevocably hostile camps—the critics and the cultists. The more aggressive camp contained the cultists, whose enthusiasm for Kipling was often as intense as it was extraliterary. The cultists, with a few notable exceptions, were people whose interest in poetry was both incidental and indirect. Their real interests were elsewhere—in politics, religion, business, or sports—and they tended to value poetry only as it sanctioned and solemnized these other interests. Poetry of the sort Kipling wrote served to put the stamp of solemnity on such normally unpoetic pursuits, and the cultists responded with an enthusiasm which they rarely displayed for poets.

One such normally unpoetic pursuit was war, and during World War I the cultists regarded Kipling's poetry as a national resource to be mobilized in the war effort. Kipling, to the cultists who reviewed *The Years*

*From *Tennessee Studies in Literature*, British Literature Issue, ed. Richard M. Kelly and Alison R. Ensor, 20 (1975):138–50. Reprinted by permission of the University of Tennessee Press.

Between in 1919, was "the Roosevelt of Poetry" and a fitting rebuke to the literary slackers who failed to respond to the war effort. W. B. Yeats's insistence that a poet "should keep his mouth shut" was denounced as "drivel," and the example of Kipling was invoked to show that "a poet can be a man of action too."[2]

Some results of the Kipling cultists' activities on behalf of their poet can be seen in the unprecedented public recognition accorded Kipling throughout his lifetime. The Nobel Prize, awarded in 1907, the Gold Medal of the Royal Society, awarded in 1926, and the founding of the Kipling Society in 1925 all attest to the zeal of Kipling's enthusiasts.[3] Yet behind the public honors there was widespread critical contempt for Kipling, and the cultists contributed, albeit indirectly, to this extreme reaction. The cultists, with their uncompromising enthusiasm, were all too often inclined to use Kipling's poetry as a rebuke to other writers of different, less congenial poetry. Kipling's poetry, as his admirers were fond of pointing out, was "masculine," practical, and patriotic in a way that made other, purer poets appear effeminate, impractical, and suspiciously internationalist.

The Kipling cultists and the Kipling critics were essentially in agreement about what they found in Kipling's poetry—imperialism, journalism, didacticism—and they differed only in their attitudes towards these extraneous subjects. The critics, outraged by Kipling's aggressive political poems, seemed to regard Kipling's imperialism as a menace to public health as well as to poetry. Thus the liberal member of Parliament, C. F. Masterman, railed against "the apostles of the new imperialism" and a conception of war "carried out in the spirit of music-hall comedy." Such a spirit of war, it seemed to Masterman, presented an obscene spectacle of "men at the close of the struggle wiping their hands which have successfully gouged out the eyes of their enemies while they hum the latest popular song."[4] In America, where passions still ran high over the Philippine intervention, critics seemed to react even more violently to the infectious imperialism of Kipling's poetry. Michael Monahan, writing in *The Philistine*, vividly described how America, surfeited with Kipling's views, "vomits its rage upon the laureate of slaughter" and rejects at last the "homicidal genius" and his poisonous poetry. "The dear American public," Monahan wrote in 1901, "gagged at last on the blood-bolted gospel of Ruddy Kipling. After so much raw meat, the d.a.p. is now expiating its gluttony by a humble attack of indigestion."[5]

The issues that divided the critics and the cultists remained relatively fixed, and throughout Kipling's lifetime his poetry received only two original and independent reviews. And these, significantly, were not written by professional reviewers, but by his peers, his fellow professional poets. Robert Bridges' observations of Kipling's style and diction were casual comments made in an article reviewing Lane Cooper's concordance to the poetry of Wordsworth. Wordsworth and Kipling, Bridges noted at the outset, were poets of immense differences who shared a common conviction that the moribund poetic diction of their times "was capable of dialectical regeneration." Kipling's use of cockney dialect was motivated, Bridges believed, by a Wordsworthian sense that the linguistic tools at the poet's disposal had been blunted and debased by artificial traditions.

Kipling's dissatisfaction with the decayed diction of his age was, then, a familiar poetic predicament. Wordsworth, Bridges recalled, had attempted to recapture the speech of common people, and, more recently, Synge had questioned whether "before verse can be human again it must learn to be brutal." Kipling's achievement was unique, though, because his "dialectical regeneration" of English diction was combined with a concomitant, distinctly modern regeneration of verse forms. This latter achievement was especially interesting to Bridges, who analyzed Kipling's portrait of Queen Elizabeth in "The Looking Glass" as an example of the poet's extraordinary sensitive orchestration of allusions. Bridges observed, first of all, that the opening line of this poem, "The Queen was in her chamber, and she was middling old," was a variation on the nonsensical nursery rhyme, "The Queen was in her parlour eating bread and honey." The echo of the familiar nursery rhyme and the expression "middling old" had the immediate effect of placing the Queen "down among the homeliest of her subjects." The result of these images and allusions, Bridges explained, was masterful: the variation of the familiar, the clash of discordant imagery and associations combined the heroic and the homely to dramatize "the vain woman's vanity and the tyrant's bad conscience."

The incongruities of imagery in this poem were of a kind that previous critics, conditioned by romantic expectations, had viewed as serious flaws. To Bridges, however, these very incongruities gave the poem a deeper dimension and precipitated a creative conflict of forces. "In spite of these things," Bridges wrote, "the whole has an irresistible force, so that our dislike of the incongruities, if we feel any, is overpowered; and this force, though it may be due to the apparent obstacles, may seem the greater for its victory over them."

Kipling's sensitive orchestration of allusions, evidenced in this and other poems, convinced Bridges that Kipling's poetry, regardless of its unpleasant politics, had much that was instructive to offer the practicing poet. Kipling, Bridges concluded, "has so true a feeling for the value of words and for the right cadences of idiomatic speech and so vast a vocabulary, that his example is generally useful to a generation whose cultured speech rhythms are so slovenly and uncertain."[6]

Robert Bridges' conclusion that Kipling's poetry had something to offer the practicing poet was confirmed in 1919 by another practicing poet of great talent. T. S. Eliot, reviewing *The Years Between* for the *Athenaeum* in an article entitled "Kipling Redivivus," suggested that Kipling was "a laureate without laurels" and a "neglected celebrity." Eliot did not undertake to provide the laurels, but he did, at least, muster the curiosity and bravery to take a fresh and relatively unencumbered look at Kipling's poetry. Eliot insisted that Kipling was no isolated phenomenon; he had antecedents, most obviously Swinburne, and he had methods which had never been sufficiently analyzed. Kipling and Swinburne, Eliot went on to note, were alike in their use of sound. Both, that is, neglected the sound value of music and attempted to employ "the sound value of oratory." Kipling and Swinburne wrote what Eliot called "the poetry of oratory," and their words were music "just as the words of the orator or preacher are music; they persuade, not by reason, but by emphatic sound." "Swinburne and Mr. Kipling," Eliot continued,

> have, like the public speaker, an idea to impose; and they impose it in the public speaker's way, by turning the idea into sound, and iterating the sound. And like the public speaker's their business is not to express, to lay before you, to state, but to propel, to impose on you, the idea. And, like the orator, they are personal, not by revelation, but by throwing themselves in and gesturing the emotion of the moment. The emotion is not "there" simply, solidly independent of the author, of the audience, there and forever like Shakespeare's and Aeschylus's emotions; it is present only as the author is on the platform and compels you to feel it.

In addition to sharing the orator's stratagems, both Kipling and Swinburne were poets of ideas. In Eliot's view, a poet who had ideas, even a few simple ideas such as liberty or empire, was distinctly inferior to that higher order of poets who had larger points of view or "worlds." Shakespeare, Dante, and Villon had "worlds," but Kipling had only ideas, and his poetry consequently appeared "to lack cohesion, to be, frankly, immature."

Kipling's ideas were inadequate, then, and so, it seemed to Eliot, were his manner and his audience. Kipling's manner, characterized by "an abuse of the English Bible," seemed to be hopelessly debased by "its touch of newspapers, of Billy Sunday, and the Revised Version filtered through Rabbi-Zeal of The Land Busy." Above all, the Biblical style seemed to resist any significant modern content. Kipling's audience, the large audience of the orator, was also scorned by Eliot, who preferred "an audience of one hypothetical man who does not exist, and who is the audience of the artist." And yet, in spite of all these specific reservations, Eliot seemed convinced, in a vague and uncertain way, that there was some indefinable greatness in Kipling's poetry. Kipling, Eliot insisted, is not an "artist," but by virtue of an "unconsciousness about him" he is "very nearly a great writer." There was, moreover, "an echo of greatness in his naive appeal to so large an audience as he addresses."[7]

Eliot, as usual, had managed to assert far more than he had demonstrated, and his 1919 review of *The Years Between* was a peculiar combination of asserted praise and documented deficiencies. Eliot, groping for definitions, seemed to sense that Kipling, if not an artist, was, in some sense, great. His readiness to measure Kipling by the standards of Shakespeare, Villon, and Dante certainly attests to the seriousness with which he grappled with Kipling's poetry. Eliot would not attempt to define Kipling's achievement with precision until his 1941 anthology of Kipling's verse,[8] but in 1919 he had already demonstrated a rare curiosity about Kipling's unique achievement.

Kipling's poet-critics, Eliot and Bridges, represented the best, that is the most original, concrete, and authentic responses to Kipling's poetry since Richard Le Gallienne's *Rudyard Kipling: A Criticism* had appeared in 1900. Originality, concreteness, and authenticity were rare qualities amidst the smug certainties of Kipling criticism, and the best critics, like Eliot and Bridges, often distinguished themselves by asking rather than answering significant questions.

Neither the Kipling critics nor the Kipling cultists were inclined to ask questions about Kipling's final volume of poetry, *The Years Between.* In 1919 Kipling was a known quantity, and most reviewers seemed satisfied that his poetry could be adequately reviewed with the platitudes of the past. Aside from T. S. Eliot's review, *The Years Between* stimulated with almost Pavlovian predictability the same stock responses that had been made twenty years earlier. Ronald Macfie, writing in *The Bookman*, praised *The Years Between* in cultist terms as "a virile volume,"[9] and the critics likewise made the familiar political objections. J. C. Squire, writing under the pseudonym Solomon Eagle, could recommend Kipling's "opinionative songs" only "to a man who thoroughly shares Mr. Kipling's opinions."[10] The anonymous reviewer of the *Dial* briefly dismissed Kipling as "reaction's most vehement spokesman,"[11] and the *London Times Literary Supplement* merely reminded readers that "the poetry of Kipling has long been anathema with field sports, Imperialism, and public schools."[12]

Yet *The Years Between* was not the standard Kipling product, and it was, in many ways, a dramatic departure from the one-dimensional homiletic poems which were customarily associated with Kipling. The new volume did contain the expected war poetry, but it was, for the first time, a war poetry which found its inspiration in a truly universal world war which had, unlike the Boer War, unified the British people in a great national crisis. The war seemed to provoke in Kipling a larger patriotism which embraced England's allies—and at times all humanity—and led to a more sensitive and specific awareness of menaced values. Kipling, as many critics have observed,[13] always expressed an almost paranoiac sense of anxiety, and his fearful insights almost always translated into angry indictments. In World War I Kipling seemed to have found an event which was at last equal to his anger. The result can be seen in the new breadth and intensity of emotion which seemed to distinguish *The*

Years Between from Kipling's earlier works. Such poems as "The Covenant," "France," "The Choice," and "For All We Have and Are" certainly express far more than the narrow militarism, specialized hatreds, and petulant partisanship which characterized *The Five Nations*. Other poems such as "A Death Bed," "En-dor," "Hyenas," and the Goyaesque "Epitaphs of War" exhibited a grim, new realism. This realism, at times bordering on the morbid, completely avoids the romantic falsifications of war which C. F. Masterman and other critics had condemned in *The Five Nations*. Kipling's references to "our dead" who "twitch and stiffen and slaver and groan / Ere the eyes are set in the head"[14] place him in the forefront of the young war poets who developed a new realistic tradition of war poetry.

In addition to this new realism and the larger, saner patriotism, *The Years Between* reflected a more mature and contemplative poetic mood which Kipling had rarely been able to articulate in his more youthful verse. The new mood is perhaps most evident in "Mesopotamia." This strange poem, written two years after Kipling lost his son in the war, was designed as a protest against the incompetence of the Indian government and the mismanagement of the first Mesopotamian campaign.[15] But because of its intensity of rage and novelty of sentiment, "Mesopotamia" transcends protest and becomes an almost pacifist poem.

Mesopotamia
1917

They shall not return to us, the resolute, the young,
    The eager and whole-hearted whom we gave:
But the men who left them thriftily to die in their own dung,
    Shall they come with years and honour to the grave?

They shall not return to us, the strong men coldly slain
    In sight of help denied from day to day:
But the men who edged their agonies and chid them in their pain,
    Are they too strong and wise to put away?

Our dead shall not return to us while Day and Night divide—
    Never while the bars of sunset hold.
But the idle-minded overlings who quibbled while they died,
    Shall they thrust for high employments as of old?

Shall we only threaten and be angry for an hour?
    When the storm is ended shall we find
How softly but how swiftly they have sidled back to power
    By the favour and contrivance of their kind?

Even while they soothe us, while they promise large amends,
  Even while they make a show of fear,
Do they call upon their debtors, and take counsel with their friends,
  To confirm and re-establish each career?

Their lives cannot repay us—their death could not undo—
  The shame that they have laid upon our race.
But the slothfulness that wasted and the arrogance that slew,
  Shall we leave it unabated in its place?

Although *The Years Between* reflected profound and dramatic changes in both the poet and the nation, most critics remained in essential agreement that Kipling was a force to be resisted and that his poetry, above all, should be scorned. Over four decades of Kipling criticism had been, with a few notable exceptions, designed to discount and discredit Kipling's reputation as a poet. The success of these hostile Kipling critics was at no time more evident than at Kipling's death in 1936. When Kipling had lain gravely ill in New York in the winter of 1899, the whole world seemed poised in anguish and anxiety while his doctors issued hourly bulletins to the huge crowds which gathered outside his hotel.[16] Now thirty-seven years after his alarming illness, Kipling's death caused scarcely a ripple in literary circles.

Few were surprised at Kipling's death, for Kipling, the poetry he wrote, and the world he had celebrated had long ago been buried beneath decades of critical contempt. Edmund Wilson had written in 1932 that Kipling "was as much a part of a definite period that came to an end with the war as Theodore Roosevelt was, and he did not, as did Roosevelt, die appropriately when it was over."[17] As early as 1924, Philip Guedalla had already undertaken to embalm Kipling in Stracheyesque irony. Kipling, Guedalla wrote, seemed "to belong to an age of fabulous antiquity. His flag, his Queen, his soldiers, are the vague figures of a mythology that is rapidly fading into folklore." Kipling's subjects had passed into deserved oblivion, and, for most critics, there was nothing in his poetry to redeem him. His widely touted contributions to poetic diction failed to impress Guedalla as they had impressed Bridges, and Guedalla, concluding with a final *bon mot*, wrote that Kipling as a poet "found the English language marble and left it stucco."[18]

Many seemed to sense that Kipling had lived beyond his time, and most of the brief and perfunctory obituary notices reflected the conviction that Kipling's poetry had long been moribund. Indeed several obituary writers, apparently unaware that Kipling had lived and worked for thirty-six years of the new century, eulogized him as a Victorian. William McFee wrote of Kipling's death as one of "the last echoes of the Victorian age,"[19] and Herbert Palmer, praising Kipling as "the father of modern outspokenness," reminded readers that Kipling had used "livid, raw-hide words, where all the other Victorian writers used dashes."[20] Henry Seidel

Canby consigned Kipling to the stagnant status of a "sterile" classic who was read "only in the underworld of readers whose imaginations still lived in the Nineteenth century."[21] R. A. Scott-James recognized the modern elements in Kipling's poetry—the "mass emotion," the colloquial language, and the violent rhythms which served "like jazz music to stir the community of feeling of the audience." It was these very elements of modernism, though, that prevented Kipling's poetry from being "a lonely adventure of the spirit, as it had been for most of the Victorian poets" and convinced Scott-James that few of Kipling's poems would be remembered.[22]

Many of the obituaries reflected the years of harsh, uncompromising conflict between the Kipling critics and the Kipling cultists. The critics repeated once again the standard clichés which had been handed down through the years since Richard Le Gallienne, Francis Adams, and Robert Buchanan had first dealt with Kipling as a menacing force in British literary life. Malcolm Muggeridge, for example, recalled Kipling's vulgarity—a vulgarity which had become in a more enlightened age "the vulgarity of the many causes he espoused."[23] Similarly, Douglas Jerrold remembered Kipling as "a voice out of the past" who served as the "sometimes inspired and always effective spokesman for a kind of imperialism no longer in fashion."[24]

The cultists, like the critics, mourned Kipling in the most predictable terms. Arthur Hood, in an angry article entitled "The Laureate of the People," summed up the feelings of those who valued Kipling as the last remaining voice of decency amidst triumphant decadence. To Hood, Kipling was, above all, a spokesman for wholesome sanity "in a world of lounge-lizards, rat-minded, would-be poets exulting in sewers, musicians imitating the savagery of banged tom-toms, and so-called artists emulating the drawing of children and bedlamites." The death of Kipling to angry idolators like Hood was obviously far more than the death of a poet; it was a social and cultural calamity which left England defenseless at a time "when the red ants of communism are untiringly busy in undermining all the long established standards of morality and honest manliness."[25]

Surprisingly enough, there were some who mourned Kipling the poet more than Kipling the imperialist or Kipling the prose writer. The *Spectator* predicted that Kipling's poems, neglected by the critics, would outlast the prose. The prose, it seemed, was already dated, but the *Spectator's* anonymous writer noted that "there is a substantial corpus of Kipling's verse that can scarcely be forgotten."[26]

Rebecca West, the novelist, also eulogized Kipling as a poet. Writing in the *New Statesman and Nation*, Miss West berated Kipling's admirers "among the rich and the great" who had promoted the poet "as an oracle of wisdom; as Shakespeare touched with grace and elevated to a kind of mezzanine rank just below the Archbishop of Canterbury." By using

Kipling as a "literary fetish," his admirers, Miss West wrote, had obscured his authentic achievements as "a sweet singer" who interpreted the mind of his age. Kipling, to Rebecca West, remained above all a "shy and delicate lyricist," and only the distortions and exaggerations of his admirers had prevented the world from recognizing that "all his life long, Kipling was a better poet than he was a prose writer."[27]

Paradoxically, it was the creative writers and the practicing poets, deeply immersed in the modern movements, who tended to eulogize Kipling as a poet. One of the most perceptive and sympathetic of these obituary assessments of Kipling was written by the promoter of avant-garde poetry in America, Harriet Monroe. Although she did register "utter amazement at the smug superiority so complacently revealed" in some of Kipling's poems, Miss Monroe was less inclined than her British counterparts to let political passions interfere with her evaluation of Kipling's poetry. Rudyard Kipling, she wrote, was "a master of rhymed eloquence" and the possessor of some enviable poetic gifts. In the "Barrack-Room Ballads" he had perfected "a variety of double quick short lines" which moved with a continually fresh "muscular facility," and Miss Monroe acknowledged that in this kind of rhyming Kipling was "pre-eminently the modern master."

In addition to the admirable metrical talents displayed in his "rhymed eloquence," Kipling was also recognized for his artistic assimilation of heretofore unacceptable topics. After quoting "McAndrew's Hymn," Miss Monroe wrote of Kipling as "one of the few modern poets (I am another) to feel the imaginative appeal of all the super power magnificence which creates a miracle every day, and to resent the narrow vision which sees in it nothing but mechanics." Yet it was Kipling's more conventionally beautiful songs which seemed to show the essence of his poetic achievement. Citing the "tragic" "Danny Deever," the superbly elegiac "Recessional," and the "delicately wistful" "Mandalay," Miss Monroe concluded that "it is upon a few songs such as these that Kipling's fame as a poet will ultimately rest."[28]

The obituaries which recorded Kipling's passing from the literary scene reflected the inability of nearly half a century to deal with Kipling's unique achievement as a poet. It was a failure due, in part, to the inherent inadequacies of the critical methods of the times. Close analysis of the text, in fact all the methodology of modern criticism, had not yet been popularized, and the many notable critics who commented on Kipling's poetry were limited to impressionistic generalizations and the search for slogans which might paraphrase rather than explicate Kipling's poetry. Consequently the best Kipling criticism from 1900 to 1936 consisted, for the most part, of isolated, undeveloped insights. Critics praised Kipling's poetry as an expression of the British character or *zeitgeist*, but none saw in Kipling's verse the more immediate product of a more specific spirit. No one, that is, looked beyond the vague generalities of the British spirit

to see Kipling as a representative writer of Edwardian "invasion literature"[29] or a pioneer in the new, realistic tradition of war poetry.

But beyond the inherent inadequacies which impoverished the criticism of all writers there were certain unique and powerful forces which
made Rudyard Kipling's reputation a special case. Kipling's reputation as
a poet had never been based entirely on literary considerations. From the
very beginning of his poetic career in 1890 Kipling was hailed as a new
star in a singularly dim literary universe, denounced as an unexpected
and alarming claimant for Tennyson's hallowed mantle as poet laureate,
and condemned as a vulgar upstart who appealed to the basest and most
prosaic interests of the newly literate reading public. As a writer of patriotic and "masculine" verse Kipling was popularly promoted as an ano-
dyne to the disease of decadence which seemed to infect British letters at
the time of Oscar Wilde's scandalous trials. Finally, Kipling as a promoter
of imperialism in general and the Boer War in particular was soon en-
snared in a variety of extraliterary irrelevancies.

Rudyard Kipling's reputation as a poet never recovered from these
extraliterary forces which aroused such violent hostilities at the very beginning of his career. The reviewers from 1903 to 1919 perpetuated the
anti-Kipling tradition of the nineties and succeeded in exiling Kipling to
the popular culture, where his poetry remained unexamined—immune
to the new critical methods which might have rescued him from uncritical idolatry. As a result, it was to the common readers that Kipling owed
his continued popularity. It was a popularity unsanctioned by taste, undisciplined by critical intelligence, and, in many eyes, totally unmerited.
Paradoxically it was also a popularity which contributed a major impedi-
ment to critical approval, for many critics, feeling perhaps that they were
pursuing the more astonishing enigma, preferred to ignore Kipling's poetry and to explain, instead, his popularity.

Yet in spite of the critics Kipling was read, and his poetry was a pervasive, if sometimes unwelcome, presence in the poetic atmosphere of his
age. It was a presence which was rarely approved and scarcely acknowledged, but it was, nevertheless, not to be ignored. For some, it was certainly a force to be resisted, and many poets, no doubt, regarded
Kipling's poetry as D. H. Lawrence regarded Ben Franklin's proverbs—as "thorns in young flesh."[30] In any event, Kipling's presence and
usefulness made it impossible for the major poets of his age to ignore him
with the smug self-assurance of the critics. It is perhaps no accident that
the best criticism of Kipling's poetry written during his long lifetime was
invariably written by poets, rather than critics, reviewers, or scholars.
Unlike the reviewers, those harried retailers of literary opinion, Kipling's
poet-critics tended to ignore both immediate political problems and ultimate Arnoldian issues and instead approached Kipling's poems with
pragmatic, technical curiosity. Such an approach, concerned with specific strategies, made Kipling a useful arsenal of artistic techniques at a

time when most critics regarded him as a museum of archaic and irrelevant ideas. It was apparent to these poet-critics that Kipling's reformation of diction was not unlike Ezra Pound's more flamboyant revolt against "Tennysonianisms" and "literaryisms,"[31] nor, as Robert Bridges recalled, was it unlike Synge's suggestion that "before verse can be made human again, it must first learn to be brutal."[32] Kipling's allusiveness, his assimilation and ironic orchestration of elements from the popular culture was not lost on Bridges, nor we may assume on Eliot. Certainly Kipling's mastery of verse exercised an evident fascination for Eliot, whose poetic dramas attempted to realize an ideal union of public and private utterance by combining the intensity of poetry with the continuity of verse.[33]

T. S. Eliot's promotion of Kipling's poetry and W. H. Auden's solemn prediction that Yeats, like Kipling, would be forgiven for his language are not, then, expressions of inexplicable eccentricity. In the context of Kipling criticism, Auden's enigmatic prophecy and Eliot's generous praise can be seen as a surfacing of a professional interest in Kipling's artistry which developed during the darkest decades of critical indifference.

Notes

1. T. S. Eliot, "Kipling Redivivus," *Athenaeum*, May 9, 1919, 297–98.

2. Charles H. Towne, "The Vanished Yeats, The Never-Vanishing Kipling, and Some Others," *The Bookman* (New York) 49 (July 1919), 618–19.

3. C. E. Carrington, *The Life of Rudyard Kipling* (New York: Doubleday, 1955), 310, 381.

4. Charles F. Masterman, "After the Reaction," *Contemporary Review* 86 (Dec. 1904), 815–34.

5. "The Kipling Blue Pill," *The Philistine* 13 (Oct. 1901), 129–36.

6. "Wordsworth and Kipling," *TLS*, Feb. 29, 1912, rpt. in *Collected Essays, Papers, etc.* (London: Oxford Univ. Press, 1927), 27–38.

7. T. S. Eliot, "Kipling Redivivus," 297–98.

8. The reception of this anthology is chronicled in my "A Choice of Critics: T. S. Eliot's Edition of Kipling's Verse," *Dalhousie Review* 52, No. 4 (Winter 1973), 572–87.

9. Ronald Macfie, "The Years Between," *The Bookman* (London), 56 (May 1919), 76–77.

10. "The Years Between," *New Statesman* 13 (April 12, 1919), 48.

11. "Notes on Books," *Dial* 66 (May 31, 1919), 571–74.

12. "Mr. Kipling Condemns," *TLS*, April 10, 1919, 196.

13. W. H. Auden, "The Poet of the Encirclement," *New Republic* 109 (Oct. 25, 1953), 579–81, and Edmund Wilson, *The Wound and the Bow* (Boston: Houghton, 1941), 105–81.

14. "En-dor," *Rudyard Kipling's Verse* (New York: Doubleday, 1940), 363.

15. Carrington, 339.

16. *The New York Journal*, reprinted in "Kipling in America," *The American Monthly Review of Reviews* 19 (April 1899), 419–22, and Carrington, 235, 225.

17. "The Post-War Kipling," *New Republic* 71 (May 25, 1932), 50–51.

18. *A Gallery* (New York: Putnam's, 1924), rpt. in *Contemporary Essays*, William Hastings, ed. (Boston: Houghton, 1928), 174–79.

19. "The Kipling who was more than the Poet of Empire," *New York Times Book Review* (Feb. 9, 1936), 2, 28.

20. "Rudyard Kipling," *Cornhill Magazine* 155 (Jan. 1937), 24–31.

21. "Kipling—The Great Colonial," *Saturday Review of Literature* 12 (Jan. 25, 1936), 3–4, 14, 16.

22. "Rudyard Kipling," *London Monthly* 32 (Feb. 1936), 373–75.

23. "Men and Books," *Time and Tide* 18 (Feb. 20, 1937), 241.

24. "Current Comments," *English Review* 69 (Feb. 1936), 139.

25. "The Laureate of the People," *Poetry Review* 27 (March–April 1936), 97–102.

26. "Rudyard Kipling," *Spectator* (Jan. 24, 1936), 118–19.

27. "Rudyard Kipling," *New Statesman and Nation* 11 (Jan. 25, 1936), 112–14.

28. "Kipling as a Poet," *Poetry* 48 (April 1936), 32–36.

29. Samuel Hynes, *The Edwardian Mind* (Princeton: Princeton Univ. Press, 1968), 15–53.

30. *Studies in Classic American Literature* (New York: Thomas Seltzer, 1923), 21.

31. Ezra Pound, a letter to Harriet Monroe as quoted by Richard Ellmann, *Eminent Domain* (New York: Oxford Univ. Press, 1967), 67.

32. Bridges, "Wordsworth and Kipling," *Collected Essays, Papers, etc.*, 28.

33. Northrop Frye, *T. S. Eliot* (New York: Grove Press, 1963), 24–26.

Kipling and India

Kipling's Jungle Eden

James Harrison[*]

> Sometimes you hear of dem in der census reports, but dey all die. Dis
> man haf lived, and he is an anachronism, for he is before der Iron Age,
> and der Stone Age. Look here, he is at der beginnings of der history of
> man—Adam in der Garden, und now we want only an Eva! No! He is
> older than dot child-tale, shust as der *rukh* is older dan der gods.[1]

This is Muller, head of the Woods and Forests of all India, speaking of
children raised by wolves[2] in "In the Rukh," the first Mowgli story to be
published.[3] Clearly his young hero's life among the animals had strong
Edenic connotations for Kipling from the outset. Along with Rousseau's
noble savage, Edgar Rice Burroughs' Tarzan[4] and William Golding's Ne-
anderthals, Mowgli takes his place as a modern Adam. The Eden he inhabits is, of course, a post-Renaissance one, and man's exclusion from it
an alienation from nature rather than from God; but such virtual meton-
ymy has become so commonplace since the Romantics as almost to pass
unnoticed, except that Kipling handles it with a difference.

Eden in "In the Rukh" is glimpsed nostalgically as a charming, in
many ways enviable, but largely irrelevant alternative or contrast to the
normal life of man. Generically such children of nature "all die" and
their sole surviver leads a peripheral, scholar-gypsy kind of existence in
the *rukh*.

Turning to *The Jungle Books* proper, however, we find that the Edenic
theme recurs too often and too centrally to be thus brushed aside. This is
almost as true of the stories in which Mowgli does not appear as of those
in which he does. In "Rikki-Tikki-Tavi," for instance, the cobra pair, Nag
and Nagaina, seek to gain possession of the garden they consider theirs
by right. And in "The White Seal," after a seven-year quest from Arctic to
Antarctic, Kotick finally discovers and leads his people to paradisal
beaches untrodden by the foot of man. Eden in "The White Seal" is assured only if the man that's foe to seals can be kept at a far remove. Similarly, in most of the Mowgli stories, the jungle is Edenic in sharp contrast

[*]From *Mosaic* 7, no. 2 (Winter 1974):151–64. Reprinted by permission.

to the world of men. Having tried both ways of life, Mowgli sums it up thus:

> Now, in the Man-Pack, at this hour, as I remember, they laid them down upon hard pieces of wood in the inside of a mud-trap, and, having carefully shut out all the clean winds, drew foul cloth over their heads and made evil songs through their noses. It is better in the Jungle.
>
> (II, 151)

In "The King's Ankus" it is man's greed for gold which, to their credit, the animals are wholly unable to comprehend. The only exception is the White Cobra, charged with keeping man's treasure. However, not only has he been rendered impotent by his long vigil over the far more virulent poison he guards, but his color bodies forth an inner corruption not of the jungle. For the first and only time it is of no avail to Mowgli to know the Master-word of the Law. "There is but one master word here. It is mine!" (II, 161) comes the reply. In "Tiger! Tiger!" and "Letting in the Jungle" the shortcomings of men are far more varied and serious, and Mowgli is throughout shown as barely tolerant or contemptuous of the villagers he comes to know. "They are idle, senseless, and cruel; they play with their mouths, and they do not kill the weaker for food, but for sport" (II, 93). In the end their treatment of his foster parents leads to a protracted destruction of the whole village which has the quality of a ritual cleansing by nature.

> I have seen and smelled the blood of the woman that gave me food—the woman whom they would have killed but for me. Only the smell of the new grass on their door-steps can take away that smell.
>
> (II, 95)

Even more incensed than the criticisms levelled against man, however, are those reserved for the *Bandar-log*, denizens of the jungle itself. The very syntax he uses betrays the difficulty Baloo finds in even bringing himself to talk of them.

> They have no law. They are outcasts. They have no speech of their own, but use the stolen words which they overhear when they listen, and peep, and wait up above in the branches. Their way is not our way. They are without leaders. They have no remembrance. They boast and chatter and pretend that they are a great people about to do great affairs in the jungle, but the falling of a nut turns their minds to laughter and all is forgotten. We of the jungle have no dealings with them. We do not drink where the monkeys drink; we do not go where the monkeys go; we do not hunt where they hunt; we do not die where they die.
>
> (I, 51–2)

Not even of Shere Khan or Tabaqui is it ever said, as of the *Bandar-log*, that they are "evil, dirty, shameful." The parallel with Swift's Yahoos suggests itself irresistibly when they drop "nuts and filth" on the heads of those beneath.

It is, of course, the unflattering parody they offer of human behavior which makes us all find monkeys in some sense less estimable than panthers, and this parallel Kipling is at pains to underline throughout both books. "Why have I never been taken among the Monkey-People? They stand on their feet as I do" (I, 51), asks Mowgli in all innocence. "The monkeys sat and talked in the upper branches . . . and the old men sat around the tree and talked" (I, 96–7), writes Kipling in seeming innocence. "Bah!" says Mowgli unequivocally, "Chatter—chatter! Talk, talk! Men are blood brothers of the *Bandar-log*" (II, 79). Most barbed of all, since it is uncertain whether men or monkeys are being disparaged, we read: "They would sit in circles in the hall of the king's council chamber, and scratch for fleas and pretend to be men" (I, 67).

Kipling's antipathy toward the *Bandar-log* is almost certainly not indicative of a total or Swiftean misanthropy. J. M. S. Tompkins finds a similarity between them and Frank Midmore's intellectual friends, the Immoderate Left, in "My Son's Wife" (*A Diversity of Creatures*).[5] An even more suggestive parallel might be with such educated, Westernized Indians as the luckless Grish Chander Dé, M.A., who has the temerity to be selected by the Viceroy to replace Yardley-Orde as Deputy Commissioner in "The Head of the District." "More English than the English," he ends up, like the *Bandar-log*, having "no speech of his own," merely "stolen words" which he has overheard—"much curious book-knowledge of bump-suppers, cricket matches, hunting runs" (*Life's Handicaps*, p. 134). Kipling shares with most colonialists a marked preference for "the real native—not the hybrid, University-trained mule" (*Plain Tales from the Hills*, p. 203), and in preferring panthers and pythons to an evolutionary halfway house like the *Bandar-log*, with their "little picking thievish hands," he is expressing a revulsion at most forms of cultural miscegenation. Man is shown as lacking much of what Kipling finds admirable about animals, but at least he has certain potential qualities of his own. Monkeys, or make-believe men, have the virtues of neither man nor beast.

Mowgli, by contrast, is true man in the jungle, and as such he must discover, by the end of the story, that this is not where he belongs. Nevertheless, so long as he does live in the jungle he is idyllically at one with its rightful inhabitants.

> The boy could climb almost as well as he could swim, and swim almost as well as he could run; so Baloo, the Teacher of the Law, taught him the Wood and Water Laws; how to tell a rotten branch from a sound one; how to speak politely to the wild bees when he came upon a hive of them fifty feet above ground; what to say to Mang the Bat when he disturbed him in the branches at midday; and how to warn the water-snakes in the pools before he splashed down among them.
>
> (I, 46)

He confirms the jungle's Edenic character, moreover, by being so clearly its Crown Prince, once if not future King, youthful Adam. It is, as Miss Tompkins notes, through the later stories the "the majestic shadow of Adam, King of the Jungle,"[6] stalks most imperiously. Indeed, the role of this fifteen-year-old can seem almost patriarchal at times.

> Those were days of good hunting and good sleeping. No stranger cared to break into the jungles that belonged to Mowgli's people, as they called the Pack, and the young wolves grew fat and strong, and there were many cubs to bring to the Looking-over.
>
> (II, 223)

But his authority is never really in question from the moment when, about to be cast out by a Pack whose members cannot look him in the eyes, he seizes the flaming branch and addresses the wolves as "*sag* [dogs], as a man should" (I, 38). Later, on his return to the jungle, when first he asserts his authority over his four brother wolves, Bagheera remarks, "There is more in the Jungle now than Jungle Law, Baloo" (II, 67).

We may note also that this authority is asserted to prevent the shedding of a man's blood, and that throughout his prolonged and terrible punishment of the village for just that offence, in "Letting in the Jungle," this is the one thing Mowgli will not permit. Cain has yet to be born. Similarly, in "How Fear Came," Shere Khan discovers that, even on the one night of the year he has power to look any man in the eyes and still attack, as granted to the First of the Tigers after he had brought death and fear into the world, he must still turn aside from Mowgli's gaze. This indicates that, within the terms of jungle mythology, Mowgli is like Adam before the Fall.

The most movingly Edenic passages are probably in "The Spring Running." Mowgli has here reached the zenith of his powers. To his foster mother, Messua, he appears like a "Godling of the Woods . . . , strong, tall and beautiful, his long black hair sweeping over his shoulders, the knife swinging at his neck, and his head crowned with a wreath of white jasmine" (II, 283). The year is at the spring, and although, as is appropriate in Paradise, "the seasons slide into one another almost without division," spring is still

> the most wonderful, because she has not to cover a clean bare field with new leaves and flowers, but to drive before her and to put away the hanging-on, over-surviving raffle of half-green things which the gentle winter has suffered to live, and to make the partly dressed stale earth feel new and young once more. And this she does so well that there is no spring in the world like the Jungle spring.
>
> (II, 268)

Nowhere else in *The Jungle Books* is there such lingering over beauty, whether of man, beast, or tree and leaf. Nowhere is so much made of burgeoning and blossom, life and fruitfulness. Yet all is touched with sadness, for Mowgli is about to close the gates of this paradise behind him.

The story is primarily, of course, an evocative account of the whole bewildering process of growing up. All the mysterious, scurrying business of the jungle at the Time of the New Talk echoes and magnifies the frightening overflow, within Mowgli, of a sexuality which has, as yet, nowhere to go. The nameless anguish of it all covers him "as water covers a log"; to run through the night till he sings at the sheer prowess and pride of bodily movement offers no more lasting relief than compulsory games at an English Public Schools; and, at the moment he is about to answer Gray Brother's question, "And now what is to be?" a girl passes by on the path, leaving Mowgli with no reply but, "And now I do not know" (II, 288–89).

To extend the Eden myth in this way, so as to include each of us individually, is common enough practice in literature, of course. But Kipling has quite clearly differentiated between Mowgli's exile from the jungle and the Fall in Genesis in a way which is not so common. Twice, indeed, he is exiled, once by the Pack and once of his own volition; yet on both occasions he has "broken no word of the Law of the Jungle" (I, 36). As Muller says, "He is older than dot child-tale." Kipling is here recording an exclusion from Eden which results from mere maturation, the individual and the species alike outgrowing a state in which the simple laws of nature suffice. Once exiled, mankind is depicted as frequently hostile toward, and destructive of, the Edenic state. So Mowgli, cast out of the jungle for being a man, is in turn cast out by men for being still in a state of Edenic innocence. But his actual departure from Eden, and the nostalgia this arouses in us, is closer in spirit to Wordsworth's "Ode on Intimations of Immortality" than to Milton's *Paradise Lost*; the loss is one which could not have been avoided, and for which there may be adequate if not abundant compensations.

So far a clear distinction seems to have emerged between an Edenic state of nature, whether found in childhood or the jungle, and the state of adult or human life. That men and man outgrow Eden is sad, since something is lost which may not be regained, but inevitable. All the animals so far discussed are free, in a wild state of nature, having little or no contact with man. And most of them, in sharp distinction to man (or surrogate man, the *Bandar-log*), are citizens, or potential citizens of Eden.

There are, however, stories in *The Jungle Books* about animals in captivity, or servitude to man. "Her Majesty's Servants," for instance, consists of a conversation about discipline between a variety of animals in the employ of Her Majesty's Indian Army. Their sleep has been disturbed for the third night in a week by the undisciplined behavior of the "savage horses" of "savage men" forming the bodyguard of "a wild king of a very wild country" before whom they are to parade the next day. In the morning the visitors from Afghanistan see, to their astonishment, a line "three-quarters of a mile from wing to wing" of men, animals and guns advance on them until "the ground began to shake," only to stop dead, salute, and disperse. On asking how this can be done with animals as well as men, they are told:

> They obey, as the men do. Mule, horse, elephant, or bullock, he obeys his driver, and the driver his sergeant, and the sergeant his lieutenant, and the lieutenant his captain, and the captain his major, and the major his colonel, and the colonel his brigadier commanding three regiments, and the brigadier his general, who obeys the Viceroy, who is the servant of the Empress. Thus is it done.
>
> (I, 273)

Here we have, seemingly, the antithesis of such free spirits of the jungle as Bagheera, Kaa, or Chil the Kite. A similar contrast between freedom and servitude is found in "Toomai of the Elephants," Kala Nag, the big black elephant who has served the Indian Government for forty-seven years, feeling the need to rejoin his wild, free brethren on the night they dance. In the words of the epigraph:

> I will remember what I was. I am sick of rope and chain.
> I will remember my old strength and all my forest affairs.
> I will not sell my back to man for a bundle of sugar-cane.
> I will go out to my own kind, and the wood-folk in their lairs.
>
> I will go out until the day, until the morning break,
> Out to the winds' untainted kiss, the waters' clean caress:
> I will forget my ankle-ring and snap my picket-stake.
> I will revisit my lost loves, and playmates masterless!

Yet discipline, servitude, law and order are not in fact disparaged. Kala Nag returns at daybreak to a camp where his duties are to help break in the newly captured wild elephants. The Afghan Chief speaks with some envy when he replies, "Would it were so in Afghanistan, for there we obey only our own wills." Even Bagheera, when telling of how he was born in captivity and escaped, admits that "because I had learned the ways of men I became more terrible in the Jungle than Shere Khan" (I, 29). And approving if ambiguous reference is made, in "Letting in the Jungle," to the English—men of law who "do not suffer people to burn or beat each other without witnesses" (II, 81). Moreover, the jungle itself, despite its lack of bars and picket-stakes, is subject to its own strict and inexorable Law.

> You will remember that Mowgli spent a great part of his life in the Seeonee Wolf-Pack, learning the Law from Baloo, the Brown Bear; and it was Baloo who told him, when the boy grew impatient at the constant orders, that the Law was like the Giant Creeper, because it dropped across every one's back and no one could escape.
>
> (II, 3–4)

Freedom alone is very far, in fact, from being the distinguishing mark of Kipling's jungle. The *Bandar-log* claim above all to be free, and it is this freedom, this lack of all law, which excludes them from jungle society. The wolves use, with more justifiable pride, the title of the Free People. But even they must learn to acknowledge, having broken the Law and been dispersed, that true freedom lies within the Law. "Lead us again, O Akela. Lead us again, O Man-cub, for we be sick of this lawlessness, and we would be the Free People once more" (I, 121). However unlikely a concomitant of innocence, it is law rather than freedom which seems to be the distinctive feature of Kipling's Eden.

Examining the nature of this Law of the Jungle more closely, we find that in certain respects, as befits a Law of Eden, it has religious characteristics. It is as elaborate and detailed as Mosaic, Mohammedan or Hindu law; it is attended by appropriate ceremonials, such as the inspection of new cubs at the Pack Council, and includes pass-words or spells for warding off danger; it is codified, versified even; its authority is beyond appeal, and its high priests are Hathi and Baloo.

On the other hand, never is it presented to the readers as having had a divine origin. (Hathi's myth in "How Fear Came" is addressed to the animals.) On the contrary, its multifarious provisions are explained or accounted for, in the best tradition of nineteenth-century religious enlightenment, on wholly rational and utilitarian grounds.

There are, at the simplest level, rules of hygiene such as also find a place in Mosaic or Mohammedan law, like "Wash daily from nose-tip to tail-tip" (II, 29). Then there are straightforward and common-sense rules of self-preservation, like "Strike first and then give tongue" (I, 30), or:

> the Law of the Jungle, *which never orders anything without a reason*, forbids every beast to eat Man . . . *The real reason* for this is that man-killing means, sooner or later, the arrival of white men on elephants, with guns, and hundreds of brown men with gongs and rockets and torches. Then everybody in the jungle suffers.[7]
>
> (I, 8–9)

Note that the "real reason" is wholly utilitarian, by contrast with the spurious, quasi-moral reason advanced by many of the animals "that Man is the weakest and most defenceless of all living things, and it is unsportsmanlike to touch him." Then again, there are rules to ensure group survival, analogous to those limitations on animal aggressiveness which Lorenz and others have since noted.[8]

> After that inspection the cubs are free to run where they please, and until they have killed their first buck no excuses are accepted if a grown wolf of the Pack kills one of them . . . *and if you think for a minute you will see that this must be so.*
>
> (I, 15–16)

> By the Law of the Jungle it is death to kill at the drinking places when
> once the Water Truce has been declared. *The reason of this* is that drink-
> ing comes before eating.
>
> (II, 7)

There are, it must be admitted, a few laws which do seem to have a
genuinely moral basis, whether at the level of schoolboy fair-play or sacred taboo.

> Your right is to kill me here on the Council Rock now. Therefore, I ask,
> who comes to make an end of the Lone Wolf? For it is my right, by the
> Law of the Jungle, that ye come one by one.
>
> (I, 35)

> "All the Jungle is thine," said Bagheera, "and thou canst kill everything
> that thou art strong enough to kill, but for the sake of the bull that bought
> thee thou must never kill or eat any cattle young or old. That is the Law
> of the Jungle."
>
> (I, 26)

However, in both these cases a child would recognize such an obvious
rightness and fitness about the injunctions that he would feel no sanction,
either adult or divine, to be necessary. The Law is still, as it were, self-
evidently justified.

Seemingly in another dimension, the Law is also used neither to pre-
scribe nor to proscribe, but merely to describe. This can be at the level of
how to tell a rotten branch from a sound one, or at a much more philosophical level. "Having cast the skin we may not creep into it afresh. It is the
Law" (II, 293), says Kaa of Mowgli's eventual realization that man has no
choice but to return to man at the last, thus encapsulating Kipling's whole
notion of the Fall from innocence being an inevitable progression.

Law of this kind makes clearer what has been implicit in the earlier
examples: that the basis of all law is something as inescapable and "natural" as biology, moral and social law being but extensions of biological
law, and as such concerned with things as they are rather than as they
might be. One is reminded, in fact, of the way Darwin and those in his
wake found biological imperatives to underly social and moral developments.

> In the case of the lower animals it seems much more appropriate to speak
> of their social instincts, as having been developed for the general good . . .
> of the species. The term, general good, may be defined as the rearing of
> the greatest number of individuals in full vigour and health, with all their
> faculties perfect, under the conditions to which they are subjected. As
> the social instincts both of man and the lower animals have no doubt been
> developed by nearly the same steps, it would be advisable, if found practi-
> cable, to use the same definition in both cases, and to take as the standard
> of morality, the general good or welfare of the community.[9]

It becomes apparent that, in making the Law of the Jungle the miscellany we have seen it to be of custom, common sense, observation, self-preservation and occasional moral insight, Kipling has created something which, from his point of view, is like religious law in ways other than were at first apparent. For religion, to Kipling, was always more a matter of consensus than of truth or falsehood, of social fact than of supernatural faith, of what exists because people believe in it than of what people believe in because it exists. Perhaps the closest to Kipling's ideal embodiment of law is the Masonic code, which, while recognizing the vital and fortifying role of ritual in helping men hold fast to the law, conceives of that law as essentially secular and social in nature. It is, as one of his characters puts it, "what everybody knows ought to be done," or "an average plan of life" (*Debits and Credits*, pp. 61, 77).

Nor should it be forgotten that *The Jungle Books* were ostensibly written for children, even though Kipling claims that their parents are his ultimate target (*Something of Myself*, p. 190). And clearly any such view of law has much in common with those inarticulate attitudes Kipling could count on in his juvenile readers towards their own equally secular tribal codes of playground and classroom. All of which, in making the Law of the Jungle more than ever self-evidently right and necessary, is greatly to his purpose, since what Kipling is preaching is not the desirability of particular laws or laws of a particular kind, so much as the bare necessity of law.

At first sight it would seem difficult for anyone to adopt a less intellectual, more authoritarianly pragmatic attitude toward the law. Yet this is precisely where lies what Noel Annan has identified as Kipling's distinctive contribution to the history of ideas.[10] Kipling, argues Annan, gives us an artist's awareness of insights which Durkheim and like-minded sociologists arrive at and express differently; that law, codified custom, a general sense of what is right and acceptable, are necessary for the functioning of human society, irrespective of whether they are right or wrong when judged by some supposedly absolute set of values. Even those who reject the moral consensus of their society, and are perhaps judged to be acting rightly in so doing, could not act at all without such a consensus. Law is necessary, quite apart from and more importantly than for its moral insights.

In many ways the clearest instance anywhere in Kipling's writings of this importance of the law, virtually for its own sake and without reference to the values it enshrines, is to be found in *The Jungle Books* themselves, in "How Fear Came." Moreover, that the story should also contain Kipling's most explicit treatment of the Edenic theme is a confirmation of the contention which prompted this rather extended analysis of the Law of the Jungle: that law is the distinguishing characteristic of Kipling's Eden. The story tells of how, for the duration of the Water Truce, a more traditionally Edenic state of affairs obtains in the Jungle, at least along the banks of the Waingunga. But in the contrast drawn by Kipling between drinking under these and more normal conditions, there is a keen sense of what has been lost by the imposition of a Water Truce, and no suggestion that this is an arrangement devoutly to be desired in perpetuity.

> In good seasons, when water was plentiful, those who came down to drink at the Waingunga—or anywhere else, for that matter—did so at risk of their lives, and that risk made no small part of the fascination of the night's doings. To move down so cunningly that never a leaf stirred; to wade knee deep in the roaring shallows that drown all noise from behind; to drink, looking backward over one shoulder, every muscle ready for the first desperate bound of keen terror; to roll on the sandy margin, and return, wet-muzzled and well plumped out, to the admiring herd, was a thing that all tall-antlered bucks took a delight in, precisely because they knew that at any moment Bagheera or Shere Khan might leap upon them and bear them down. But now all that life-and-death fun was ended, and the Jungle people came up, starved and weary to the shrunken river,—tiger, bear, deer, buffalo, and pig, all together,—drank the fouled waters, and hung above them, too exhausted to move off.
>
> (II, 7–8)

What Kipling does find to praise in the situation is that the jungle, in its hour of need, is "working under the Law" (II, 4).

Within this setting of a latter-day truce between hunter and hunted, we then have Hathi's myth of the beginning of things, when "there was no drought, and leaves and flowers and fruit grew on the same tree, and we ate nothing at all except leaves and flowers and grass and fruit and bark" (II, 17). This is the traditional, milk-and-honey, seasonless, pacific infancy of the earth that so many mythologies portray before accounting for the coming of dearth and death. But Bagheera clearly speaks for the author when he responds, "I am glad I wasn't born in those days . . . Bark is only good to sharpen claws." For, in Hathi's version of the Fall, this state of unremitting ease merely leads to debilitating idleness and all the disputes of idleness. And the toothless, clawless law of the word of the First of the Tigers, mere eater as yet of "fruit and grass with the others" (II, 18), whom Tha, the First of the Elephants and Lord of the Jungle, has left in charge, is clearly unequal to keeping the peace.

One day, goaded by a too quarrelsome buck, the First of the Tigers loses his temper and inadvertently brings death into the jungle. He flees the scene of his crime, and there follows a period of anarchy under the rule of the Gray Ape, until Tha decides "it is time there was a Law, and a Law that ye must not break. Now ye shall know Fear, and when ye have found him ye shall know that he is your master, and the rest shall follow" (II, 20). Fear turns out to be man, and the First of the Tigers' attempt to kill Fear merely teaches man how to kill tigers.

Ostensibly the myth explains, in a traditional manner, the coming of meat-eating and death into a perfect world; for subsequently the tiger, branded with stripes by the creepers to mark his shame, no longer eats of their fruit but revenges himself on the deer who occasioned that shame. In fact, the idyllic quality of the earth's initial perfection is quite passed over, if not actually denied. The whole story leads up to, and seems intended to demonstrate, the need for law, for fear as a sanction of law, and for man (who plays no role in Eden prior to this) as the rightful dispenser of fear.

It may seem, at this point, that the Eden Mowgli grows up in is more like an anti-Eden—a justification as well as a portrayal of nature and things much as they are. And there is certainly no blinking the fact that it is no vegetarian paradise. The tone is set by the epigraph to the very first story.

> Now Chil the Kite brings home the night
>   That Mang the Bat sets free—
> The herds are shut in byre and hut
>   For loosed till dawn are we.
>
> This is the hour of pride and power.
>   Talon and tush and claw.
> Oh hear the call!—Good hunting all
>   That keep the Jungle Law—

It is a song for predators, among whom Mowgli moves almost exclusively, and of whom he is clearly one. "I have never killed a goat but I wished it had been a buck; nor a buck but I wished it had been a nilghai" (II, 151). Even the Law, embodiment of the underlying principles of this paradisal state of nature, counsels its followers to such policies as "Strike first and then give tongue."

Yet even were the Law less Darwinianly practical and realistic, to argue that law is an essential feature of Kipling's Eden, but to suggest no other more positive qualities, would be to adumbrate a singularly unrapturous kind of Eden, and in fact to do an injustice to the life led by Mowgli as Kipling portrays it. But if Kipling's notion of law places more stress on the existence *per se* of some kind of law than on its precise nature or the values informing it, much the same can be said of the more positive or dynamic factors he depicts. The essential is that there be some manifestation of a life force which is as a rule youthful and vigorous, frequently crude, at times even anarchic. Something there must be that doesn't love a law, that wants it down. This is then held in check by law of one sort or another, but its existence is a constant safeguard against the law becoming a mere dead letter.

Thus "Toomai of the Elephants" is neither a simple plea for freedom, nor a straightforward vindication of law and discipline. Old Toomai remembers nostalgically the plains, with their "brick elephant-lines, one stall to each elephant, and big stumps to tie them to safely, and flat, broad roads to exercise upon, instead of this come-and-go camping" (I, 209–

210). Little Toomai, on the other hand, much preferring the excitement and uncertainty of hunting wild elephants in the hills, remembers only "the long hours when there was nothing to do except watch Kala Nag fidgeting in his pickets." And Kala Nag himself, responding for a night to the call of the wild, return the next morning to his picket-stake.

In the Mowgli stories, however, the main characters already have their freedom. They are very much creatures of the wild, who, for all that they talk to one another, hunt and kill swiftly and without remorse. Indeed, that Bagheera is no stuffed, nursery panther is a great part of the fascination and excitement of jungle life, as well as of its need for law.

> He loved better than anything else to go with Bagheera into the dark, warm heart of the forest, to sleep all through the drowsy day, and at night to see how Bagheera did his killing. Bagheera killed right and left as he felt hungry, and so did Mowgli—with one exception. As soon as he was old enough to understand things, Bagheera told him that he must never touch cattle because he had been bought into the Pack at the price of a bull's life . . . "That is the Law of the Jungle."
>
> (II, 25–26)

Moreover, in the description of drinking at the banks of the Waingunga, Kipling extends participation in this "life-and-death fun" to the hunted as well as the hunters. In other words, if one's Eden is a jungle, and if its animal inhabitants are presented honestly and not sentimentally, then the only vital and potentially anarchic forces available (apart, in this case, from Mowgli's youth) as a foil to the restrictions of the law are precisely those harsher aspects of nature which seem least Edenic. And Kipling was predisposed, by temperament, to relish rather than recoil from the paradoxes of so post-Darwinian a paradise.

That such unpromising material can be transformed into a paradise of sorts is best seen in "Red Dog," that account of a territorial dispute between the wolf pack and dhole. Early in the story we have what seems to be a boy's unthinking view of suffering and death in Mowgli's anticipation of battle.

> "But Oh, Kaa"—here Mowgli wriggled with sheer joy,—"it will be good hunting. Few of us will see another moon."
>
> (II, 231)

However, as Miss Tompkins has noted,[11] the story employs such a range of conventionally evocative heroic devices that it succeeds in bestowing on its unlikely protagonists an astonishingly authentic archaic quality, and Mowgli's words, in retrospect, seem scarcely less appropriate than any spoken before the Battles of Brunanburh or Maldon. The primitive, "Edenic" quality here captured is that of an Old Germanic, even a Homeric, warrior innocence.

Before searching for the same balance of power between the irruptive and the restraining elsewhere in Kipling's writings, it may be helpful to remember that, in the jungle, the sternest upholders of the Law, and the only completely reliable animals—like Baloo the Bear, Bagheera the Panther, Kaa the Python and Chil the Kite—are members of solitary species. Wolves, red dogs, monkeys (to say nothing of men), in other words the social animals, are all untrustworthy to some extent. This is an acknowledgement, perhaps, that law in the jungle is still largely biological and instinctive rather than social and learned. It confirms what might be gleaned elsewhere: that Kipling is most certain of his Edenic values when life is at its simplest. For there is a sense in which Kipling always felt safest with children, Pathans or hillmen, and private soldiers. When children grow up—"that process which Kipling, for all his cult of adult masculinity, dreaded most"—,[12] when native peoples begin to acquire western ways, when Mulvaney earns so much as a corporal's stripes, their Edenic incorruptibility is threatened by the responsibilities that crowd in on them.

Thus, in *The Jungle Books*, transitionally social stages like wolves, monkeys and native villagers fall sadly short of the ideal seen in Baloo and Bagheera. Ostensibly, of course, Kipling is not advocating no form of existence other than the Edenically simplest. Man has his role to play in the scheme of things, and the distant glimpse of men who are more successful at living by the law, offered by the Englishmen whom Mowgli's foster parents seek protection from, is presumably meant to reassure. But throughout Kipling's work, though we are so often asked to admire the White Man or his equivalent, the man who accepts and is equal to his civilizing responsibilities, his "burden," Kipling never quite trusts him as he does the child or the loyal native. His distaste flashes out in an aside such as:

> I was silent, reviewing that inexhaustible matter—the more than inherited (since it is also carefully taught) brutality of the Christian peoples, beside which the mere heathendom of the West Coast nigger is clean and restrained.
>
> (*Traffics and Discoveries*, p. 316)

Perhaps Kipling's disgust at the *Bandar-log* is indicative of a more deepseated ambivalence towards mankind in general, or all but its simplest souls, than was allowed for earlier.

At all events, when we move to Kipling's other writings, we shall not be surprised to find the Edenic balance less uniformly maintained in the complex lives of men than in the jungle. Nevertheless, there is still very much in evidence the notion of balance (witness the titles of such volumes as *Action and Reactions, Debits and Credits, Limits and Renewals*), and of a tension between youth, energy, that which makes for freedom or anarchy on the one hand, and law on the other. There are the impossibly pink young heroes of "Only a Subaltern" (*Soldiers Three*), "The Tomb of His Ancestors," "The Brushwood Boy" (*The Day's Work*), and "A Deal in Cotton" (*Actions and Reactions*), or the irrepressibly youthful Mulvaney, all of whom, by submitting willingly or unwillingly to the traditions of the regiment or its equivalent, are strengthened by belonging to something greater than themselves, while at the same time reinvigorating such agencies of law. There are the anarchic impulses which prompt Stalky and all Kipling's other practical jokers, and which, in Stalky's case, are eventually employed in the simultaneous enforcement and rejuvenation of the law, but in that of "The Village that Voted the Earth was Flat" (A Diversity of Creatures) come hilariously and in the end terrifyingly close to overthrowing a law that has ossified. There is the perpetual youth of England, personified in Puck, working its way out through history and tradition, or the youthful Kim preparing for the role he must play in the Great Game. It is as though the law were the gnarled, twisted form of the tree through which the sap of Eden rises; yet, though year after year the sap must take upon itself the tree's deformed configuration, it does not thereby cease to be sap, nor could it otherwise transfigure the tree to blossom.

Mention of Kim calls to mind an instance of this balance between law and the impulse to freedom which is about as far removed from the Mowgli stories as one could imagine, and which therefore illustrates very clearly that what matters to Kipling is the balance itself rather than the nature of the impulse or the law. Kipling seems to offer his young hero a choice between the Way and the Great Game, between a higher and a more earthly law. And it is certainly true, in one sense, that what the lama seeks is a kind of spiritual law. His equivalent in The Jungle Books, Puran Bhagat, when asked by a native policeman not to obstruct the traffic, "salaamed reverently to the Law, because he knew the value of it, and was seeking for a Law of his own" (II, 41). Yet there is also a sense in which the quests of both these holy men are for an escape from a life that has need of law, for freedom.

The lama tells Kim, "Yea, my Soul went free, and, wheeling like an eagle, saw indeed that there was no Teshoo Lama nor any other soul . . . By this I knew the Soul had passed beyond the illusion of Time and Space and of Things. By this I knew that I was free" (Kim, p. 411). And of Puran Bhagat we learn:

> He would repeat a Name softly to himself a hundred times, till, at each repetition, he seemed to move more and more out of his body, sweeping up to the doors of some tremendous discovery; but, just as the door was opening, his body would drag him back, and, with grief, he felt he was locked up again in the flesh and bones of Puran Bhagat.
>
> (II, 45)

However, surprising and remarkable as is the author's sympathy with these Buddhist and Hindu ideals of freedom from the body and all earthly matters, there is still a sense in which, ultimately, he regards them as irresponsible. For both these seekers of a higher life achieve it, in fact, by a last minute renunciation of their professed ideals of detachment and passivity. The lama, apparently at the point of highest fulfillment, seeming to have reached the Great Soul and "meditated a thousand, thousand years, passionless" (*Kim*, p. 412), remembers his *chela*, and, withdrawing "from the Great Soul with strivings and yearnings and retchings and agonies not to be told," returns lest Kim miss the Way. And only then does he find the River which has been the object of his search throughout.

Similarly, Puran Bhagat, being warned by the animals that the mountain is falling, asks, "And yet—why should I go?" Here, without action or striving on his part, is the consummation he desires. But only for a moment does he hesitate, before descending to warn the villagers who have fed him daily since his arrival. "He was no longer a holy man, but Sir Puran Bass, K.C.I.E., Prime Minister of no small State, a man accustomed to command, going out to save life" (II, 53).

Even more clearly than does the lama, Puran Bhagat—who has lived two lives, one of law and the concerns of this world and his fellow men, and one of the contemplative quest for freedom from this world— reconciles this duality at the end. But both men feel the claims of this world and of their fellow men, and therefore of a kind of earthly law, at the very moment they seem to have attained the freedom they seek, and by acknowledging those claims attain their freedom all the more completely. Kipling, by reconciling the ideals of East and West, achieves the same kind of Edenic balance as *The Jungle Books* posit at the level of a child's life among animals: a balance between that which liberates and that which constrains.

To perceive this same recurring theme elsewhere in Kipling's work helps explain another feature of Kipling's Eden. For though Eden is irrecoverably lost at the end of "The Spring Running" in the sense that the childhood of a man or of the species cannot be re-experienced, yet Mowgli, unlike Adam, does retain the right of re-entry to his paradise at will. That precise, primitive, and perhaps most perfect poise that belongs to a state of nature may be irretrievable. But all such balance is not lost for ever.

This is why Kipling does not take us back to the temporally remote Edens of *Genesis, Paradise Lost*, or even William Golding's *The Inheritors*. This is why his paradise does not need to be shielded from all contact with the outside world, as do those in W. H. Hudson's *A Crystal Age*, James Hilton's *Lost Horizon*, or the fourth book of *Gulliver's Travels*.[13] The jungle can co-exist with a fallen world; men may live on its outskirts, monkeys in its tree-tops, wolves in its innermost caves. Kipling's Eden is in this respect essentially post-lapsarian, his conscious vision almost as robust (despite his secret misgivings) as he hoped the children he wrote it for would be.

Notes

1. Rudyard Kipling, *Many Inventions* (London: Macmillan, 1899–). pp. 229–230. All subsequent quotations from Kipling's works are taken from the Macmillan Uniform Edition, and the references included in the text.

2. "India is probably the cradle of wolf-child stories, which are here universally believed and supported by a cloud of testimony, including in the famous Lucknow case of a wolf boy the evidence of European witnesses.": John Lockwood Kipling, *Beast and Man in India* (London, 1891), pp. 313–14.

3. Charles Carrington, in a footnote (p. 209) in *Rudyard Kipling: His Life and Work* (London, 1955), claims that "The adult story, 'In the Rukh,' published before 'Mowgli's Brothers,' " was nevertheless "written after it." He gives no reason for this assertion, and Kipling, in *Something of Myself* (London, 1937), p. 113, states clearly: "It chanced that I had written a tale about Indian Forestry work which included a boy who had been brought up by wolves. In the stillness, and suspense, of the winter of '92 some memory of the Masonic Lions of my childhood's magazine, and a phrase in Haggard's *Nada the Lily*, combined with the echo of this tale. After blocking out the main idea in my head, the pen took charge, and I watched it begin to write stories about Mowgli and animals, which later grew into the *Jungle Books*.:" Clearly at least an early draft of "In the Rukh" was the first to be written.

4. *Something of Myself*, pp. 218–19, ". . . bear serenely with imitators. My *Jungle Books* begat Zoos of them. But the genius of all the genii was one who wrote a series called *Tarzan of the Apes*."

5. *The Art of Rudyard Kipling* (London, 1959), p. 67.

6. *Ibid.*, p. 68.

7. My italics in this and extracts immediately following.

8. Konrad Lorenz, *On Aggression*, tr. Marjorie Kerr Wilson (New York, 1966), p. 109 ff.

9. Charles Darwin, *The Descent of Man*, 2nd edn. (London, 1906), pp. 184–85.

10. "Kipling's Place in the History of Ideas." *Kipling's Mind and Art*, ed. Andrew Rutherford (Edinburgh, 1964), pp. 100–102, 104 ff.

11. *The Art of Rudyard Kipling*, p. 70.

12. George Shepperson, "The World of Rudyard Kipling," *Kipling's Mind and Art*, p. 128.

13. That not everyone regards the land of the Houyhnhnms as paradisal does not alter the fact that it is presented, perhaps ironically, as such.

Kipling and Fantasy   Peter Havholm[2]

Boris Ford voiced the opinion of many when he wrote: "Except for children, there seems little to be said on behalf of [Kipling's] imagination; but of course, though children probably do enjoy *Puck of Pook's Hill* and the *Jungle Books*, Kipling rather hoped that adults would like them too."[1] I object both to this view of Kipling's prose fiction and to another, less

[2]*From *Children's Literature*, annual of the Modern Language Seminar on Children's Literature and the Children's Literature Association, 4 (1975):91–104. Reprinted by permission.

harsh judgment found on the crowded critical battlefield that spreads around this most evaluated of writers. The other view is that Kipling did not really come into his own until he developed what is commonly referred to as his "late manner" after 1900.[2] There is a third view which embraces all of Kipling and dismisses his negative critics as the victims of political prejudice,[3] but measured rejection on the one hand and equally measured selection of the mature work on the other mark the bounds of worthwhile Kipling criticism.

Indeed, these views are trying to get at the same thing in Kipling, but they share an error of interpretation that has so far not been pointed out. Both Ford and those who boost the later work as mature take a superficial view of stories "children probably do enjoy." Ford assumes that grownups ought not to enjoy such stories. Those who take the other side seem to agree with him because they look for a maturity they do not find in early Kipling. On one side, simplicity of substance is rejected because it is not complex; on the other, simplicity is virtually ignored on the ground that it disappears later on.

Through an examination of a few of Kipling's works, I wish to show that while there is reason to believe he could not achieve the particular kind of complexity we associate with tragedy, he did achieve brilliantly a kind of simplicity we associate with some stories "children probably do enjoy." "Complex" and "simple" are appropriate (though all too value-tinged) words because the kind of story at which Kipling fails and the kind at which he succeeds require our assent to different views of human possibility. The view I call complex assumes that the great challenges in life are within us. More simple is the view that human beings are either good or bad, and that consequently great challenges come always from outside the self. Thus, measured on the single scale of human possibility, the simple assumption is that we can do only what evil outside us and a limiting Providence will allow. The complex view is that we can do what we will. The simple view is that we are what we are made. The complex view is that we are what we make ourselves.

This pronouncement should not be taken very broadly; I am concerned only with what Kipling could and could not do well. I have no wish to argue either that children cannot enjoy the kind of complexity Kipling could not create or that such complexity is always absent from stories commonly considered "for children."

My argument runs as follows. In *The Light that Failed*, there is evidence Kipling was trying to write a species of tragedy. He fails because he cannot adopt the complex view of human possibility. But in certain of the Mowgli stories in the *Jungle Books*, we find Kipling succeeding brilliantly at an effect quite as soul-shaking in its way as is successful tragedy. J. R. R. Tolkien has called this effect "The Consolation of the Happy Ending" in his discussion of fairy stories.[4] Once Kipling adopts the convention of fantasy, a kind of heroism that has nothing to do with blameable human error is available to him, and he uses the gift of joy, Tolkien's *eucatastrophe*, again and again in his later work. I shall show in detail how it operates in "They," a story very much in Kipling's "late manner."

Kipling could accomplish one thing superbly despite his inability to accomplish another, and it is not very fruitful to look in his work for the complex. But it is futile to damn him for succeeding in stories "children probably do enjoy." Adults have always been able to enjoy such stories, and will not, I hope, lose the capability. If we understand one of the things Kipling can do in the proper light, evaluation of his work will become both more temperate and more accurate.

I am not the first to be disappointed by *The Light that Failed*.[5] Edmund Gosse summed up contemporary critical response in 1891: "I confess that it is *The Light that Failed* that has wakened me to the fact that there are limits to this dazzling new talent, the *eclat* of which had almost lifted us off our critical feet."[6] Max Beerbohm, reviewing a dramatic version in 1903, suggested scathingly that because there is so much effeminate man-worship in the story "Rudyard Kipling" might well be a woman's pseudonym.[7] With the assistance of Charles Carrington's authorized biography, Mark Kinkead-Weekes concluded in 1964: "Kipling cannot finally see beyond his own private agonies and violences; this means that he is less and less able to achieve any real focus at all."[8]

Though the novel is still in print, it might be well to give a brief summary here. We meet Dick Heldar and his nemesis, Maisie, as children in a grim foster home. There occur puppy love and a nasty powder burn on Dick's forehead. We next meet Dick as a rough, knockabout vagabond artist whose chosen subject is men at war. In the Sudan (he is following Kitchener's expedition to Khartoum), he is taken up by Torpenhow, a war-correspondent, and begins to send his sketches to Torpenhow's paper. Dick's work is a great hit at home, though it is thought too violently and dirtily "realistic" by some. The first wonderful flush of success causes him to use callously as a model one Binat, an alcoholic ex-painter in Port Said, to mistreat violently a rapacious publisher in London, and to paint for gold a much-prettified picture called "His Last Shot." His journalist friends attempt to set him straight, but he remains desperately cynical about his public. In the meantime, however, he has met Maisie again and again fallen in love with her. But Maisie is determined to achieve popular success with her own pallid paintings and cares nought for Dick except as a sort of footman-teacher. After a good deal of painfully unrequited love, Dick begins to go blind as a result of the old powder burn overlaid by a sword cut in the Sudan. He suffers a last, terrible double disappointment when Maisie rejects him even though he is blind and Bessie (an ex-prostitute, whom he has prevented from vamping Torpenhow) ruins the masterpiece finished just before his blindness becomes complete. Finally, Dick goes to the Sudan, where all his journalist friends have gone to cover another military campaign, and makes his way to the front just in time to die in Torpenhow's arms, shot through the head.

One could dismiss all this as mere autobiographical rambling or as a pathetic story of the most obvious kind were it not for a very important aspect of the novel only partly apparent in my summary. This aspect is pointed to by critical comments about how unlikeable Dick is (readers who feel they are meant to pity Dick have difficulty in doing so unreservedly because he is so obnoxious in the middle chapters)[9] and by Lionel Trilling's remark: "If [as a boy] one ever fell in love with the cult of art, it was not because one had been proselytized by some intelligent Frenchman, but because one had absorbed Kipling's credal utterances about the virtues of craft and had read *The Light that Failed* literally to pieces."[10]

I think Kipling meant the credal utterances and Dick's arrogance to indicate that Dick's prolonged suffering is the result of his own error. Indeed, Dick sees his blindness as a punishment visited upon him by a "very just Providence." Soon after he has been told he will be blind within the year, he prays, "Allah Almighty! . . . Help me through the time of waiting, and I won't whine when my punishment comes" (p. 197). Later, when he has finished the *Melancolia*, his masterpiece, he says "Just God! what could I not do ten years hence, if I can do this now!" (p. 209).

The reason God is just, taking this line of interpretation, is that Dick has thought the very hard life he has led means he is *owed* success. That he is quite wrong to make such demands on Providence, to say nothing of his Public, is clear from Torpenhow's remark just after Dick has re-met Maisie, fallen in love with her again, and realized "there's everything in . . . [her] face but love" (p. 82): "It's no business of mine, of course, but it's comforting to think that somewhere under the stars there's saving up for you a tremendous thrashing. Whether it'll come from heaven or earth, I don't know, but it's bound to come and break you up a little. You want hammering" (pp. 85–86). We are meant to see Maisie, the blindness indirectly caused by her, and even the destruction of the *Melancolia* as a "tremendous thrashing" administered in return for Dick's arrogance in making demands on Fate and his Public.

The novel was meant to proceed in a manner not entirely unlike Thomas Hardy's *Mayor of Casterbridge*. In such a story, the protagonist suffers because of his own error and then, through defiant action in the teeth of that error's train of vicious consequences, redeems himself in our eyes. Such a story differs from the ordinary, pathetic, have-a-nice-cry-dearie tear-jerker in that the protagonist is sufficiently noble in character both to be responsible for his own suffering and to be able to achieve redemption through his own effort. Fate may operate malevolently, but we never lose our sense that Fate has been given its cue by the victim's own mistakes.

J. M. S. Tompkins, in the best full-length appreciation of Kipling, seems to agree with this estimate of what *The Light that Failed* was meant to be:

> There is, however, one design . . . which holds the book together . . . by a genuine though unmatured life that runs throughout all its parts. This is the question of degradation, the possible degradations of art, of love, and of life. It is from these that Dick is to be saved, by Torpenhow, by Maisie, and finally even by Bessie's spite in destroying the *Melancolia*, so that he cannot traffic in it to buy an inglorious physical comfort . . . [In the book's last chapters, Dick] has "paid for everything" and is free of self-pity. He is back among the sounds and smells of the East . . . and in Dick's last words—"Put me, I pray, in the forefront of the battle,"— Kipling's excited Muse, under the cover of quotation, reached for the proud amplitude of Jacobean speech. The allusion is to Uriah, and the unspoken words as "that I may be smitten, and die." (*Art*, pp. 15–16)

I think the pattern is there in embryo. Dick wastes his art on "His Last Shot," his love on Maisie, and nearly his life on Bessie and the imagined profits from the *Melancolia*. Kipling means Dick to save himself from all of this by the realization that such waste is unworthy and by the consequent journey back to the Sudan. Providence keeps after him until he realizes what he *must* do, and turns to that rather than what he *will* do.

But the novel as Kipling finally wrote it refuses to allow Dick really to be to blame for what happens to him. Moreover, Kipling childishly makes sure that everyone who hurts Dick is thoroughly punished for what he has done. Neither of these lapses is consistent with the apparent "design" of the novel. Together, they ruin it.

We cannot blame Dick because the train of misfortune that overwhelms him is too clearly linked to the independent malevolence of Maisie and Bessie and God. Despite Kipling's excuses for Maisie, she ends up a thoroughly selfish tease. Yes, she tells Dick several times that his romantic hopes are baseless. Yes, "His Last Shot" proves that success can make even the best of artists do trivial, Maisie-like things. And yes, Dick himself reminds us that he has shown Maisie a ruined canvas as his best work. But all this falls into the background at her exit from the novel:

> There she sat in the almost dismantled drawing-room and thought of Dick in his blindness, useless till the end of life, and of herself in her own eyes. Behind the sorrow, the shame, and the humiliation, lay fear of the cold wrath of the red-haired girl when Maisie should return. Maisie had never feared her companion before. Not until she found herself saying, "Well, he never asked me," did she realize her scorn of herself.
>   And that is the end of Maisie. (p. 254)

Few heroines have received quite so vehement a dismissal.

It would have been consistent with her insensitivity to have had Maisie quite unaware of her fault in the matter. But Kipling cannot let her go unpunished. It would have been equally appropriate to have Bessie, the agent of a "just Providence," remain unaware of the ruined *Melancolia's* value. But Kipling must have her aware of how much money she has lost—"she knew the value of money" (p. 287)—and then heap further contempt upon her: "Now through a slip of the tongue, and a little feminine desire to give a little, not too much, pain, she had lost the money, the blessed idleness and the pretty things, the companionship, and the chance of looking outwardly as respectable as a real lady" (p. 293). These punishments indicate that Kipling really does not believe Dick's suffering is fair. Since Kipling cannot believe it, he cannot convince his reader, and we are left with what seems like chapter after chapter of excessive pity for Dick.

The final departure for the Sudan is motivated not by "a very just Providence" but by "a very just Providence *who delights in causing pain*" (pp. 290–91, italics mine). Such a Providence must take Its place alongside Maisie and Bessie as the real cause of Dick's misfortunes, leaving Dick a hounded, bathetic victim.

In his short stories at about this time in his career, Kipling created a number of very successful victims: Learoyd in "On Greenhow Hill," Holden in "Without Benefit of Clergy," Georgina in "Georgie Porgie," and Punch in "Baa Baa, Black Sheep." They are "successful" because the stories in which they suffer are designed only to make us pity their innocent pain at the hands of outside forces—and we do, we do. But when Kipling tries to make Mulvaney a tragic hero in "The Courting of Dinah Shadd" (in which are evoked the images of Mulvaney as Hamlet and as Prometheus), he again comes a cropper.[11] Mulvaney's "error" in the story is twenty minutes' drunken flirtation with another woman once he has become engaged to Dinah Shadd. The result, perhaps assisted by an alcoholic curse from the other woman's mother, is the loss of his only child, a life of alcoholism, and no promotion. The punishment so overwhelms the youthful indiscretion that we must see the notions of human responsibility in this story and in *The Light that Failed* as similar.

Kipling's notion for the novel was to give his protagonist a heroic glory through suffering brought on by his own pride. That Kipling cannot bring off redemption through suffering results not only from his own real suffering at the hands of Florence Garrard, Harper Brothers, and the British critics in 1890, but also from his inability to imagine a good man committing a blameable wrong. Instead, in Kipling's cosmos, if a good man doesn't watch out he will be struck down by a Providence who "delights in causing pain." Clearly, such an attitude cannot produce the kind of tragedy I have called "complex," for such a work depends upon the possibility of terrible error in the best of men.

Dick Heldar's story ends with a whimper. But in a thoroughly different vein, Kipling's fiction finds in many readers a response nearly as strong as that he seems to have wished for *The Light that Failed*. We first find this achievement in the non-didactic Mowgli stories in the *Jungle Books.*[12]

I specify non-didactic because critics have a tendency to treat all the Mowgli stories as if they were fables like "How Fear Came" and "The King's Ankus."[13] But if "Red Dog," for instance, were fable rather than adventure, someone would surely have demanded by now that children not be allowed to read it. For the story opposes Mowgli and the Pack against the Hun-like Red Dog of Dekkan, who are anathematized not just because they kill needlessly but also because they produce larger litters than the wolves. Mowgli "despised and hated them because they did not smell like the Free People, because they did not live in caves, and, above all, because they had hair between their toes while he and his friends were clean-footed" (p. 225). Following the fabular line, Mowgli's leading the dholes through the bee-cliffs is the atrocity made "necessary" by the threat to the civilized tribe. The story would then end with genocide: "But of all the Pack of two hundred fighting dholes, whose boast was that all Jungles were their Jungle, and that no living thing could stand before them, not one returned to the Dekkan to carry that word" (p. 256).

What actually happens is that Kipling finds in fantasy the absolute evil that makes blameable human error as the prerequisite to glory quite unnecessary. In the "real" world, where Kipling places Dick Heldar and Terence Mulvaney, we know absolute evil is hard to find—and we are unwilling to find it in Maisie, Bessie, and the carefully low-class Sheehy women of "Dinah Shadd." But the world of fantasy is a different matter.

G. K. Chesterton points out in "The Ethics of Elfland"[14] that the "philosophic manner of fairy tales" assumes all connections between discrete physical events to be magic. Thus, in the context of fantasy, Cinderella's midnight transformation is no more improbable than the appearance of an apple on a tree. Chesterton uses the example to proclaim the apple as much a miracle as the disappearing ball gown, but it can be turned the other way. Once magic begins to operate openly, the consequences of overstaying the fairy godmother's time limit are as natural as the fairy godmother herself: we accept the laws of magic in precisely the same way we accept the laws of nature once we realize an author is operating within the fantasist's convention.

This goes far enough to produce rather abrupt moral imperatives. Some frogs may turn into princes, but there are certain trolls and a witch or two who are better off eliminated. The creation of animals who are evil by definition is merely a special form of the fantasist's miraculous laws. From the wolf who is out to get Little Red Riding Hood to the dholes who threaten the Pack is a short step indeed. By definition, by law, by magic, the troll or the witch or the slavering wolf or the dhole is inherently evil.

Once such a simplification is accepted, all Mowgli's heroism and invention in "Red Dog" at the expense of the dholes achieve a wonderfully straightforward glory of the kind unavailable to Dick Heldar.

A good argument could be made that fantasy is almost by definition wish-fulfillment. At least it must be a major temptation for the artist who takes on the freedom to organize the world to fit his notions of how it ought to be. Such a possibility brings to mind Edmund Wilson's suggestion in "The Kipling that Nobody Read":

> This increasing addiction of Kipling to animals, insects and machines is evidently to be explained by his need to find characters which will yield themselves unresistingly to being presented as parts of a system. In the *Jungle Books*, the animal characters are each one all of a piece, though in their ensemble they still provide a variety, and they are dominated by a "Law of the Jungle," which lays down their duties and rights. The animals have organized the Jungle, and the Jungle is presided over by Mowgli in his function as forest ranger, so that it falls into its subsidiary place in the larger organisation of the Empire. (pp. 50–51)

What happens, however, is that the notions Wilson extracts from the stories (notions that were certainly Kipling's) fall into place as sections of the background for Mowgli's adventures. In "Red Dog," Mowgli's final triumph in no way depends upon Kipling's organization of the jungle in the sense Wilson means.[15] Instead, Mowgli's stature ultimately depends upon the same love and innocent courage that motivate most of the behavior in the *Jungle Books*.

Victorious over the dholes, running to help cut off their retreat, Mowgli falls to his knees beside the dying Akela: " 'Said I not it would be my last fight?' Akela panted. 'It is good hunting. And thou, Little Brother?' " Mowgli replies: " 'I live, having killed many,' " and the wolf goes on, " 'Even so. I die, and I would—I would die by thee, Little Brother' " (p. 254). Akela tells Mowgli to return to his own people, but the boy refuses to go until "Mowgli drives Mowgli."

> "There is no more to say," said Akela. "Little Brother, canst thou raise me to my feet? I also was a leader of the Free People."
> Very carefully and gently Mowgli lifted the bodies aside, and raised Akela to his feet, both arms around him, and the Lone Wolf drew a long breath, and began the Death Song that a leader of the Pack should sing when he dies. It gathered strength as he went on, lifting and lifting, and ringing far across the river, till it came to the last "Good hunting!" and Akela shook himself clear of Mowgli for an instant, and leaping into the air, fell backward dead upon his last and most terrible kill. (pp. 255–56).

In his last words Dick Heldar reaches through "the proud amplitude of Jacobean speech" for a noble death. The notion of a "good death" in the sense that it meets standards of decorum arising from a life of battle is pretty much lost to us now except in Western movies (which have abundant fantasy conventions of their own to depend upon). And Dick's last words, ending a life whose keynote is pathetic innocence, seem silly rather than noble. But in the admittedly brutal, necessarily simple Jungle, the Lone Wolf finds such a death. Even more significantly, he is as innocently strong as Dick is innocently weak.

In the "real world," we adults have difficulty considering noble a person incapable of doing something blameably wrong. But what about a wolf? Or a boy? To understand the very strong emotional force of Akela's "I die, and I would—I would die by thee, Little Brother," we must turn to what J. R. R. Tolkien has called the "Consolation of the Happy Ending" or the *eucatastrophe* of fairy tales ("On Fairy-Stories," pp. 68–69).

Tolkien explains the affective power of the *eucatastrophe* as analogous to "The Christian joy, the *Gloria*" (p. 72), which is the ultimate and true consolation. But I prefer to stop at the place where he describes the feeling:

> The consolation of fairy-stories, the joy of the happy ending: or more correctly of the good catastrophe, the sudden joyous "turn" . . . : this joy, which is one of the things which fairy-stories can produce supremely well, is not essentially "escapist," nor "fugitive." In its fairytale—or otherworld—setting, it is a sudden and miraculous grace: never to be counted on to recur. It does not deny the existence of *dyscatastrophe*, of sorrow and failure; the possibility of these is necessary to the joy of deliverance; it denies (in the face of much evidence, if you will) universal final defeat and in so far is evangelium, giving a fleeting glimpse of Joy, Joy beyond the walls of the world, poignant as grief.
>
> It is the mark of a good fairy-story, of the higher or more complete kind, that however wild its events, however fantastic or terrible the adventures, it can give to child or man who hears it, when the "turn" comes, a catch of the breath, a beat and lifting of the heart, near to (or indeed accompanied by) tears, as keen as that given by any form of literary art, and having a peculiar quality. (pp. 68–69)

This passage describes accurately the feeling we have when Akela asks to die by Mowgli.

It is Akela's good death by Mowgli's side that is the climax of "Red Dog," not Mowgli's defeat of the dholes. And "heroism" is the wrong word for Mowgli's stature when Akela asks to die by him. In fact, Mowgli has risked nothing. There is the possibility of his doing so when he has committed himself to the fight, but Kaa's plan for leading the dholes through the bee-cliffs effectively solves the problem. Mowgli makes a jump from those cliffs he tells us is not so terrible as others he has made before, and Kaa waits for him in the river. When Mowgli fights the dholes, he has his four wolf brothers ranged round him for protection.

There is no indication in the story that Mowgli has "earned" Akela's tribute except by being the same good person he was when, barely able to stand, he was first found by Mother and Father Wolf. The triumph of innocent goodness is no triumph in the "real world" where, as we all know, innocence is often a liability. But in a fantasy designed to make it not a liability but a glory, it is a wonderful possibility the side of our minds Tolkien associates with Christian *Gloria* can accept happily.

In the last of the Mowgli stories, "The Spring Running," Mowgli discovers (somewhat belatedly at seventeen, the "realistic" critic might comment) that, in what the animals call "The Time of the New Talk" in the Spring, the jungle holds no pleasure for him. A series of events leads him to decide to return to people, and he wishes to tell all the jungle at Council Rock of his decision. But because it is Spring, no one comes except his four wolf brothers, Kaa, old Baloo, and finally Bagheera.

Mowgli's last adventure is no adventure at all, but ends with a boy sobbing, "with his head on the blind bear's side and his arms around his neck, while Baloo tried feebly to lick his feet" (p. 292). As he walks to the village of men, he hears the song of the Three behind him, ending: "Jungle-Favor go with thee!"

"Jungle-Favor" is the love of the Three, the love Mowgli has earned as a child "earns" love—by being innocently good-hearted. What Mowgli goes to is not suffering; what he leaves he does not leave by his own choice. But in going, he receives another tribute like the one Akela gave him. It is a dream of loving fealty, with all the emphasis on love. The term "Master of the Jungle" becomes an endearment when Baloo uses it. Indeed, Mowgli is proved no master (though again, that is not his fault) by the appearance only of his brothers and the Three at his last and most urgent call.

Precisely the same limitations can be found in Mowgli's character as in Dick Heldar's. But in Mowgli, they are not flaws because he aspires no higher than innocence. Dick is no boy; Maisie, Bessie, and the Head of the Central Syndicate are no animals, and we cannot accept the paces Kipling puts them through. But in the Jungle of Kipling's fantasy, animals and a boy succeed or fail depending upon their strength against enemies and Fate.

"A fleeting glimpse of Joy, Joy beyond the walls of the world, poignant as grief," describes our response to the wonders Kipling aims at in a number of stories written after the *Jungle Books*. Repeating the pattern of "Red Dog," Kipling's masterpiece *Kim* ends with a tribute to its boy hero from his mentor, the Lama. Kim has "deserved" the Lama's care from the beginning as Mowgli "deserved" that of the Three: by being the "Little Friend of all the World." Chance and Providence intervene in Kipling nearly as often as they do in Hardy, but in Kipling's later stories, their intervention is likely to be benign. That the gift of joy is occasionally preceded by a good deal of suffering makes it no less a type of the *eucatastrophe*. In "An Habitation Enforced," "The House Surgeon," "In the Same Boat," "Friendly Brook," and " 'My Son's Wife,' " those who do good help, are helped by, or are rewarded by remarkable coincidence or the frankly otherworldly. Christ appears in "The Gardener" to help relieve the protagonist of her burden of guilt. "Uncovenanted Mercies," a kind of apotheosis in this vein, pulls a reversal by finding a happy ending through the "intervention" of human love in Hell.[16]

One of the very best of Kipling's stories in the "late manner" is "They," published in 1904.[17] It is the story of a man who discovers a house prepared by its owner to be a refuge for dead children not quite ready to leave this world. The climax of the story is the narrator's realization—at his own dead daughter's remembered touch—that this is what the house is and why he is in it.

I first read the story when I was about twelve, but I did not understand it until much later. On first reading, I was awe-struck by the bravura descriptions of the Sussex countryside, the beautiful house, and its owner, but I did not know what it was the story's narrator "knew" at its end—despite a very real sense that there was much there teasing me on to realize something not stated outright. I should have had no problem with the explicit idea of a dead child wishing to say goodby to her father, but Kipling's elliptic style, always hinting and never relaxing into straightforward statement, left me baffled. Because of the way the story is told, I think few children today could do any better.

Out for a drive, the narrator comes on the house by mistake and nearly drives onto its lawn before he is stopped by a clipped yew "horseman's green spear laid at my breast." The pointing spear becomes significant only at the story's climax when we realize that the narrator's discovery of this house is no accident.

Once the narrator has met the house's owner, a beautiful blind woman, the hints proliferate. In her second speech, she says, "You—you haven't seen any one, have you—perhaps?" We know he has seen two children, but the hesitation in her speech might be over "seen" because she is blind. This supposition seems confirmed a little later by "Oh, lucky you! . . . I hear them, of course, but that's all. You've seen them and heard them?" But the confirmation is made ambivalent again by her odd introduction of the narrator to her butler, Madden: "Is that you, Madden? I want you to show this gentleman the way to the cross-roads. He has lost his way but—he has seen them."

This is one line of clues, the line which leads to our knowledge (and the narrator's) of what is going on in the house. In this line is Madden's questioning of the narrator about *whether* he has seen the children rather than which children or where. Later is the business of "Jenny's turn to walk in de wood nex' week along" when Jenny's child is dying and the wood is the one surrounding the house. Finally, on the narrator's last visit to the house, there is the animal fear of the tenant farmer when he is forced to enter the house at night.

The other line of clues begins with the lady's question: "You're fond of children?" and the narrator's description of his response: "I gave her one or two reasons why I did not altogether hate them." Why such reticence? Why not "I told her I had two of my own," or something similar?

Perhaps it is because there is something more to tell than that. What that something might be is hinted when she comments, "And they tell me that one never sees a dead person's face in a dream. Is that true?" (why does she ask him as if he might know?), and the narrator replies:

> "I believe it is—now I come to think of it."
> "But how is it with yourself—yourself?" The blind eyes turned to-ward me.
> "I have never seen the faces of my dead in any dream," I answered.

"My dead" and "How is it with yourself—yourself" imply a bond already made, an understanding between the two that the reader has somehow missed. Perhaps it occurred in the "one or two reasons why I did not alto-gether hate them."

The two lines of clues come together at the story's climax:

> The little brushing kiss fell in the centre of my palm—*as a gift on which the fingers were, once, expected to close*: as the all faithful half-reproachful signal of a waiting child not used to neglect even when grown-ups were busiest—*a fragment of the mute code devised very long ago.*
> Then I knew. And it was as though I had known from the first day when I looked across the lawn at the high window.

The words I have italicized above are as impersonal (note "of *a* waiting child") as all the other clues in the story, yet they culminate the two lines of hints such that, if we have followed the story carefully, we have the same rush of discovery as its narrator at the line: "Then I knew." What he knows, what we "know" at this lovely moment is "The Consolation of the Happy Ending" as Tolkien describes it: poignant as grief.

Though there must be some ten-year-olds somewhere for whom tragedy at the level of *The Mayor of Casterbridge* is moving, I suspect many of them are more intrigued by the kind of glory Mowgli finds. That adults can respond with equal fervor to this kind of glory is apparent in critical response to stories like "They" and "The Gardener" among Kipling's later work. In these stories, Kipling finds new and frequently quite complex ways of producing the *eucatastrophe* effect, but he does not abandon it. And only the way in which a story like "They" is presented makes it relatively unavailable to children. There is nothing complex about its matter.

The joy of such stories is always given, whatever the struggles that precede it. Indeed, as Tolkien hints, it derives some of its power as a liter-ary device from its other worldly connections. Mowgli's innocence and good heart are given him. The narrator in "They" is given the joy of knowing: the yew horseman's spear at his chest singles him out for it at the story's beginning. On the other hand, the affirmation of tragedy as-sumes our knowledge that the ultimate hazard is within rather than without, and the greatest glory our ability to transcend our very human limitations unaided and against the most tremendous odds.

One thing we mean by the word "child" is "a being growing into complexity." Such a definition avoids substantively the flat assumption that a child is simple. But it suggests that there are some complexities about which a child is still learning. And since tragedy in the classic sense is something we spend our adult lives learning about, it is no great criticism to say that a child cannot appreciate it in the way an adult can.

We could criticize Kipling for never achieving the tragedy he falls so far short of in *The Light that Failed*. Or we could proclaim the complexity of manner in "They" as complexity of matter. But in either case, we imply that, because the *eucatastrophe* is not so complex as the end of tragedy, it must be rejected. I can imagine the Olympian heights from which such an argument might be made, but I prefer to remain on a level from which I can respond—along with the children—to the glimpses of joy Kipling gives us in his best work.

Notes

1. In "A Case for Kipling?" reprinted from *The Importance of Scrutiny*, ed. Eric Bentley, in E. L. Gilbert, ed., *Kipling and the Critics* (New York: New York University Press, 1965), p. 62.

2. The View is most clear in Edmund Wilson's "The Kipling that Nobody Read," reprinted from *The Wound and the Bow* in Andrew Rutherford, ed., *Kipling's Mind and Art: Selected Critical Essays* (Stanford: Stanford University Press, 1964), pp. 17–69. See particularly pp. 63 and 69. J. M. S. Tompkins, though she has a perceptive appreciation for all of Kipling, suggests the same view in *The Art of Rudyard Kipling* (2nd ed.; London: Methuen, 1965), pp. ix–x, 115–18. The assumption underlies C. A. Bodelsen's *Aspects of Kipling's Art* (Manchester: Manchester University Press, 1964).

3. See Roger Lancelyn Green's "Introduction" to his *Kipling: The Critical Heritage* (New York: Barnes and Noble, 1971), pp. 1–33, particularly pp. 1–2.

4. "On Fairy-Stories," in *Tree and Leaf* (Boston: Houghton, 1965), pp. 3–84.

5. My text is that in Vol. IX of the "Outward Bound" edition of *The Writings in Prose and Verse of Rudyard Kipling* (New York: Scribner's, 1897–1937).

6. "Rudyard Kipling" in Green's *Critical Heritage*, p. 116, reprinted from *Century Magazine*, XLII (1891), 901–10.

7. Max Beerbohm, "Kipling's Entire," in *Around Theatres* (New York: Knopf, 1930), pp. 314–18.

8. In "Vision in Kipling's Novels," *Mind and Art*, p. 210. Carrington discusses the close relationship of life to art in *The Life of Rudyard Kipling* (New York: Doubleday, 1955), pp. 130–33, and in "Some Conjectures about *The Light that Failed*," *Kipling Journal*, XXV, no. 125 (1958), 9–14.

9. See Gosse, p. 116, and J. M. Barrie, "Mr. Kipling's Stories," in *Critical Heritage*, p. 85.

10. In "Kipling," reprinted from *The Liberal Imagination* in *Kipling and the Critics*, p. 91.

11. "Georgie Porgie" and "Baa Baa, Black Sheep" were first published in 1888 and first collected in *Life's Handicap* (1890) and *Wee Willie Winkie* (1888), respectively. "On

Greenhow Hill," "Without Benefit of Clergy," and "The Courting of Dinah Shadd" were all first published in 1890 and first collected in *Life's Handicap*.

12. Collected in Vol. VII of the "Outward Bound" edition, to which my page numbers refer.

13. The first is a story of animal original sin which places Fear in control of the jungle. The second is a cautionary tale about the consequences of human greed.

14. In *Orthodoxy* (New York: Dodd, Mead, 1908), pp. 81–118.

15. Wilson depends too much on the notion that "In the Rukh," in which Mowgli becomes a forest ranger, is the climax of Mowgli's story. In fact, it preceded "Mowgli's Brothers" in composition and was the product of a different line of inspiration. See Roger Lancelyn Green, "Two Notes on *The Jungle Book*," *KJ*, XXV, no. 128 (1958), 12–15, and C. E. Carrington, "Casual Notes on the Mowgli Stories," *KJ*, XXVI, no. 129 (1959), 23–24.

16. *Kim* was published in 1900. "An Habitation Enforced" (1905) and "The House Surgeon" (1909) were collected in *Actions and Reactions*. "In the Same Boat" (1911), "Friendly Brook" (1914), and " 'My Son's Wife' " (1917) were collected in *A Diversity of Creatures*. "The Gardener" (1926) was collected in *Debits and Credits* and "Uncovenanted Mercies" (1932) in *Limits and Renewals*.

17. Collected in *Traffics and Discoveries*, Vol. XXIV of the "Outward Bound" edition, pp. 132–56. I have not given page references because the story is so short.

An Attempt at Soul Murder: Rudyard Kipling's Early Life and Work
Leonard Shengold, M.D.[*]

The term *soul murder* appeared in psychiatric literature after its use by the psychotic Daniel Paul Schreber, whose *Memoirs*, written in 1903, were the subject of extensive study, most notably by Freud (1911).

The earliest use of *soul murder*, however, appeared in a popular book of the middle nineteenth century entitled *Kaspar Hauser: An Instance of a Crime Against the Life of the Soul of Man* by Anselm von Feuerbach. Kaspar Hauser, a cause célèbre in his time, had spent the first seventeen years of his life in a dark dungeon, cut off from all human contact except for an occasional glimpse of his jailer (pathetically called by Kaspar "the man who was always there"), and was fed only on bread and water. Feuerbach wrote: "How long soever he may live, he must for ever remain a man without childhood and boyhood, a monstrous being, who, contrary to the usual course of nature, only began to live in the middle of his life. . . . he may be said to have been the subject of a partial soul murder. . . . the life of a human soul was mutilated at its commencement" (1832, pp. 56–57). Feuerbach was a distinguished judge and his work

[*]From *Lives, Events and Other Plays*, ed. J. T. Coltrera, M.D., Downstate Psychoanalytic Institute Twenty-fifth Anniversary Series (New York: Jason Aronson, Inc., 1981), 243–51. Reprinted by permission of the publisher. © 1981, Jason Aronson, Inc.

might very well have been read by his fellow jurist Schreber. (I am grateful to Professor Jeff Masson for directing me to Feuerbach's book.)

The term was used by Strindberg in an 1887 article on Ibsen's *Rosmersholm*, entitled "Soul Murder." *[Because the major part of this article, pp. 203–43 in the original, is biographical in its emphasis, I have omitted it. However, the concept of "soul murder," as defined in these pages, is crucial to an understanding of the "Summary and Conclusions" section. Dr. Shengold concentrates on Kipling's childhood experiences. "It is easy to kill the soul of a child," he writes (p. 205). Kipling at Southsea, in the House of Desolation, felt abandoned by his parents. In addition to external insults, the absence of protection, and his awareness of the impossibility of rescue, he could not understand what he had done to deserve his fall from the bliss of his earliest years in India. The consequences—trauma and a bitter feeling of helplessness—may be traced in "Baa, Baa, Black Sheep," The Light That Failed, numerous stories about children filled with a longing for good father figures, Stalky & Co., and the autobiographical fragment Something of Myself. The death of Wolcott Balestier, his beloved brother figure, led directly to his decision to marry Wolcott's sister, Carrie, but the "soul murder" had been committed two decades earlier.—The Editor.]* Kipling was scarred by the soul murder. His intense hatred was a burden adversely affecting his art as well as his life. His marvelous talent for seeing and knowing (he was one of the greatest describers in English literature) was often inhibited by the simultaneous need to attack and to justify the established order. He escaped overt homosexuality, but married a domineering, masculine woman. In some ways this was a narcissistic choice since he too had identified with "Aunty Rosa" with a lifelong bent for the Harrys—the doers and bullies of this world. But the relationship with his wife was close and contained much happiness. Kipling was a loving father to his children, and suffered terribly when two of them died. He was subject to moods of depression and irritability, but also could laugh, occasionally even at himself, and make others laugh. He became a great success, a public figure, the most widely read author in English since Shakespeare. Following the first World War, his critical reputation plunged. The intellectual generation that grew up in the twenties was disinterested or hostile to the poet of patriotism and imperialism. Except for his books for children, he had become the "Kipling that nobody read" (Wilson 1941). There was a group of devoted readers he never lost. But the artistry of his later short stories went largely unrecognized until a revival of critical interest in his work occurred in the 1940s.

SUMMARY AND CONCLUSIONS

The psychoanalyst who is only a reader has no special source of insight. His view of the author's childhood is of necessity superficial. On the surface, Kipling's childhood is portrayed as six years of bliss followed by six years of hell. The crucial first six years of his life must have provided Kipling with the strength to survive the soul murder in the "House of Desolation;" he says so himself. How much did these early years also provide the seeds of his undoing? The reader can only speculate, reconstructing from what Kipling wrote, and basing his shaky structure on a general knowledge of human development. Seemingly there was an overwhelming acceptance of the boy's importance. He was a wanted child, perhaps too much wanted. There was little curbing of his aggression which was freely displayed in the nursery world. Although his parents may have been distant at times, his *ayah* and bearer were physically close and very indulgent. In his memoirs and stories, Kipling depicts the narcissistic vulnerability that can accompany the grandiosity of the overindulged child. It would be important to know more about the specifics of his relationship with his parents, especially with his mysterious mother. It must be meaningful that Trix wrote of herself in Lorne Lodge as having had "no least recollection of" (1937, p. 168) her mother, while "remember(ing) that dear *ayah* known and loved all my short life in India" (1937, p. 170).

Fears about his anger and sexual feelings must have been evoked in Rudyard by the births of his sister and the stillborn sibling. These births were probably linked to fantasies about parental intercourse and the first trip to the "dark land": England. The lifelong, obsessive metaphors of light and darkness, vision and blindness show the importance of primal scene fantasies for Kipling, fantasies that had exciting and terrifying connotations. Another evidence for his fixation is his lifelong, intense curiosity and need to be "in the know"—mysteriously transmuted into his creative gifts as an observer, describer, and evoker of realistic detail.[1]

During the time of the attempted soul murder (ages six to twelve), Kipling had to face three terrible psychological dangers: the loss of his parents; the soul murder proper (the overstimulation and overwhelming rage which threatened his identity and inner stability, his self- and object-representations); castration anxiety—Rudyard was, at six, at the height of his oedipal development. At Lorne Lodge, there was the situation (perhaps prefigured in his first years in India too) of domination by a cruel, all-powerful woman, with the much-needed, protective father at a distance.

The trauma of the desertion was made more terrible by the boy's being completely unprepared for it.[2] Suddenly, the children were in Hell. Their fate resembles that of children studied and cared for by Anna Freud who were suddenly separated from their parents during the emergency evacuations from London in the Blitz of World War II.

> The child experiences shock when he is suddenly and without preparation exposed to dangers which he cannot cope with emotionally. In the case of evacuation the danger is represented by the sudden disappear-

ance of all the people he knows and loves. Unsatisfied longing produces in him a state of tension which is felt as shock. . . . In reality it is the very quickness of the child's break with the mother which contains all the dangers of abnormal consequences. Long drawn-out separation may bring more visible pain but it is less harmful because it gives the child time to accompany the events with his reactions, to work through his own feelings over and over again, to find outward expressions for his state of mind, i.e., to abreact slowly. Reactions which do not even reach the child's consciousness do incalculable harm to his normality. [A. Freud 1939-1945, vol. 3, pp. 208–209]

Rudyard, at six, was more able than the three-year-old Trix to face the loss, since images of both parents and the predominantly loving servants were firmly established as part of the structure of his mind. He had achieved "object constancy;"[3] as long as he could remember and think, his parents couldn't be completely lost. He could use his mind and his creative imagination to fight against that part of himself that turned toward, gave into, and identified with Aunty Rosa and Harry.[4] And his power to know and to remember was specifically attacked by their brainwashing techniques. Reading and writing were crucial skills, and reading (so tied to the forbidden seeing) became the subject of conflict and symptoms. Apparently there were occasional letters from the parents which helped reinforce the children's memories.[5] Rudyard could fight his passive entrapment with an active ordering of, and playing with, the bad reality in fantasies and memories (with Trix as his eager listener-participant). When Rudyard was small, his father had written a nursery rhyme that had consoled him after an attack by a hen. In Lorne Lodge, Rudyard could identify with his protective father's humor and creativity, to try to ward off the attacks by the Woman. There was, after his near-blindness and the breakdown, a flowering of Kipling's creative writing in the predominantly male atmosphere of school. He emerged as a writer and poet, specifically as a master of rhyme. The ambition to become a writer crystallized in adolescence at a time when there must have been a renewal of conflict over masturbation. He was using the writer's hand to keep away (to use the metaphor from his childhood memories) the severed child's hand. In his struggle with his fear of and fascination for castration, he needed to identify with his father to try to conquer the bad Woman—to conquer her in himself, and outside himself.

Since Rudyard was in the midst of his oedipal development he was subject to intense shifting ambivalence toward both parents. The desertion and subsequent sadomasochistic overstimulation made for libidinal regression and a terrifying access of rage. This enhanced his parricidal (especially patricidal) impulses at a time when the boy needed good parents desperately to fight off his own bad inner imagos. Anna Freud is describing children of about Ruddy's age (six) when she says of the desertion involved in school phobias:

> . . . the distress experienced at separation from mother, parents or home is due to an excessive ambivalence towards them. The conflict between love and hate of the parents can be tolerated by the child only in their reassuring presence. In their absence, the hostile side of the ambivalence assumes frightening proportions, and the ambivalently loved figures of the parents are clung to so as to save them from the child's own death wishes, aggressive fantasies, etc. [1965, p. 113]

This need to preserve the internal images of good parents, so intense for the wartime evacuees at the Hampstead nurseries where the parental substitutes were good and understanding, becomes desperate under conditions of soul murder, where hatred is deliberately cultivated. And how devastating if the parental substitutes, with the fanaticism of the religiously righteous and the power of concentration camp commandants, suppress rather than understand the child's thoughts and feelings, and operate to prevent the child from registering what has happened.

The subjection to Aunty Rosa as the Woman—with Harry as her phallic extension—threatened Rudyard's masculinity. He needed a strong father to take her away. Kipling continued to seek for fathers and older brothers in his work and in his life. The fear of the Woman, the need to submit to the phallic parent, the need to deny his parricidal urges, made homosexuality a continuing danger. The ongoing good external relationship with his father in later life must have helped stave off his strong latent homosexuality. (One can see in his life and work a conflict-ridden range of wishes involving wanting to be, and to have—a man, a phallic woman [the ranee-tiger from childhood], and a woman.)

The presence of his sister at Lorne Lodge helped strengthen Kipling's masculinity and also his identity. Toward her he was able to feel and act like the protective parent that both so needed. Trix was grateful for and craved his care. She was the living link to his home, his parents, and his past. His memory and his gift for storytelling allowed him to become the author of, and Trix his primal audience for, a Family Romance based on real events. He could identify with Mother and Father and the *ayah,* and so both children could hold on to them.[6] Trix's devotion continued the love from and for a female that was not swept away by Rudyard's hatred for the Woman. Together the two children could retreat from the desolation and persecution of their daily life to the sanctuary created by the boy's imagination. To create a wonderful and sometimes a terrible world for abandoned children made Rudyard a god who need not fear abandonment. He could know what was what, reward the deserving and punish the wicked. Throughout his long writing career he was obsessed with the family romance,[7] and what began with Trix continued in his books.

I have speculated that there may have been sexual play between Trix and Rudyard which had some saving effect on his masculinity. He did manage a heterosexual life, despite his aversion for women. There was no real loving sexual woman in his early fiction. Sex was never treated as joyous; at best it was a guilt-ridden pleasure followed by punishment.

The effects of the soul murder on Kipling's subsequent life were intermittently present and complicated by a struggle against them. There was a need to repeat the sadomasochistic experiences in the House of Desolation. Kipling's predominant position as victim had enforced an identification with the persecutors, presumably out of the child's need for "dear kind God." The destructive hatred had to be turned toward others; he required and found enemies: strangers. Boers, Boches, "the lesser breeds outside the law." But he could also remember what it was to have been the victim, and in some of his best work his empathy for and identification with the underdog catches the reader's emotions. He was successful in bringing to sympathetic life the Indians and the Lama in *Kim*, the natives in many of the early stories, the British privates and noncommissioned officers in his prose and verse, and, above all, the abandoned and neglected children.

But persecutor raged against victim within Kipling; making him subject to attacks of depression. Just as he split the images of himself, he needed to split the mental pictures of his parents into good and bad. With intolerable rage aimed against those he loved and needed, he was forced to deny his hatred. The denial—the need not to know—existed alongside his driving curiosity. The denial made the split registration possible: contradictory images and ideas could exist side by side in his mind without blending, as with Orwell's doublethink. This kind of compartmentalization is a way of dealing with overwhelming feeling, but it is paid for by sacrificing the power of synthesis that is needed for joy, love, and the feeling of identity.[8] The ease with which this splitting was possible is not entirely explainable by the defensive need to ward off hatred and fear from the mental images of his good parents. Even before the assumption of parental roles by the bad Holloways, Kipling had lived through the intense experiences involved in having two sets of parents—white and black, light and dark—as a child in India. It was common in the British colonies for the servants in the family to be closer to the children than the natural parents. The mere existence of the complicated split mental representations of self and parents doesn't involve pathology. That depends on how the splits are used. The crucial question is: can the contradictory mental representations be synthesized, can they be brought together and taken apart again so that they can be worked with in a flow of thought and feeling; or, must they exist for most or all of the time isolated and beyond criticism, as with Kipling (see Shengold 1974a). Beneath the fragile seeming clarity of the bad Aunty Rosa and Harry, and the good Mother and the good Father, was a terrible ambivalent fragmentation and confusion. This is beautifully described by Jarrell: "As it was, his world had been torn in two and he himself torn in two: for under the part of him that extenuated everything, blamed for nothing, there was certainly a part that extenuated nothing, blamed for everything—a part he never admitted, most especially not to himself" (1962, p. 144).

There is a depiction of "being torn in two" in madness, or at least in a dream of madness, in a poem called "The Mother's Son" that Kipling (1928) wrote when he was in his mid-sixties. The speaker is in an asylum and is looking into a mirror, that metaphor for split images.

> I have a dream—a dreadful dream—
>   A dream that is never done.
> I watch a man go out of his mind,
>   And he is My Mother's Son. . . .
>
> And it was *not* disease or crime
>   Which got him landed there,
> But because They laid on My Mother's Son
>   More than a man could bear. . . .
>
> They broke his body and his mind
>   And yet They made him live,
> And They asked more of My Mother's Son
>   Than any man could give. . . .
>
> And no one knows when he'll get well
>   So, there he'll have to be.
> And, 'spite of his beard in the looking-glass,
>   I know that man is me!
>   [1928, pp. 398–399]

Here the blaming of the mother is not conscious; it appears in the repeated characterization of the self as "My Mother's Son," with Kipling's characteristic accusatory capitalization. The "too-much-ness" is attributed to an impersonal bad They (again capitalized), a projection of the bad self and transference of the bad parents, as in the familiar *They* of the paranoid. For Kipling it means: not me, not the Mother or the Father, but the Holloways. The poem's last line—"'spite of his beard in the looking-glass" (vile verse!)—implies that the bearded man is looking for a beardless self in the glass. Kipling developed facial hair very early. The adult victim of unbearable strain is surely expecting to see the image of himself as a boy in the House of Desolation.

Kipling was most comfortable when the separation of the split mental images operated to suppress hatred. This could happen when he was active and in control, at one with his Daemon so that his creative energy could flow; and when in life he felt he had achieved that perfect ordering of things, that discipline that ruled out sudden desolation: the good could not suddenly become the bad. Here is the image with which he ends *The Jungle Books*—he had begun them with Mowgli abandoned to the mercy of the tiger. Animals and men take part in a magnificent review before the Viceroy, and a native officer responds to a stranger's asking how it was done:

> The animals obey, as the men do. Mule, horse, elephant, or bullock, he obeys his driver, and the driver his sergeant, and the sergeant his lieutenant, and the lieutenant his captain, and the captain his major, and the major his colonel, and the colonel his brigadier commanding three regiments, and the brigadier his general, who obeys the Viceroy, who is the servant of the Empress. Thus it is done. [1894, p. 421]

In such a well-regulated world, the Empress, the Great Mother, watches over all. The Jungle has lost its terror.

I have described an attempt at soul murder directed against Rudyard Kipling as a child. His years in the House of Desolation left effects that continued to inhibit Kipling's ability to feel joy and to love, and that sometimes flawed his art. Yet, the soul murder was far from completely effected: Kipling's identity was preserved, and he became a great artist. The struggle to fight off the soul murder and its effects strengthened him, and gave him motive and subject matter for his writing. I have connected those terrible years of his childhood to his flaws and to his greatness. Kipling's story touches on the mysteries of the origin of mental sickness and of creativity. The explorer must be prepared for contradiction and complexity.

Notes

1. Randall Jarrell (1963) quotes a wonderful description of a drugstore from Kipling's short story, "Wireless," and adds, "One feels after reading this: well, no one ever again will have to describe a drugstore; many of Kipling's descriptive sentences have this feeling of finality" (p. 269). Elsewhere (1962) he says, "Knowing what the peoples, animals, plants, weathers of the world look like, sound like, smell like, was Kipling's *métier*, and so was knowing the worlds that could make someone else know" (p. 137).

2. I am grateful to Drs. Charlotte and Joseph Lichtenberg for pointing out to me the instance of soul murder in Kipling's short story "Lisbeth" (from *Plain Tales from the Hills*, 1888). The story shows the destructive effect of not saying goodbye and lying about a desertion, seemingly with good motive, at the instigation of a bad woman. It reflects Rudyard's childhood experience.

3. About the crucial attainment of object constancy, Anna Freud says, "It is only after object constancy . . . has been reached that the external absence of the object is substituted for, at least in part, by the presence of an internal image which remains stable; on the strength of this achievement temporary separation can be lengthened, commensurate with the advances in object constancy" (1965, p. 65). Speaking of a three-and-a-half year old

(that is a child of about Trix's age where object constancy is not firmly established), she states:

> Distress and *desolation* are inevitable [in the young child who needs to separate from the mother on going to nursery school] . . . only if developmental considerations are neglected. . . . if the child has reached object constancy at least . . . separation from the mother is less upsetting. Even then, the change has to be introduced gradually, in small doses, the periods of independence must not be too long, and, in the beginning, return to the mother should be open to choice. [1965, pp. 89–90; italics mine]

4. Trix: "Ruddy at six always understood the realness of things, and his parents knew that his frequent phrase, when three years old, 'Don't disturv me, I'm finking', had a very real meaning" (1937, p. 170).

5. One would like to know more about these letters. They could have meant a lifetime for Rudyard's identity and contributed to his own drive to be a writer. In his memoirs Kipling describes his writing as specifically motivated toward communication with his parents: "I think I can with truth say that those two made for me the only public for whom then I had any regard whatever till their deaths, in my forty-fifth year" (1937, p. 89). How often did the parents write? What did they say? Were the children allowed to read the letters or answer them? In *Something of Myself*, Kipling tells of the (perhaps fictional) "parting in the dawn with Father and Mother, who said that I must learn quickly to read and write so that they might send me letters and books" (1937, pp. 4–5). The books sent by his father are mentioned by Kipling, but at six the parents had not yet taught him to read. Indeed he resisted learning from Aunty Rosa and this also could have involved spite against his parents. Trix tells of Aunty Rosa treating as a crime the children's "crying like 'silly babies' when she read us letters from Bombay" (1937, p. 168). But neither Rudyard or Trix has more to say about the existence or the impact of what should have been a vital correspondence.

6. The sharing of the past in the House of Desolation is reflected in Kipling's two collections of historical tales for children: *Puck of Pook's Hill* (1906) and *Rewards and Fairies* (1910). In these stories exciting scenes from the history of England and America are told to two children, Dan and Una, brother and sister. Under the magic guidance of Puck, they meet people from the past who observed and participated in the events. So brother and sister travel through history together, denying their alienation and exile from the great figures and happenings of the past; together they master the primal scene.

7. Randall Jarrell: "To Kipling the world was a dark forest full of families; so that when your father and mother leave you in the forest to die, the wolves that come to eat you are always Father Wolf and Mother Wolf, your real father and mother; and you are—as not even the little wolves ever quite are—their real son. The family romance, the two families of the Hero, have so predominant a place in no other writer" (1962, p. 148).

8. Another evidence for splitting can be seen in Kipling's attribution for his writing not to himself, but to his Daemon: "My Daemon was with me in the Jungle Books, Kim, and both Puck books, and good care I took to walk delicately lest he should withdraw" (1937, p. 210). Jarrell (1963) describes Kipling as possessed "by both the Daemon he tells you about, who writes some of the stories for him, and the demons he doesn't tell you about, who wrote some others" (p. 140). Kipling talks of having a "contract" with his Daemon (which evokes soul murder à la Schreber) and gives this advice to writers: "*Note here*. When your Daemon is in charge, do not try to think consciously. Drift, wait, and obey" (1937, p. 210). Kipling describes here the creative benefits of passive subjection to his Daemon; he was splitting off what it meant to be in subjection to that "Devil-boy," Harry.

Orality in Kipling's *Kim*

David H. Stewart[*]

Recent studies of the oral or performative element in literature provide novel methods for understanding the work of Rudyard Kipling. In this essay, I shall review Kipling's peculiar approach to the creative process, demonstrates its applications to *Kim*, and note some ways of modifying critical response to Kipling and perhaps other writers.

Everyone concedes Kipling's exploitation of the visual possibilities of print. Many of his poems and pages of prose foreground the typesetter's paraphernalia: dashes, leaders, apostrophes, quotation marks, exclamation marks, and uncommon capitalizations appear constantly. The word "telegraphic" is often used to describe his style. He was delighted to include his father's illustrations to enhance the visual appeal of his books. Having mastered the journalist's craft at an early age, he sensed the power and romance of highspeed presses and made print-technology serve his ends, so that critics often credit him with helping initiate the enhancement (or subversion) of literature by incorporating journalistic techniques.[1]

But this conventional sense of Kipling's procedure cannot be reconciled with his own statements. Late in life, he described his early efforts as a writer:

> I made my own experiments in the weights, colours, perfumes, and attributes of words in relation to other words, either as read aloud so that they may hold the ear, or, scattered over the page, draw the eye. There is no line in my verse or prose which has not been mouthed till the tongue has made all smooth, and memory, after many recitals, has mechanically skipped the grosser superfluities.[2]

Here the emphasis is clearly on the acoustic element in his work, although he acknowledges the importance of visual and other sensory elements. His is an excellent example of writing that poses problems for readers in our century because, according to Walter Ong, literary criticism ignores auditory, olfactory, gustatory and tactile imagination and imageries. We are "addicted" to the visual—and thereby "impoverished."[3]

The importance of the oral-aural elements in Kipling can be demonstrated in a number of ways. He once admitted that "three generations of Methodist Preachers lie behind me—the pulpit streak will come out!"[4] Probably the moralizing strain was foremost in his mind, but this is inseparable from the oral medium of evangelical, indeed of Christian, tradition. How this tradition affected Kipling can be witnessed in a negative and positive way by noting his childhood experiences, first in the House of Desolation, where fundamentalist piety took venomous forms, and

[*]From the *Journal of Narrative Technique* 13, no. 1 (Winter 1983):47–57. Reprinted by permission.

second in the presence of his mother and his sisters, women with an uncommon "command of words" inherited directly from a Methodist environment.[5]

Kipling spoke often of his "Daemon." "My Daemon was with me in the *Jungle Books, Kim,* and both Puck books, and good care I took to walk delicately, lest he should withdraw. . . . When your Daemon is in charge, do not try to think consciously. Drift, wait, obey."[6] In some sense, Kipling believed that he "heard" what to write and transmitted the message. To whom was he listening? Psychologists might say, "to his alter ego or subconscious;" but he also conversed about and read his work to his parents. Another hypothesis claims that it is small groups of orally bonded individuals who create all literature. Writers must listen and speak before they write. Until populations became too large, you simply asked an author or his acquaintances what he meant if his poem puzzled you. The coffeehouse or salon provided appropriate settings. Literary works existed within an oral network that obviated explication. When the network broke down, as it did at first between dominant critics and Wordsworth or Kipling or Faulkner, wild allegations began to fly; but the normal fabric of communication ordinarily restored itself and conversation resumed. Isolated writers such as Emily Dickinson or Kafka, who worked somewhat outside the network, remained enigmatic until critics brought them inside. In our century, local networks continue to function (for example, the Inklings at Oxford, the Black Mountain poets, the New York Review of Books coterie), but there is no general network, hence every author requires a biographer and dozens of academic explicators. This situation gives credence to the alternative hypothesis that books are made not from living language but from reading (or *mis*reading) other books, which seems unsatisfactory when applied to Kipling, although he read widely all his life.

That Kipling chose isolation by listening to his Daemon and by using as a sounding board his parents rather than contemporary writers is confirmed in another way when he told Rider Haggard that "we are only telephone wires;" that is, we transmit messages rather than originating them. He amplified this by explaining that neither he nor Haggard actually wrote anything. "*You* didn't write *She* you know; something wrote it through you!"[7]

Given this assumption about the genesis of his fictions, we can understand why he confessed to writing not from notes but from memory. "I took down very few notes except of names, dates, and addresses. If a thing didn't stay in my memory, I argued that it was hardly worth writing out."[8] Moreover, we can imagine why Kipling's reading his tales aloud was such a compelling experience for the auditor.[9] He became a rhapsode, as Plato would have it, disclosing messages to the souls of those who can hear rightly and respond beneficially. At the very end of his life, when he revised his work for the definitive Sussex and Burwash editions, the only significant change he made in the text of *Kim* was italicizing key words, evidently to guide the voice of his reader toward correct rhythms, accents, and intonations.

Perhaps this helps explain the violent reactions of readers to Kipling from the first. Of course, his imperial posturing and anti-intellectualism can account for the intelligentsia's repudiation of his work; but the unique vehemence of this repudiation suggests that something in Kipling triggers extraordinary responses. Working by ear as well as by eye, he breaks into our consciousness in ways that prevent our keeping the text at arm's length. Nietzsche called the ear "the organ of fear," and Kipling assaults our ears. The "voices" of *Kim* occupy us, so that we become bridges threatened by the marching feet of a verbal legion, glass strained to the shatter-point by the pitch of words. His books talk in ways that force us to answer, and we try to reduce the stress of invading language by talking back—by humming along or humming against.

How is it that a writer so expert with typographic conventions manages to neutralize them, to elicit continually an aural as well as a visual response? As critics recognized when Kipling's career began, his writing is like speech or music. Already in 1890, Barry Pain wrote a parody of Kipling that included the observation that

> when we speak . . . , we often put a full stop before the relative clauses— add them as an afterthought. . . . But when we write we only put a comma. The author of *Plain Tales from the Hills* saw this, and acted on the principle. He punctuated his writing as he did his speaking; and used more full stops than any man before him. Which was genius.[10]

George Moore claimed that Kipling's language is rhetorical, "copious, rich, sonorous. . . . None since the Elizabethans has written so copiously."[11] And T. S. Eliot believed that, like Swinburne's, Kipling's work "has the sound-value of oratory, not of music. [His] is the poetry of oratory; it is music just as the words of orator or preacher are music; they persuade, not by reason, but by emphatic sound."[12] That this is equally true of Kipling's prose seems clear from the testimony of Henry James and other critics who sought musical analogs to describe Kipling's style.[13]

Of greater importance than these impressionistic responses is an approach through Kipling's use of colloquialism, which many critics mistook for journalism. Richard Bridgman examined the rise of colloquialism in American literature, tracing the slow and clumsy process by which authors discovered how to convey dialect and direct speech in a convincing way. He concludes that Kipling's contemporaries, Twain and James, were the first writers to succeed and that, except for James' experiments, "nothing very clear or purposeful happened to the vernacular in literature for a quarter of a century following the publication of *Huckleberry Finn*."[14] Bridgman refrains from noting the parallels between Twain and the so-called "regional" writers all over Europe during this period, from

Leskov in Russia to the practitioners of *Heimatkunst* in Germany;[15] nor does he call attention to the similarities between Twain and Kipling as uneducated ex-journalists who expanded the literary lexicon by successfully importing colloquial language. He does not ask the obvious question: Would English and American literature have diverged so significantly in the twentieth century if English writers had capitalized on Kipling's stylistic explorations as American writers did on Twain's?

Approaches to Kipling through dichotomies between journalism and "true art" or between imperialist vulgarity and compassionate humanism can be productively supplemented by examining the tension between oral and literate strategies. To be sure, others have noted what we may call the "gestic" component in Kipling's language. Even in German translation, Berthold Brecht evidently heard "vividness and epigrammatic directness of speech" in Kipling's diction, which can be called gestic.[16] R. G. Collingwood described Kipling as the one who shocked late nineteenth century aesthetes by reviving "magical art," dead since the Middle Ages. It is an art that has strong vocal overtones which he calls "speech-gestures."[17]

Kim invites us to hear how Kipling conveys orality through print. In chapter seven, there are two descriptions that provide entry to the book in a new way. First, Colonel Creighton explains Kim's future in school and as a government servant. "Kim pretended at first to understand perhaps one word in three of this talk. Then the Colonel, seeing his mistake, turned to fluent and picturesque Urdu, and Kim was contented."[18] The second passage is a description of the language of schoolboys at St. Xavier's:

> And every tale was told in the even, passionless voice of the native-born, mixed with quaint reflections, borrowed unconsciously from native foster-mothers, and turns of speech that showed that they had been that instant translated from the vernacular. Kim watched, listened, and approved. This was not insipid, single-word talk of drummer-boys.

Both passages remind readers that the novel is mainly "oral" (three-fourths is direct discourse) and also that it is a "translation." *Kim* contains four "languages," each with its own distinctive style. First there is Kipling's (or the omniscient narrator's) style, that encyclopedic, confiding, emphatic, and often elliptical language that was his trademark. We hear it, with all its commas, dashes and foreign words, in the first paragraphs of the novel and from time to time thereafter. For some readers, it obtrudes, as Thackeray's voice does. For most readers, however, it is a supple instrument with astonishing versatility that enables him to present superb descriptions, for example of the Grand Trunk Road in chapter four. It also provides him the latitude to adopt the second person singular ("Therefore, you would scarcely be interested in Kim's experiences as a St. Xavier's boy . . . ," chapter seven), the first-person plural (". . . almond-curd sweetmeats (*balushai* we call it) a fine-chopped Lucknow tobacco," chapter eight), the imperative mood (the Babu: "Behold him. . . . Watch him, all babudom laid aside, smoking at noon . . . ," chapter 15), and the ironic voice (the Babu: "Never was so unfortunate a product of English rule in India more unhappily thrust upon aliens," chapter 13). One added trait of this "narrator's language" is the high incidence of compounds, frequently hyphenated: "*fiend-embroidered* draperies," "*brow-puckered* search," "*many-times-told* tale," "*quick-poured* French," "*de-Englishised*," "*be-ringed*," "he . . . was *bad-worded* in clumsy Urdu." In addition to these verbs and verbals, compounding can be found in other parts of speech; and it led one critic to speculate that this is an important source of Kipling's epic flavor and fairy-tale quality.[19] Certainly it is Kipling's "deviant language" in *Kim* (whether the narrator's or some character's) that makes his idioms so emphatic and that gives the novel a kind of deep-structure that takes us back to Anglo-Saxon word-formation.

The second language of *Kim* is the voice of the homeland (*Balait*, as Kim calls it). Creighton, the Reverend Bennett and Father Victor, even the drummer boy from Liverpool speak "standard English"—more or less. That is, each speaks his own dialect of English, always signaled by the appearance of contractions: " 'em" for them, " 'an" for and, " 'ud" for would, "amazin' " for amazing. Moreover, Kipling distinguished Victor's Irish from Bennett's English.

It is this conglomerate "normative language" that gives special flavor to what might be called "native English," the third language of the novel. This is Kim's "tinny saw-cut English" ("oah yess") before he attends school. It is the English of the bazaar letter-writers, for example "*Sobrao Satai Failed Entrance Allahabad University*" who added *P.M.* (sic) to the lama's letter to Kim: "*Please note boy is apple of eye, and rupees shall be sent per hoondie* [cheque] *three hundred per annum. For God Almighty's sake*" (chapter six). This is also the Babu's English, which Kipling exhibits frequently: "the best of English with the vilest of phrases" (chapter 13). For example, in chapter 12, the Babu describes himself to Kim in English: "By Jove! I was such a fearful man. Never mind that. I go on colloquially. . . ." Then he switches to Urdu, which Kipling translates into standard English. But the signal for this switch is not buried for most readers. The compulsory examination for British officers in Hindustani was called the "colloquial."[20] Kipling provides an aural sign for the switch between languages.

It is in this third language that Kipling often devises colloquial deformations that accentuate an aural response to words. When the Babu says that something "is creaming joke" or refers to "locks, stocks and barrels," we must "sound out" the right meaning, as we do when Huck Finn describes a subject taught by the Duke as "yellocution." Kipling was especially adept with deviant verbs. Thus a scribe, writing English translated from the lama's dictation in imperfect Urdu, records: *"Then Almighty God blessing your Honour's succeedings to third and fourth generation and ... confide in your Honour's humble servant for adequate remuneration ..."* (chapter six). The most dramatic example of Kipling's foregrounding of verbs occurs in chapter three when Kim converses with Father Victor:

> "They call me Kim Rishti-ke. That is Kim of the Rishti."
> "What is that—'Rishti'?"
> "*Eye*-rishti—that was the regiment—my father's."
> "Irish, oh I see."
> "Yes. That was how my father told me. My father, he has lived."
> "Has lived where?"
> "Has lived. Of *course* he is dead—gone out."

Incorrect present perfect "has lived" is exactly right in place of a past tense or the verb "died" for conveying the un-Western blur of life with death. It is this "translated" Urdu and Hindi (for example, the boys' talk at St. Xavier's) that comprises perhaps ten percent of the novel.

Finally there is *Kim's* fourth language in which over half of the book is written. It is "actual" Urdu, often spoken with an accent. Kipling performs an impressive feat here by making English sound (and look) non-English. He does it by leaving remnants of the original vernacular, single vocables, sometimes translated in parentheses but always italicized as if inviting us to sound them aloud, however senseless and alien. He does it by "Germanic" capitalizations, a typographic trick which accentuates nominals. He does it by studding the language with borrowed, sometimes inflected words (usually mispronounced) from English, for example *te-rain* (for "train"—"Quick: she comes!"), *Berittish* (for "British"), *tikkut* (for "ticket"), *takkus* (for "taxes"), *Ker-lis-ti-an* (for "Christian"), and a number of corrupted proper names. He does it by punning—in both English and Urdu and once in Pushtu.[21] He does it with archaic and Biblical constructions: "We *be* craftsmen," "the gates of his mouth were loosened," "if so be thou art woman-born," "whoso bathes in it washes away all taint and speckle of sin," "thou wast born to be a breaker of hearts." Finally, he does it with a variety of malformations. In chapter seven, Kim leaps from a cab to greet the lama. The driver exclaims, "What is to pay me for this coming and recoming?" A moment later the lama explains his own sudden appearance: "perceiving myself alone in this great and terrible world, I bethought me of the *te-rain* to Benares." "Recoming" and "bethought" are little surprises in Kipling's rhetorical armory that make his language vitally oral.

In addition to these four distinct languages of *Kim*, there are several other features of the text that enhance its aural appeal. The poetic epigraphs for each chapter serve as a musical parados. Kipling's habit of radical excision and compression of his manuscripts (*Kim* "as it finally appeared was about one-tenth of what the first lavish specification called for")[22] has the paradoxical effect of accelerating the reader's vocalization by forcing him to fill in the gaps. Kipling's prodigal descriptions seem all the more copious because they are rare. They are show pieces set in a tale that advances almost exclusively by laconic dialog. More importantly, Kipling's visual imagery is usually random and non-cumulative. Except for such obvious links as between Kim and a colt or horse and the recurrent allusions to the Wheel, River and Road as metaphors of life, Kipling's images rise momentarily to the surface and then vanish. By no means does this minimize Kipling's appeal to the eye (or indeed the other senses). His repeated use of horizontal lighting to intensify physical descriptions gives *Kim* its visual brilliance. But Kipling never organizes and unfolds his texts the way Joyce, for example, does. As Hugh Kenner has observed, Joyce depends on "technological space;" that is, on the printed page exclusively, on "the antithesis between the personal matrix of human speech and the unyielding formations of the book as book."[23] *Ulysses* strives for a kind of simultaneity in which incremental repetitions and recurrences call attention to themselves. We must refer constantly to the text to see them. *Kim* inhabits the aural recesses of memory, creates echoes in addition to visions.

Still more important in *Kim* is the constant "translation" from the vernacular, which creates an unusual aural medium. For example, characters "speaking" Urdu at times use an "elevated vocabulary that would be inappropriate in plain English. Kim tells Colonel Creighton, "it is *inexpedient* to write the names of strangers." The Jat farmer says of his sick son, "he *esteemed* the salt lozenges." Later when Kim scolds him for meddling, he says, "I am *rebuked*." Kim describes the ash in the farmer's pipe as "*auspicious*." Such diction is incompatible with these characters' vocabularies in English, but here in "translation" it seems normal, therefore doubly suggestive.

A second example: the novel is full of oral formulas ("let the hand of Friendship turn aside the Whip of Calamity;" "I am thy sacrifice") that are unknown in English yet familiar because they conform to the structure of maxims. A speaker of Urdu can actually translate some of them back into the original, so that he may read "I am thy sacrifice" but hear "*Main tum pe qurban jaoon*," a Moslem oath of fidelity. An English reader hears, instead, echoes from an archaic, perhaps Biblical, past that authenticates such statements. Curses ("Room for the Queen of Delhi and her prime minister the gray monkey climbing up his own sword!"), oaths ("I am thy cow!"), and proverbs ("For the sick cow a crow; for the sick man a Brahmin") abound in *Kim*. The structure is unmistakable although the words are strange, so that meaning comes as emphatically through rhythm and intonation as through diction. The continual appearance of conventionalized and formulaic locutions makes *Kim* rhetorical, dialogic. Its compressed style, confiding narrator, and loquacious characters everywhere reinforce an apothegmatic quality that transforms the book into a sustained enthymeme which, as students of rhetoric know, forces auditors to participate in and contribute to verbal transactions.[24]

A final striking characteristic of *Kim* is the appeal to our ears through frequent use of exclamations and the imperative mood that they create.[25] Hear and obey! Let all listen to the Jâtakas! The search is sure! Hear the most excellent Law! It is found! Be Quiett! These are cries that leap above the "surface noise" of Indian life and Kipling's high volume prose. The mood is so strong that it deflects the narrator's voice from its normal indicative mood. For example, in chapter five, there is a description of the Maverick regiment's setting up camp for the night, pitching tents, unpacking equipment, "and behold the mango-tope turned into an orderly town as they [Kim and the lama] watched!" In chapter 15, after summarizing Hurree Babu's hoodwinking the foreign agents, the narrator's voice suddenly rises: "Behold him, too fine-drawn to sweat, too pressed to vaunt the drugs in his brass-bound box, ascending Shamelegh slope, a just man made perfect." The epigraph of chapter one and the second sentence of the novel ("Who hold Zam Zammah, that 'fire-breathing dragon,' hold the Punjab . . .") are emphatic generalizations that sound like a Commandment.

If it is true that Kipling managed his typographical medium in a way that recreates the illusion of hearing rather than reading, then perhaps we can explain *Kim's* "magical" appeal to readers and also its peculiar isolation as a modern classic. It speaks to us from an oral-aural world not only of nineteenth century Anglo-India but of childhood. It seems to short-circuit the alphabetical print medium and operate in terms of the seven features of oral cultures that Walter Ong has listed:

(1) stereotyped or formulaic expression, (2) standardization of themes, (3) epithetic identification for "disbambiguation" of classes or of individuals, (4) generation of "heavy" or ceremonial characters, (5) formulary, ceremonial appropriation of history, (6) cultivation of praise and vituperation, (7) copiousness.[26]

Illustrations from *Kim* for each of these come to mind at once and suggest the profoundly conservative tendency of the novel. Formulaic language, cliches, incantatory and exclamatory expressions withdraw us from the abstract, objective world of print, according to Ong, and reintroduce us to a world of matter, potency, indistinctness and subjectivity.[27] This occurs because voice "signals the present use of power," sound being "more real or existential than other sense objects, despite the fact that it is more evanescent."[28]

Like Twain and other American vernacular writers, Kipling transcribed English that was under the stress of an alien environment, which wrenched it with new words and accents, as well as novel concepts. Anglo-Indian English was as different as American English from the language of the homeland.[29] Kipling's typographical medium captured the sense of adventure and expansiveness that rapid language modification conveys as it assists us in the struggle to assimilate new experience. His lexical and syntactic innovations explain in part why *Kim* is a valuable book for people learning to read.

To the triumph of print technology, Kipling reacted one way, Joyce another. Both of them listened diachronically to language and tried to transmit the word they heard. But Kipling's creed said, "drift, wait, obey," which meant that he affirmed traditional wisdom. Joyce followed a more romantic and modern path, preferring what Ong calls the "irenic" stance and avoiding the "free dialogic struggle with an audience,"[30] which was the older, perhaps more venerable, way to speak.

Notes

1. Emile Legouis and Louis Cazamian, *A History of English Literature* (New York: Macmillan, 1927), p. 458; William York Tindall, *Forces in Modern British Literature: 1885–1946* (New York: Knopf, 1947), p. 65; Cyril Connolly, *Enemies of Promise* (New York: Macmillan, 1948), p. 19. The best survey of English criticism is in John J. Rouse, "The Literary Reputation of Rudyard Kipling: A Study of Kipling's Works in British Literary Periodicals from 1886 to 1960," Diss. New York University, 1963.

2. *Something of Myself* (Garden City: Doubleday, 1937), p. 78.

3. *Interfaces of the Word* (Ithaca: Cornell University Press, 1977), p. 131. Kipling recalled that his Anglo-Indian audience in the early days was not interested in his dreams and ideals but in the "accuracy" of his stories. "My young head was in a ferment of new things seen and realized at every turn—that I might in any way keep abreast of the flood—it was necessary that every word should tell, carry, weigh, taste and, if need were, smell." (*Something of Myself*, pp. 222–23.) Kinaesthesia in Kipling's work is examined by Antonio Gräffin Spee, "Der Sinnesimpressionismus bei Kipling," Diss. Bonn, 1934.

4. A letter to his cousin Florence MacDonald in the *Methodist Times*, 23 January, 1936; quoted in Arthur R. Ankers, "The Kiplings of Yorkshire," *The Kipling Journal*, XLVI (Sept. 1979), 9.

5. A W. Baldwin, *The MacDonald Sisters* (London: Peter Davis, 1960), pp. 36 and 40.

6. *Something of Myself*, p. 227.

7. *Rudyard Kipling to Rider Haggard*, ed. M. Cohen (Rutherford, N.J.: Fairleigh Dickinson University Press, 1965), p. 100.

8. *Something of Myself*, p. 247.

9. As a child, Angela Mackail heard Kipling read: "The *Just So Stories* are a poor thing in print compared with the fun of hearing them told in Cousin Ruddy's deep unhesitating voice. There was a ritual about them, each phrase having its special intonation which had to be exactly the same each time and without which the stories are dried hunks. There was an inimitable cadence, an emphasis of certain words, an exaggeration of certain phrases, a kind of intoning here and there which made his telling unforgettable." Charles E. Carrington, *The Life of Rudyard Kipling* (Garden City: Doubleday, 1955), p. 221.

10. "The Sincerest Form of Flattery," in *Kipling: The Critical Heritage*, ed. R.L. Green (New York: Barnes and Noble, 1971), p. 63. Recent linguistic studies of T-Units and syntax shed surprisingly little light. John C. Schafer, "The Linguistic Analysis of Spoken and Written Texts," in *Exploring Speaking-Writing Relationships*, ed. B.M. Kroll and R.J. Vann (Urbana: NCTE, 1981), pp. 11–12.

11. "Kipling and Loti," *Kipling: The Critical Heritage*, pp. 288–89.

12. "Kipling Redivivus," *Kipling: The Critical Heritage*, p. 323.

13. James called *Seven Seas* "all prose trumpets and castenets and such—with never the touch of the fiddlestring or a note of the nightingale." (Letter to Jonathan Sturges, 5 November, 1896, *Ibid.*, p. 69). By 1901, when he wrote Kipling about *Kim*, James disapproved of Kipling's artistry; nonetheless "the quality, the prodigality, the Ganges-flood [of *Kim*] leave me simply gaping. . . ." (Leon Edel, *Henry James: The Treacherous Years* [New York: Lippincott, 1969], p. 53.) For Dixon Scott, Kipling's "tunes" lacked "glides and gracenotes" (*Men of Letters* [London: Hodder and Stoughton, 1917], p. 56), and Humbert Wolfe tried to explain Kipling's "sound-control" by analogs with saxophone, fiddle, oboe, and flute playing. (*Dialogues and Monologues* [1929; rpt., New York: Books for College Libraries Press, 1970], pp. 78–9.)

14. *The Colloquial Style in America* (New York: Oxford University Press, 1966), p. 131.

15. I tried to sketch the complex history of this problem in "Faulkner, Sholokhov, and Regional Dissent in Modern Literature," in *William Faulkner: Prevailing Verities and World Literature*, ed. W.T. Zyla and W.M. Aycock (Lubbock: Texas Tech University, 1973), pp. 135–50.

16. James K. Lyon, *Berthold Brecht and Rudyard Kipling: A Marxist's Imperialist Mentor* (The Hague: Mouton, 1975), p. 23.

17. *The Principles of Art* (Oxford: Clarendon, 1938), pp. 70 and 243.

18. Margaret P. Feeley notes that these sentences replace two others in the manuscript: "Kim understood perhaps one word in three of this talk to which he listened politely, one eye on the dusky landscape of the Northwest. The Colonel spoke always in Urdu." "Kipling's *Kim*: Introduction and Annotations," Diss. City University of New York, 1976, p. 556.

19. W. Leeb-Lundberg, *Word-Formation in Kipling* (Lund: Ohlsson, 1909), pp. 45–49.

20. *The Reader's Guide to Rudyard Kipling's Works*, ed. R.L. Green and A. Mason (Canterbury: Gibbs and Sons, 1961), I, 263. One measure of Kipling's success in transcribing Bengali English is to compare it with Arnold Wright's *Baboo English as 'Tis Writ* (London: T. Fisher Unwin, 1891).

21. Shamsul Islam, "Kipling's Use of Indo-Pakistani Languages," *The Kipling Journal*, XXXVI (Sept., 1969), 15–19.

22. *Something of Myself*, p. 149. Kipling recommended three re-readings of a text, the last one "aloud alone and at leisure," with a camel hair brush and Indian Ink for excisions. "The magic lies in the Brush and the Ink." *Ibid.*, p. 225.

23. *The Stoic Comedians: Flaubert, Joyce, and Beckett* (Berkeley: University of California Press, 1974), pp. 47–48. The origin and development of "spatial form" in criticism, beginning with Joseph Frank's well-known essay (1945), are surveyed in *Spatial Form in Narrative*, ed. J.R. Smitten and A. Daghestany (Ithaca: Cornell University Press, 1981).

24. Lloyd F. Bitzer, "Aristotle's Enthymeme Revisited," *The Quarterly Journal of Speech*, XLV (Dec., 1959), 399–408.

25. The exclamation mark may be the most distinctive part of Kipling's stylistic signature in *Kim*. It occurs far more often here than in his stories or journalistic writing. Two sections of *Stalky & Co.*, dated 1898 and 1899, are full of exclamations, but the language is the elliptical jargon of schoolboys, "single-word talk" that Kipling avoided in *Kim*. For comparison, I checked seven other "adventure" stories: G.A. Henty's *In Times of Peril: A Story of India* (1881), Stevenson's *Treasure Island* (1883), Twain's *The Adventures of Huckleberry Finn* (1894), Haggard's *King Solomon's Mines* (1885) and *She* (1886), Flora Annie Steel's *On the Face of the Waters* (1896), and Conrad's *The Nigger of the Narcissus* (1897). Only Steel's novel and chapters 20-33 (the duke and Dauphin passage) of Twain's approach *Kim* in fre-

quency of exclamations, but their effect is different because the narrator's voice in the former remains unimplicated and the narrator of the second is Huck himself.

26. *Interfaces of the Word*, p. 102.

27. *Ibid.*, pp. 136–37.

28. *The Presence of the Word* (New Haven: Yale University Press, 1967), pp. 111–12.

29. Phiroze E. Dustoor makes an interesting comparison of English in India and America: *The World of Words* (New York: Asia Publishing House, 1968), pp. 101–102; and, of course, one must always consult Yule and Burnell's *Hobson-Jobson*.

30. *Interfaces of the Word*, pp. 222–23.

The Mature Craftsman

The Mature Craftsman
J. I. M. Stewart*

There is a celebrated essay by Mr. Edmund Wilson called "The Kipling that Nobody Read," and it is the achievement of this Kipling—an artist in full maturity—which remains to be considered. That people simply ceased reading Kipling during this phase of his career is, of course, rather a long way from being literally true. But as his art, in Mr. Wilson's words, "became continually more skilful and intense" he certainly lost many of those readers who had enjoyed chiefly the simple, emphatic, and pictorial side of his writing. It is hard to imagine his own William, for example, making much of the subtle and elusive clues which are the reader's sole guide through some of the later stories. What may appear surprising is that Kipling entirely failed to impress in a new way either the professional critics or the more sophisticated "common readers." Yet there is nothing really perplexing about this, since the history of literature and the arts presents many illustrations of the fact that a man's early achievement, if striking enough, may "type" him for good, so that few, even among the more sensitive and discerning, much notice or admire what later generations may acknowledge as an enlarged and deepened vision. Rembrandt is a classic instance of this.

Further factors were at play. Kipling lived and worked in privacy, and it would not have occurred to him to cultivate the society of persons likely to be influential in recommending him to the continued regard of the public. Again—and this is more important—a great deal remained unchanged alike in Kipling's tone and in his fundamental assumptions. His later writing, it is true, can now be discerned as bearing the stamp of suffering to which no clue is afforded us by any word of Kipling's own—and only an imperfect clue by what we have come to know of his personal history. The fruit of this suffering is compassion, disillusion, and courage to face nakedly "the gods of things as they are." Yet these qualities are brought to us still defiantly parcelled up with passions and prejudices as old as Beetle's while he wields the cricket stump, or the brash young

*From *Rudyard Kipling* by J. I. M. Stewart (New York: Dodd, Mead & Co., 1966), 189–219. © 1966 by J. I. M. Stewart. Reprinted by permission of the publisher.

Anglo-Indian journalist's when he believes himself to descry the pitiful inadequacy of San Francisco's seaward defenses. To the end, that is to say, Kipling retains the power and will to irritate those "liberal" sentiments which have tended to make most of the running among English-speaking writers and intellectuals during the present century. When Professor Lionel Trilling, anxious to say a favourable word, remarks that Kipling's poetry can be read through "in two evenings, or even in a single very long one," he is testifying quaintly to Kipling's talent here. Let us consider something of this sustained power to irritate through the medium of the short story.

"An Habitation Enforced" (*Actions and Reactions*) will make a good beginning. A wealthy American businessman, George Chapin, falls seriously ill "at the very hour his hand was outstretched to crumple the Holz and Gunsberg Combine," and his doctors pack him and his wife Sophie off to Europe for a couple of years. They drift around, staring at the things tourists stare at, "from the North Cape to the Blue Grotto at Capri." Chapin feels frustrated, and longs to get back to work. It is true, he tells Sophie, that he has between four and five million:

> "But it isn't the money. You know it isn't. It's the principle. How could you respect me? You never did, the first year after we married, till I went to work like the others. Our tradition and upbringing are against it. We can't accept those ideals."

The Chapins go to England, and an acquaintance sends them to lodge in a farmhouse in one of the southern counties, promising that they will find there "the genuine England of folklore and song." This is still tourist brochure stuff—but what the Chapins actually find is an empty and dilapidated Georgian mansion, along with an estate of half-a-dozen neglected farms. The house is called Friars Pardon, and when Sophia falls in love with it her husband buys it—reflecting that he "could double the value of the place in six months." Actually George Chapin is almost as sensitive as his wife to the social pitfalls surrounding wealthy Americans who buy English landed properties. But they learn quickly, for the most part from their servants and tenants. On one occasion, just before their purchase of the estate, Sophie, entering the derelict home farm, finds the old man who lives there sitting dead in his chair. She feels that she must not run for help, but must watch with the body until somebody else happens to turn up. A few days later, she also feels that such a newcomer as herself (although now become the lady of the manor) would be taking a liberty if she attended his funeral. Much of this sort of thing in the Chapins is marked and silently approved. Moreover, since they are well-bred and unassuming, they are received by the local gentry—a privilege denied an even wealthier newcomer, Mr. Sangres, who is Brazilian and vulgar.

When the Chapins go to church for the first time as the owners of Friars

Pardon they are ushered with ceremony into the Pardon's Pew. Sophie finds this an ordeal—but it is an ordeal with a strange culmination:

> "*When the wicked man turneth away.*" The strong alien voice of the priest vibrated under the hammer-beam roof, and a loneliness unfelt before swamped their hearts, as they searched for places in the unfamiliar Church of England service. The Lord's Prayer—"Our Father, *which art*"—set the seal on that desolation. Sophie found herself thinking how in other lands their purchase would long ere this have been discussed from every point of view in a dozen prints. . . . Here was nothing but silence—not even hostility! The game was up to them; the other players hid their cards and waited. Suspense, she felt, was in the air, and when her sight cleared, saw indeed, a mural tablet of a footless bird brooding upon the carven motto, "Wayte awhyle—wayte awhyle."
>
> At the Litany George has trouble with an unstable hassock, and drew the slip of carpet under the pew-seat. Sophie pushed her end back also, and shut her eyes against a burning that felt like tears. When she opened them she was looking at her mother's maiden name, fairly carved on a blue flagstone on the pew floor:

> Ellen Lashmar. ob. 1796. aetat. 27.

Wondering at this strange coincidence, Sophie writes to an aunt for information on her family history:

> Her Aunt Sydney of Meriden (a badged and certificated Daughter of the Revolution to boot) answered her inquiries with a two-paged discourse on patriotism, the leaflets of a Village Improvement Society, of which she was president, and a demand for an overdue subscription to a Factory Girls' Reading Circle.

Whether or not Aunt Sydney's ignorance is to be judged plausible, it is through some transatlantic correspondence among very humble folk that the truth appears and is revealed to Sophie. Her mother's family did indeed come from these parts, and were of an ancient and honourable stock. Socially speaking, Sophie now has a trump card, but she remembers the family motto, "Wayte awhyle," and refrains from playing it. She has her reward. When her first son is born, an august neighbor, Lady Conant, who has also worked out the truth, sends her an antique christening mug which had been in the Lashmar family for generations—simply adding as a postscript to her note: "How quiet you've kept about it all!"

"What does she mean about our keeping quiet?" George Chapin asks his wife.

> Sophie's eyes sparkled. "I've thought that out too. We've got back at the English at last. Can't you see that she thought that we thought my mother's being a Lashmar was one of those things we'd expect the English to find out for themselves, and that's impressed her?" She turned

the mug in her white hands, and sighed happily. " 'Wayte awhyle—
wayte awhyle.' That's not a bad motto, George. It's been worth it."

To "An Habitation Enforced" there is appended a poem, "The Recall,"
which begins:

> I am the land of their fathers,
>   In me the virtue stays:
> I will bring back my children
>   After certain days.
>
> Under their feet in the grasses
>   My clinging magic runs.
> They shall return as strangers,
>   They shall remain as sons.

Let us leave this story without comment for the moment, and turn to
"My Son's Wife" (*A Diversity of Creatures*). This too is about somebody
whose ways of feeling, thinking and behaving are changed by the impact
of English country life. In one respect Frankwell Midmore has less far to
go than the Chapins, since he is an Englishman. But essentially he has to
go further. George Chapin, although represented at the start as suffering
more than bodily sickness as a consequence of the pressures of a sterile
competitive life, is a mature and straight personality, and his wife owns as
alert a sensitiveness as one of Henry James's American heroines.
Midmore, on the contrary, has all the appearance of being a hopelessly
rubbishing character. His main activity, fairly broadly intimated to us, is
an undignified sexual promiscuity carried on beneath the cloak of disinterested moral and social reform:

> He and a few friends had rearranged Heaven very comfortably, but
> the reorganization of Earth, which they called Society, was even greater
> fun. It demanded Work in the shape of many taxi rides daily; hours of
> brilliant talk with brilliant talkers; some sparkling correspondence . . .
> and a fair number of picture galleries, tea fights, concerts, theatres,
> music halls, and cinema shows; the whole trimmed with love-making to
> women whose hair smelt of cigarette smoke. Such strong days sent
> Frankwell Midmore back to his flat assured that he and his friends had
> helped the World a step nearer the Truth, the Dawn, and the New Order.

We have met these objectionable people before. They are the "long-haired
things" of those first contemptuous verses sent back from London to the
Civil and Military Gazette. They are, for that matter, the *Bandar-log*.

Midmore unexpectedly inherits a house and some land in the country, and we are given his first "sparkling" letter about it. He has nothing
but ridicule for the place and its people, and is determined to sell out as
soon as a purchaser can be found. But then his current love affair
collapses—with rather more serious nervous consequences than one

might judge probable. He takes refuge in his new house, and is cared for by an old family retainer called Rhoda, who remembers him as a child:

> It was not a dignified entry, because when the door was unchained and Rhoda exclaimed, he took two valiant steps into the hall and then fainted—as men sometimes will after twenty-two hours of strong emotion and little food.
>
> "I'm sorry," he said when he could speak. He was lying at the foot of the stairs, his head on Rhoda's lap.
>
> "Your 'ome is your castle, sir," was the reply in his hair. "I smelt it wasn't drink. You lay on the sofa till I get your supper."
>
> She settled him in a drawing-room hung with yellow silk, heavy with the smell of dead leaves and oil lamp. Something murmured soothingly in the background and overcame the noises in his head. He thought he heard horses' feet on wet gravel and a voice singing about ships and flocks and grass. It passed close to the shuttered bay window.
>
> > But each will mourn his own, she saith,
> > And sweeter woman ne'er drew breath
> > Than my son's wife, Elizabeth . . .
> > Cusha—cusha—cusha—calling.

The singer, the daughter of a neighbour returning from hunting, is the girl Midmore will marry when his full salvation is accomplished. To detail in terms of psychological realism the course of such a salvation is beyond the scope of a short story, and also beyond Kipling's range. So the thing is done in terms of a bold shorthand. Midmore finds himself reading the hunting novels of Surtees and recognizing his new neighbours in them; he secretly learns to shoot and ride; he finds satisfaction in countering the wiles of his tenant at the home farm and getting on terms with him. This would not in itself produce anything very memorable: only a fable about an English and grown-up Harvey Cheyne. But Kipling also has other devices at his command ("horses' feet on wet gravel"); and the climax of the story comes when a dam bursts, and the stream which has murmured in the background of the story overflows its banks with an effect both of practical challenge and symbolic purification. Already, while his new life has been gaining on him, he has viewed his former associates with clearer sight and judged that their "old tricks were sprouting in the old atmosphere like mushrooms in a dung-pit."

Both these stories–"An Habitation Enforced" and "My Son's Wife" —require a certain radical sympathy in the reader if they are not to appear bullying performances. They are emphatic statements of persuasions which can readily present themselves as prejudices; we may feel that we are being faced with arguments in which one side is allowed to have things all its own way. Yet they do faithfully reflect elemental facts of human life, and they touch us at depths of our own nature where the "clinging magic" does run. Nor must we be misled by the mere social overtones of the stories. The fact that Sophie Chapin, *née* Lashmar, is a Lashmar draws only trivial significance as affecting her place in relation to an existing English class structure; what Sophie (like Midmore) is really discovering is that the present must acknowledge and contain the past, if life itself is to be rightly known as a sacred flame. Both stories, then, deal with something very primitive. So, in a simpler and even more impressive way, does a third. It, too, has a brook in it. Indeed, it is called "Friendly Brook" (*A Diversity of Creatures*).

Here there are no social complications whatever. The characters are all simple countryfolk, such as would be called "peasants" on the continent of Europe. Two old men are hedging and ditching—and nearby there is a brook beginning to flood. In the course of their talk we simply learn why another countryman, Jim Wickenden, insists on building his haystack so low down in the meadow that the brook looks like sweeping it away as it swells. One of the old men rounds off the tale:

> "Well, well! Let be how 'twill, the brook was a good friend to Jim. I see it now. I allus did wonder what he was gettin' at when he said that, when I talked to him about shiftin' the stack. 'You dunno everything',' he ses, 'an' if she's minded to have a snatch at my hay, I ain't settin' out to withstand her.'"

The good turn which the brook did Jim Wickenden was to drown his enemy, a city blackguard who had the legal power to take away Wickenden's beloved (although not very loving) adopted daughter, and who had been practicing blackmail on the strength of this. Here the story in itself is, in a sense, nothing; what is remarkable is the power of the dialogue to carry us into remote modes of feeling, in which it is taken for granted that the brook has its own life, and is fitly to be rewarded and propitiated with a "snatch" of hay, should it be minded to take one.

The pagan feeling commanded in "Friendly Brook" derives its effectiveness, at least in part, from being given expression in a tale with a contemporary setting; the old men who discourse in it could have been met with in any corner of Kipling's Sussex, and might indeed be so met with today. There are other stories in which the historical imagination operates without a "frame" of this sort, and notable among these is "The Eye of Allah" (*Debits and Credits*). The setting is an English monastery in the thirteenth century, and we are introduced to an artist, John of Burgos, "burnishing a tiny boss of gold in his miniature of the Annunciation for his Gospel of St. Luke." This, and later other of John's illuminations, are exhibited to us in brilliant detail, and we find eventually that the effect of the story depends upon this. John travels about Europe, and will presently be revisiting Spain; we are told, again in detail, of the various pigments and rare substances he is commissioned to bring back for the use of the monastery's Scriptorium—and also of drugs and salves which both the Infirmarian and the Abbot Stephen himself (for Stephen is passionately interested in medicine) similarly ask for. John, at the moment, is wholly absorbed in the problem of visualizing and depicting devils and evil spirits in inexhaustible variety, for without these how shall his Great Luke deal worthily with the Miracle of the Magdalene and the Miracle of the Gadarene swine? John's prompting is wholly the artist's; to him men are "but matter for drawings"; when once he has achieved his devils, devils will cease to interest him. He does achieve them, bringing back from Spain "wholly a new sort." Kipling's description of them, leading our mind gropingly as it does towards the heart of the story, is surely one of his most astonishing achievements:

> Some devils were mere lumps, with lobes and protuberances—a hint of a fiend's face peering through jelly-like walls. And there was a family of impatient, globular devillings who had burst open the belly of their smirking parent, and were revolving desperately toward their prey. Others patterned themselves into rods, chains and ladders, single or conjoined, round the throat and jaws of a shrieking sow, from whose ear emerged the lashing, glassy tail of a devil that had made good his refuge. And there were granulated and conglomerate devils, mixed up with the foam and slaver where the attack was fiercest. . . .
>
> The border to the picture was a diaper of irregular but balanced compartments or cellules, where sat, swam, or weltered, devils in blank, so to say—things as yet uninspired by Evil—indifferent, but lawlessly outside imagination. Their shapes resembled, again, ladders, chains, scourges, diamonds, aborted buds, or gravid phosphorescent globes— some well-nigh starlike.

It is the Infirmarian who sees the relationship between border and picture: "These lower shapes in the bordure may not be so much hellish and malignant as models and patterns upon which John has tricked out and embellished his proper devils among the swine above there!"

But where has John seen his models? The answer is: through the eye of what we should call a microscope—an instrument of "art optical" which he has obtained from a Moorish source, and which he now produces and places on the Abbot's after-table. The after-table is important to the total effect produced by the story. Stephen has been entertaining distinguished guests to dinner in his parlour; John and a few of the brethren have been bidden to meet them; it is at the after-table that the company takes its place for dessert: "dates, raisins, ginger, figs, and cinnamon-scented sweetmeats set out, with the choicer wines." This touch brings us very close to these thirteenth-century people; in polite society—aristocratic, learned or ecclesiastical—manners and customs do not much change (Kipling, as a matter of fact, must have met something very like this scene when he "dined with the tutors and so on at Balliol College"); and we thus have rather remote habits of mind telescoped with manners, and a mode of conversation, which are familiar.

Soon the whole company is looking in turn through the lens of the microscope at a drop of puddle water from the monastery roof. Thomas the Infirmarian's mind takes a leap at a tremendous truth. "As in the water, so in the blood must they rage and war with each other . . . Think on it again! Here's the Light under our very hand!" Earlier in the evening Abbot Stephen has taken off his ring and dropped it into a silver cup— this in token that, for the time, he is simply a gentleman in the society of his equals. He puts his ring on again, and takes the microscope. He has known about the invention already, having been on an unsuccessful Crusade and held captive by the Saracens. He knows that "man stands ever between two Infinities—of greatness and littleness." But he knows, too, that in the Europe of the Mediaeval Church John's microscope is like an untimely birth, and anybody who appears to discern a million devils in a drop of water will merely go to the stake. The Infirmarian pleads: "The little creatures shall be sanctified—sanctified to the service of His sick." But Stephen knows what he must do. He asks John for his dagger, and smashes the microscope with its hilt.

The power of this great story cannot be adequately suggested in summary and quotation, since it derives in large part from the detail poured into it from a vivid and concretizing imagination. But at least it can be seen as a story deliberately inviting us to look into the future as well as the past. In the future, as at the present, science will offer men gifts they are unready for.

John, the artist in "The Eye of Allah," is uninterested in doing the same thing twice; and Kipling declares himself to have had a compact with his Daemon never simply to follow up a success. (It was the Daemon, incidentally, who bade him, when "The Eye of Allah" wouldn't come right, "treat it as an illuminated manuscript," thus turning failure into success.) There is a rule here not easy for a prolific writer of short stories to keep, but Kipling commonly contrived to find at least a new slant on familiar material. "The Church That Was at Antioch" (*Limits and Renewals*) is another exercise of the historical imagination, being a close-up and intimate view of St. Peter and St. Paul wrestling with the situation briefly recounted in the eleventh chapter of the Epistle to the Galatians. But the events are shown us through the eyes of a young Roman officer, Valens, who has all the firmness, tact and tolerance which a first-class English subaltern might be expected to show in face of some more or less incomprehensible communal squabble in British India. The effect is contrived in the main by setting Valens and his uncle the Prefect talking in an idiom which constantly hints such a modern analogy. "My objection to fancy religions," the Prefect says, "is that they mostly meet after dark, and that means more work for the police." And, again: "I've got to see Paulus and Petrus when they come back, and find out what they've decided about their infernal feasts. Why can't they all get decently drunk and be done with it?" This in itself would make only a superficial achievement. The story takes depth from the contrasted characters of Peter and Paul, and from a great moment at which Peter, hitherto troubled, hesitant, and apparently out of his depth, suddenly, and in a flash of spiritual perception, towers over the accomplished, intellectual, and commanding Apostle to the Gentiles. Moreover Valens, when mortally wounded on duty, lays upon his uncle an injunction to mercy and forgiveness. "Don't be hard on them," he says. "They get worked up . . . They don't know what they are doing." The echo of Christ's words gives us a sudden sense of a whole pagan world moving unknowingly towards one of the new "fancy religions."

Kipling himself was not a man who found forgiveness easy. That he was incapable of "personal hate" we may believe; there is, as we have seen, his own word for it, and he was not a man who would record about himself any untruth whatever. Political animus, often bitter and deep, was another matter. Throughout his adult life there was seldom a time when he was quite safe from it. In particular his country's involvement in war was liable at once to trouble and to barb his art. "A Sahibs' War" and "The Comprehension of Private Cooper" (*Traffics and Discoveries*) are two stories prompted by the conflict with the Boers both of which hold something disturbingly unassimilated into the imaginative structure aimed at. A third, "The Captive" (*Traffics and Discoveries*) is better; it is about an American inventor, Laughton O. Zigler, who has been interned by the British after equipping the Boers with a new type of field gun. Zigler is allowed a fair run for his money—less because Kipling has any liking for him than because his sardonic American manner affords his creator an admirable medium in which to convey his own scorn and anger over the large incompetence of the British campaign. Zigler turns up again in "The Edge of the Evening" (*A Diversity of Creatures*), a story first published in 1913, and which serves curiously as a prologue to Kipling's writing about the Great War which began a year later. It instances again the uncertainty of Kipling's feelings towards America.

Zigler, having acquired great wealth, has rented a very splendid English country house, and filled it with guests from among his compatriots. These are far from sympathetically regarded; nor is Zigler himself, as long as he is in this milieu. It turns out, however, to be unimportant: a "frame" for the main story, which is recounted by Zigler himself. He tells how, returning from his private golf course with three English guests, he finds an aeroplane in his park. It has grounded while being flown by two German spies—and it is another invention of Zigler's, the Rush Silencer, which makes technically possible what they have been about: "a bird's-eye telephoto-survey of England for military purposes." We have at least to admit that Kipling is looking faithfully into the future here. But the rest of the story is implausible. The grounded spies, in order to have some chance of escape, at once attempt to kill their discoverers—but in fact their discoverers kill them: Zigler braining one with a golf club, and an English high-court judge breaking the neck of the other with a lethal football tackle. Between them they hoist the bodies back into the plane, which Zigler gets going with its controls so set that it will disappear into the English Channel. We are left with the impression that Zigler has acted less badly in marketing his silencer where he can than has the British Government in not being alert to secure it. We are also told that Zigler's English companions have placed themselves in a dangerous position, since their Government would not back them up if the fatal incident became public. The latter part of this story is admirably told, but we may feel that only an impatience to express political feeling would have hurried Kipling into a recital of improbabilities which could find acceptance only in a boys' magazine.

The most famous, or notorious, of Kipling's stories of the First World War is "Mary Postgate" (*A Diversity of Creatures*), published in 1915. This too has an aeroplane in it, and two dead men. The first of these is Wynn Fowler, who went straight into the Flying Corps and got himself killed in a trial flight. Wynn had been an unlovely and graceless orphan, brought up by an aunt who cared little for him, and in his turn caring little for his aunt's paid "companion," Miss Postgate, a dim-seeming woman who had been devoted to him, and whom, whether as boy or young man, he had never treated other than with breezy contempt. There is only Miss Postgate to be affected by his death:

> "I never expected anything else," said Miss Fowler; "but I'm sorry it happened before he had done anything."
> The room was whirling round Mary Postgate, but she found herself quite steady in the midst of it.
> "Yes," she said. "It's a great pity he didn't die in action after he had killed somebody."

This sounds the dire note that is to come. Miss Postgate has the grim experience of chancing upon a child killed by a German bomb. Hard upon this, and while destroying in the gardening incinerator Wynn's old toys, books, motoring journals and other personal possessions, she comes upon something else: a wounded man, "in a uniform something like Wynn's." He is an injured German airman, and he begs for help. Miss Postgate returns to the house, not for help but for a revolver. She has no need to use it. The man is groaning in his death-agony. "Stop that!" Mary says, and stamps her foot. "Stop that, you bloody pagan!" It is Wynn's sort of language. The man dies. That evening, Miss Fowler notices that her dim and repressed companion is looking, for once, "quite handsome."

It is easy to see that in "Mary Postgate," as in one or two other war stories which are less successful, Kipling begins from a passion of hate which he believes himself to share with his countrymen at large: a hate that is "impersonal" in the sense of being directed not against an individual but against the evil-doing of the German nation. He even adds as tail-piece a poem called "The Beginnings":

> It was not part of their blood,
>   It came to them very late
> With long arrears to make good,
>   When the English began to hate. . . .

But the story is not about the English beginning to hate, nor about Kipling beginning to hate, either. It is about something that happens to a particular woman when wrought upon by forces some of which she is quite unconscious of. This is what makes "Mary Postgate" not merely a shattering story but a tragic story as well—one full of pity and terror. For nowhere else in Kipling are we so powerfully confronted with a horror which we are made to recognize as proceeding from an authentic exploration of human character in depth. All the emotion behind the story has been transfused into its action. Dreadful though it be, this is why it remains a work of art.

"The Gardener" (*Debits and Credits*) is another war story about a woman, and one looking forward, in some respects, to the final phase of Kipling's work. Its key word, spoken once only, is "compassion." Helen Turrell has had an illegitimate son, Michael; and she has cleverly contrived to avert scandal, although at the cost of living out a lie. When her pregnancy could no longer be concealed she had gone to the South of France, invented various explanations to account for her long absence, and returned with the baby and the assertion that she has adopted the child of a brother who had lately died in India. The story is so told by Kipling that we may ourselves be misled by the untruth as we read—and on a rereading (so subtle is his narrative art) we cannot be certain whether or not Helen's friends and neighbours have similarly been deceived. When war breaks out Michael Turrell gains a commission, is thrown into the line after the Battle of Loos, and is soon posted as missing. Later (unlike John Kipling) his body is recovered and identified, and Helen eventually goes to visit his grave in a vast military cemetery in Flanders. In her hotel she meets another Englishwoman who tells an improbable story of frequent visits to the cemetery simply on behalf of bereaved friends, but who then breaks down and confesses that it is to the grave of one whose mistress she had been that she is drawn back again and again:

> "I'm so tired of lying. Tired of lying—always lying—year in and year out. When I don't tell lies I've got to act 'em and I've got to think 'em always. You don't know what that means . . . I can't go to him again with nobody in the world knowing."

Helen tries to comfort this woman, but without admitting her own secret, so that the woman is obscurely repelled by her insincerity, and repulses her.

The next day Helen makes her way through the thousands and thousands of graves. She loses her bearings, and looks around for help:

> A man knelt behind a line of headstones—evidently a gardener, for he was firming a young plant in the soft earth. She went towards him, her paper in her hand. He rose at her approach and without prelude or salutation asked: "Who are you looking for?"
>
> "Lieutenant Michael Turrell—my nephew," said Helen slowly and word for word, as she had many thousands of times in her life.
>
> The man lifted his eyes and looked at her with infinite compassion before he turned from the fresh-sown grass toward the naked black crosses.
>
> "Come with me," he said, "and I will show you where your son lies."
>
> When Helen left the Cemetery she turned for a last look. In the distance she saw the man bending over his young plants; and she went away, supposing him to be the gardener.

In St. John's Gospel it is Mary Magdalen who supposes that the risen Christ "must be the gardener."

After writing "The Church That Was at Antioch" Kipling had not done with St. Peter and St. Paul. They appear severally in two sharply contrasting stories in his final collected volume, *Limits and Renewals*. "The Manner of Men" is almost a nautical companion piece to the earlier story, being based upon the voyage and shipwreck described in the twenty-seventh chapter of *The Acts of the Apostles*. Here is a wonderfully convincing close-up view of seafaring in the ancient Mediterranean, carrying for us echoes from as far back as "The Finest Story in the World." To the mariners gossiping in these pages, Paul is no more than an odd philosopher, casually encountered; or rather he is at once this and a little man of unaccountable and unforgettable power.

"On the Gate" presents a very different Peter from the struggling saint of "The Church That Was at Antioch." He now holds the keys of Heaven, and it is in Heaven that the story is set. Kipling was not a professing Christian, and there is something disconcerting at first—in appearance, indeed, almost frivolous—in his presentation of Death and Judgement, Salvation and Damnation, as matters transacting themselves through the machinery of something like an earthly Government Department. The story has a subtitle, "A Tale of '16," and what we are shown is this machinery almost breaking down under the strain imposed upon it by the mounting war casualties of that year. Only Peter himself can cut through the red tape which, hour by hour, impedes the operation, and we are tempted to see him at once as a first-class Indian Civil Servant. The similitude is enhanced by his situation. Above him is a remote and inscrutable Power, not unlike the Government of India. Below him, and flooding in upon him, are helpless and driven millions. Like Scott who milked the goats in "William the Conqueror," he must do what he can. But he is the authentic Peter of the Gospels in that he is the disciple of Christ (Who is not mentioned in the story), dedicating his will and intellect to an endless labour of mercy. The letter killeth, but the spirit giveth life; and Peter's job is really to circumvent the letter with all the guile of an experienced subordinate. It is this, rather than the lightness of fantasy and constantly hovering comedy, that imports something equivocal into the story. What Kipling himself saw as overarching this earth was not Heaven, but a void—and into that void he is here injecting something for which his heart hungers, but which is unsanctioned by his belief. There is a point at which Peter is made to cry out "Samuel Two, Double Fourteen." When we make the reference, we find the words of the Wise Woman of Tekoah. King David has been at fault in not calling home again his banished son. For it is otherwise with God: "For we must needs die, and are as water spilt on the ground, which cannot be gathered up again; neither doth God respect any person; yet doth he devise means, that his banished be not expelled from him." Kipling's story has the validity of poetry, not of theological belief. Peter, hard at work wresting the frame of things to "devise means," has the limitations of something merely yearned for, not known. Yet "On the Gate" is a deeply serious story. And St. Peter is its hero essentially because (to make one final return to "William the Conqueror") he is among those "who do things." This places the fable in the full stream of Kipling's final writings. In these the constant threat is of acquiescence in hopeless, because passive, suffering. Kipling casts actively about for help and healing to the end.

The theme of healing is not confined entirely to Kipling's last period. It makes an appearance (in a sufficiently crude form) in as early a story as "The Mark of the Beast"; in one or two places in *Puck of Pook's Hill*; and in a curious story called "The House Surgeon" in *Actions and Reactions*. It will be remembered how the Kiplings, on returning from Vermont, found something mysteriously depressing in what appeared to be a delightful house at Torquay. In the actual house the mysterious blight seems to have been permanent, since Kipling found it just as bad when he revisited it thirty years later. But in "The House Surgeon" such a house undergoes a cure. Its manner of afflicting with an unaccountable depression all who live there is found to be occasioned by their telepathic rapport with a former inmate who believes that her sister committed suicide in it. When the belief is proved to be erroneous the house ceases to be depressing.

This is a trivial story, but has interest as hovering between the supernatural and theories of psychopathology and psychotherapy which were to become increasingly current during the first quarter of the twentieth century. There is no evidence that Kipling knew much about Freud (whose *Die Traumdeutung* appeared in 1900); it is unlikely that he would have heard him talked about by the eminent and conservative English physicians who were among his acquaintances in later life; and there is much in Freud's ideas which he would have violently disliked. Nevertheless certain of the stories seem to touch on Freudian psychotherapy as it came to be popularly conceived: some traumatic experience which has been "repressed" is successfully restored to consciousness and confronted in a fashion from which a cure results. Kipling's tentative explorations here are likely to suffer from our associating them with mediocre novels and films which make facile play with this kind of thing. Some of them are remarkable, nevertheless. A prewar story called "In the Same Boat" (*A Diversity of Creatures*) is an example. Here a man and a woman have severally consulted their doctors when suffering from constant and insupportable nightmares. Manoeuvred into each other's company on a railway journey, they establish a sympathetic relationship from which each derives strength and support, until finally it is discovered that the mother of each suffered some alarming experience during pregnancy. The result of this prenatal illumination is "unspeakable relief." We are not very convinced by this story (in which we discern a distant relationship with "The Brushwood Boy"). But it has a curious historical interest, and at the same time points forward to related postwar stories in which we feel Kipling's imagination to be much more deeply engaged.

A few of these stories are very obscure, particularly when they continue to hover indecisively between a psychological and a supernatural interpretation of their material. Thus "The Dog Hervey" (*A Diversity of Creatures*) is a tale, or fantasy, on the true meaning of which there is still no agreement. Miss Sichliffe is an unattractive maiden lady, whom nobody has ever liked except a wealthy man who has, however, disappeared from her life. Miss Sichliffe now loves only a dog (an unattractive dog), and eventually the Spiritual Form of this dog (as the poet Blake might have called it) appears to her former lover in circumstances not in themselves edifying—but with the consequence that a subsequent chain of events reunites the lovers, and they are married. The oblique and opaque character of "The Dog Hervey" seems to reflect some area of its creator's mind resistant to the power of his art. Kipling wrote only one other story which is at once haunting and hopelessly mysterious. This is the much earlier "Mrs. Bathurst" (*Traffics and Discoveries*), the theme of which appears to be sexual passion in its destructive aspect.

There is another dog in one of the late stories of healing, "The Woman in His Life" (*Limits and Renewals*). John Marden, a sapper during the war, has returned from some stiff experiences—below ground and above—and has rapidly built up a flourishing engineering business. Quite suddenly he suffers a severe nervous breakdown, and this worsens when he takes refuge in drink. "A Fear leaped out of the goose-fleshed

streets of London between the icy shop fronts, and drove John to his flat."
His condition grows yet worse, so that he becomes subject to hallucinations; among these is a small black dog, pressed against the skirting board of his room; he believes that if the animal leaves this position the whole universe will come crashing down. Marden's manservant, also an ex-soldier, introduces a real black dog into the flat, a dwarf Aberdeen bitch. Marden, now that the spectral dog has become a real dog ("the woman in his life" is in fact the bitch Dinah), begins to recover. Eventually Dinah, by a strange chance, is trapped in a tunnel much as Marden had once been during the war. Marden stands up to a supreme nervous challenge, saves Dinah, and his cure becomes complete.

We may feel this to be rather a sentimental story. Most dog stories are. But it shows a mind sensitively aware of the agony of neurotic illness precipitated by experience in battle: "shell shock," as it was then termed. Kipling was quick to see the possibilities of occupational therapy, and the need to integrate such sufferers within a sympathetic social group. Seeking a means of achieving both these ends, he turned to Free Masonry, in which he had always been interested, and wrote several stories to illustrate how it might help, alike through the bracing effect of ritual and through practical activities. "I cured a shell-shocker this spring by giving him our jewels to look after," one Mason is made to report. There is no doubt something a little overconfident about this, and these stories sometimes betray an uncertainty of tone, such—we may say—as one unaccustomed to the visitation of the sick may at times exhibit. Ritual of a sort plays its part in "The Janeites" (*Debits and Credits*), in which the members of an English battery in Flanders keep a grip on themselves by elaborating a convention of ceaseless allusive reference to Miss Austen's novels: this serves its purpose, for they hold out until the battery is destroyed and most of them are killed. "Fairy-Kist" (*Limits and Renewals*) has some sort of irregular Masonic setting, and begins on a note of cozy dining and yarning not very happily knit to the horror of the central situation: Wollin, another war casualty, released from a mental hospital, surviving only after submission to voices which bid him wander the countryside planting flowers, involved in complex events which seem likely to result in his being convicted of murder—and finally saved by more amateur psychotherapy in which we do not quite believe.

In *Something of Myself* Kipling records what was to him, as a child, "the loveliest sound in the world—deep-voiced men laughing together over dinner." In his stories celebrating the mysterious power of laughter (there are plenty of them, but few seem very funny when merely summarized) women are commonly allowed a very small part. The place for laughter—significant laughter—is among men, and "deep-voiced" men at that. Kipling's is very much a man's world, and he saw the essential masculine principle as best embodied in the ability of men to labour together to some impersonal end within the brotherhood of one or another profession, craft, or service. Hence Kipling's unceasing need to be "in the know" whenever the spectacle of men working together came his way. C. S. Lewis makes a shrewd observation here:

> In the last resort I do not think he loves professional brotherhood for the sake of the work; I think he loves work for the sake of professional brotherhood . . . To belong, to be inside, to be in the know, to be snugly against the outsiders—that is what really matters.

That this is not a wholly adequate judgement appears most clearly in those final stories in which it is the brotherhood of doctors and the work of healing which constitute the "Inner Ring" (as Lewis calls it) to which, by an imaginative projection, Kipling seeks to "belong." It is very probable that as a man moves through his sixties he will have increasing personal need to consult physicians and give thought to their art. Here was no doubt the occasion of Kipling's final look at an "Inner Ring." But when we consider in this context Lewis's further generalization that "the spirit of the Inner Ring is morally neutral" we may feel that it stands in need of qualification. Kipling saw great sanctity as attaching to the Hippocratic Oath, and his doctors (like his Indian Civilians, for that matter) are dedicated to purposes not reasonably to be described as "morally neutral." Like all men with stiff assignments, they are liable to have grown a tough skin or hard shell. But that is another matter.

"The Tender Achilles" (*Limits and Renewals*) takes its title from the legend that, when the Greek forces were being mustered for the Trojan War, the young Achilles, the future hero of the campaign, hid among women. Kipling's Achilles is Wilkett, a brilliant bacteriologist, whose work is essential to the progress of the "Great Search" going on in the biological laboratories of St. Peggotty's Hospital. (The Great Search is Kipling's term for cancer research.) During the war Wilkett has been an army surgeon; and now, like Marden in "The Woman in His Life," he suffers from the result of delayed shock, and breaks down. "Everything that a man's brain automatically shoves into the background was out before the footlights," one of his colleagues records—and goes on:

> "Of course, I argued with him, but you know how much good that is against fixed notions! I told him we were all alike, and the conditions of our job hadn't been human. I said there were limits to the machine. We'd been forced to go beyond 'em, and we ought to be thankful we'd been able to do as much as we had. Then he wrung his hands and said, 'To whom much has been given, from the same much shall be required.' That annoyed me. I hate bookkeeping with God!"

Wilkett's breakdown results in his giving up his work and sheltering weakly with his mother. But he has a physical as well as a nervous wound, and a group of his colleagues make this the basis of a stratagem to get him back, showing him that a faulty diagnosis of his own physical trouble could not have occurred had he himself been doing his proper work. Again we may not be very impressed with the statement that an absolute cure has been achieved. But the Wilkett whose experiences in an S.I.W. (hospital for self-infected wounds) have pushed him beyond the "breaking strain" is convincing and moving enough.

"Unprofessional" (*Limits and Renewals*) is also about the medical profession, and takes its title from a group of research workers who go outside what their colleagues would regard as the admissible boundaries of science in their method of studying and treating cancer. The basic idea of this story relates it to "The Eye of Allah," and more particularly to a poem entitled "Untimely," which serves as prologue there:

> Nothing in life has been made by man for man's using
> But it was shown long since to man in ages
> Lost as the name of the maker of it. . . .

It is certain of the beliefs of mediaeval physicians that Kipling in "Unprofessional" represents as embodying scientific truth which now has to be discovered anew. When working on "Dayspring Mishandled" he must have read how Chaucer's Doctor of Physic

> was grounded in astronomye.
> He kepte his pacient a ful greet del
> In houres, by his magik naturel.

This means that the Doctor was careful his patients should receive their treatment at hours when the disposition of the stars was favourable. The doctors in "Unprofessional," as a result of prolonged and lavish use of every technique known to modern science, find that their mediaeval forerunners were on the right track, since our bodily tissues prove subject to a minute but all-significant "tidal" action arising from the motions of the stars. Thus the time of day at which a specimen of such tissues is scrutinized under the microscope may validate or invalidate a diagnosis, and compass bearings are vital in an operating theatre. In the course of the story a woman who would otherwise have died is in fact healed by this neo-astrological medicine. There is surely something inartistic in the triumph within the fable of a therapy we know to have no existence outside it. Kipling, perhaps conscious of this, soft-pedals his conclusion. Nothing has really been achieved, one of the team says, except, perhaps, "some data and inferences which may serve as some sort of basis for some detail of someone else's work in the future." On this professional rather than unprofessional note the story comes to an end. Although Kipling has used all his accustomed command of detail to render the characters and their milieu convincing, we shall probably conclude that "Unprofessional" is the work of a man who no longer has much impulse to elaborate "realistic" fiction.

If this is so, it must have been deliberately that Kipling placed last in his last book of stories a companion piece to his earlier fable "On the Gate." "Uncovenanted Mercies" is about the problem of pain—where pain takes the form of spiritual anguish inscrutably imposed, and inscrutably deepened and prolonged. Since hope deferred is the direst torment of all, the "full test for Ultimate Breaking Strain" takes place in a supernal railway terminus in which men and women are made to wait through eternities for some beloved person who never turns up. It is a strangely powerful and haunting image, which may remind some readers of Kafka, and some of Sartre. But in English literature, too, there is an apposite comparison: with *The Dynasts* of Thomas Hardy. Hardy's "Overworld," with its Spirits Sinister and Ironic, but also with its Spirit of the Pities, has some affinity with this last region of Kipling's imagining. But Kipling, once again, plucks something affirmative from the abyss. The test for ultimate breaking strain represents only Satan's carrying out the last of the tasks appointed him among the soul of the damned; and survival means that a soul has been "reconditioned for reissue." *He that endureth to the end shall be saved.* This was Kipling's final reading of life.

The False Structure   John Bayley*

Kipling's remarks on his art are few, but not reassuring. They mostly come in *Something of Myself.* There is the daemon of course, on whose attendance he waits, and whose status is such that Kipling the man can accept no honours for the work done. There is the joy of creating, and the awareness that what is created may turn out pretentious or false, on which "Hal o'the Draft" is eloquent, learning the ironic lesson that for strictly non-artistic reasons bad work may be more richly rewarded than good. There are the metaphors of a three-decker masterpiece, matured like a ship's timbers, sumptuously gilded and carved. There are the overlapping tints and textures, whose import is graduated to the age and discernment of the reader. Art displays its ingenuity in its modes and levels of instruction.

Yet none of this sounds quite real. Partly because it has nothing to do with the impact the writing actually makes, its absolute and unique appeal; and the paradox, often noted, on which that appeal is based: that here is an immensely popular author whose prose has nonetheless the air of being written for an in-group, for a few connoisseurs of craftsmanship and style. More pungent, perhaps more meaningful, is what is implied in two of the stories—"A Matter of Fact" and "The Finest Story in the

*Reprinted from *English Literature in Translation, 1880–1920* 29, no. 1 (1986):19–27, by permission.

World." The message of these, pushed to the edge of self-parody, is that the best narrator is the one who, as the sailor Pyecroft was later to say, can relate "solely what transpired," or, as the poem puts it, the "unvarnished accident" as it "actually occurred." Having been a slave at the oars of the galley that was sunk, or having seen the sea-monster from the steamer's deck, he alone can give the entirely authentic account which constitutes true art.

The absolute authority of the young man who can recall episodes from his past lives is cunningly transmitted to us by Kipling the narrator. The principle is the mirror image. Absolute truth gives absolute art: therefore absolute art is absolute truth. The artist who has actually seen a sea-monster rising out of the depths nonetheless decides to write the experience as fiction, for truth is a naked lady, and, if she appears, right-minded men avert their eyes and swear they did not see. The facetious image tells us that people will accept the truth if properly clothed. They will accept what Kipling wants to tell them—his version of the truth—if it is concealed as art.

This paradox may explain the strange air of unreality which grows more and more marked in Kipling's stories, becoming their point and justification, virtually the sign of their success. The more "authentic" the narrator, the more marked the unreality. There is of course a simple nemesis which waits for all highly imaginative writers whose imaginations are deeply involved in politics. Their political and social pictures tend to become wholly fictive. In *Bowen's Court*, her biography of an Irish house, Elizabeth Bowen remarks on the fact that when the IRA occupied it during the troubles their young men were fascinated by a Collected Works of Kipling, and pored over his tales with absorption. Kipling's vision or his ideal army and empire does indeed have something of that potent fictive unreality, however much less legendary, more detailed and more clear-cut, which attended the growth of Irish nationalism. The two visions were roughly contemporary; and though the British Empire itself had a vast, solid, and objective existence, it was inevitably a dream to Kipling's daemon, to his creating mind.

He could be quite aware of this. In his earlier writings he can even be amused by it. "His Private Honour" shows Kipling having a dream about the ideal British army in India, lying on the mud wall of a fort, from which he wakes to find the actual British army getting into small personal difficulties on the parade ground below him. (Even here we might notice, Ortheris's private honour, how it is impugned and how restored, seems itself a fantasy, although the tale affects to set down "solely what transpired.") But "The Army of a Dream," a story from the time of the Boer War, is much more serious, a Kipling fantasy of the most practical kind, with all the meticulous bitterness of which a disappointed day-dreamer is capable.

As his readers know, the Boer War made a crisis in Kipling's life and art. The absoluteness of authenticity claims more, and assumes a more positive function. *Puck of Pook's Hill* (1906) and *Rewards and Fairies* (1910) claim the authority suggested, and in some degree parodied, in "The Finest Story in the World." The characters called up by Puck to tell their experiences to the children are a sort of perfected version of the young man in "The Finest Story," whose total but temporary authority over past events is dissolved by all the sentimental illusions of present calf lovers.

The past in these stories seems as casual as a good conjuring trick. The weight of truth falls on the area of contrivance; truth is palpably at one with artifice. Kipling's authenticity has a very special status of its own, an aesthetic status comparable to the uniform individuality of a Braque or a Mondrian. If we compare dialogue and detail in any Kipling story with those, say, in Conrad's *The Nigger of the "Narcissus,"* it is clear that Conrad has left such matters in the area of literariness which the reader quite simply takes for granted: that is to say the part of narrative that does not bear its thrust of mastery and meaning. In Kipling, on the other hand, every last word of description or dialogue is intended to convey the casual but overwhelming impression that this is exactly it, the words, the gesture, the event "that actually occurred," with every touch in place. When the reader recovers, so to speak, he realises that it is like looking at a painting, where what matters is the opacity and totality of the painter's style. There is no distinction between what is true and less true, or between the feeling of truth and the feeling of contrivance. There is only the absoluteness of Kipling's verbal, or—as it might be—painterly, personality.

Authenticity is in the look of the thing. Kipling would be a good example of Gombrich's thesis in *Art and Illusion*—a thesis itself deduced from the theory and practice of modern painting—that nothing on the surface of art is in itself true or false. The point involved, so cogent where paint is concerned, has a different application with words, but it concerns words themselves becoming like brush strokes or small blobs of art. There is a modern parallel, too, with the art work of film or television, which is vowed to a seemingly complete authenticity of construction, as music recordings are dedicated to total fidelity.

Critics have pointed out that in early Kipling his displays of knowingness and of offhand power over his material disguise getting away with utter implausibility. In "The Return of Imray," for instance, events and properties are as inherently fantastic as in Conan Doyle's story "The Speckled Band." Because of the personalities of Holmes and Watson the reader accepts them there in a different spirit: they do not have to be swallowed in a lump, as with Kipling. (How, after all, could the corpse of Imray have remained in the room where it was without being "nosed," as Hamlet said of Polonius?) What we pass over as the area of contrivance in a thriller or detective story—and many of Kipling's tales, early and late, have close affinities with the genre—is here laid before us with a kind of emphatic insolence, as if the falsity itself were a kind of superior truth. In the last story of *Rewards and Fairies*, "The Tree of Justice," the broken old man who turns out to be Harold of England, sits by the fire with knees on elbows and his face in both hands, "Saxon-fashion," where a Norman, we are informed, sits with one hand on his chin. This is to create one's own truth. The painting analogy is again opposite. When asked whether an object in one of his paintings was a man's front or back, Delacroix is said to have replied: "Neither—it's painting." Kipling's arbitrary assignments of physical distinction have something of the same bravura effect.

This kind of thing can militate against the thrust of the moral in the tale. In a previous story in *Rewards and Fairies* about Bishop Wilfred and the conversion of the South Saxons, the moral is to be loyal to the beliefs and customs one was brought up in, and not to abandon them for personal or political advantage. Meon the Saxon king is a noble figure, and Kipling cleverly suggests the ideals of heroic society, but in this case the touches of authenticity, instead of being merely a function of a style which "overbore unbelieving," sharply suggest a potent if irrelevant area of truth which, like so much in Kipling, can, on re-reading, bring tears unexpectedly to the eyes. It is one of Kipling's jokes, for the benefit of his young and not so young listeners, that when Meon and the two Christian priests are dying on a little island of starvation and exposure, their savior is a tame seal that brings them fish and alerts Meon's retainers to their plight. The joke is that Meon will not desert Wotan in his last extremity, and calls on him in what Wilfred describes as "that high shaking heathen yell which I detest so."

In prompt answer to this prayer the seal shoots out of the water with a fish in its mouth. To the priest Eddi, it is a miracle, and miracles can only be Christian, but it might just as well be credited to Wotan. Wilfred, and Kipling, forbears to comment, and when he is safe back in his hall Meon is baptised, with his people. Wilfred's comment on Meon, a wonderful man who "never looked back—never looked back," has the true ecclesiastical flavour, and there seems something curiously convincing about the high shaky heathen yell. Perhaps Kipling was thinking of the call from the Muezzin or some other intonation of the east.

However that may be, a touch in a Kipling story that strikes one as true has the same status as one that is obviously bogus, like the different sitting pose of a Norman and a Saxon. Both belong to the same area of created and hypnotic actuality, in which lies and truth form a seamless whole. In most of the stories there is a meaning and a moral which imposes itself, sometimes gently and persuasively, sometimes with sarcasm and force. But good or bad these are never relevant to the impact of the story and its memorableness. The truffle-hunting dog story, "Teem," has the curious phrase, quoted by Angus Wilson: "Outside of himself an artist must never dream." This, I think, attaches itself to the implications suggested very much earlier in "The Finest Story." The morals and meanings are, as it were, a dreaming outside the story, whose authenticity is also in its totality of manufacture. The stories try to have it both ways. They insist on their absolute authenticity, but they also seek to point a moral, and the two directions are, often, incompatible. The truth / contrivance contrast is a perfectly harmonious one in other kinds of writing, but in Kipling the magic of contrivance is quite alien to the emergence of any truth independent of art. This artist is compelled to dream outside himself, but then his dreaming becomes false because his art cannot control it, and the reader is left in both a state of total acceptance and an equally total scepticism.

It may be that one's appreciation of Kipling's "lies" militates directly against acceptance of his truths, however unexceptionable these may be. This seems often to be the case in the later stories. The Bible itself takes on an air of unreality from its deft use at the end of "The Gardener" and "The Church that Was at Antioch." The obstinacy of love, the sublime idea of which is cunningly groped toward in "The Wish House," "They," and "A Madonna of the Trenches," projects embarrassingly from the rich concoction of Kipling's own magic falseness. In doing so they help to explain the unusual relation between Kipling's dream world—inside himself—and the sources of his popularity. The undoubted creepiness of the "Token" in "The Wish House," the other self that may be of the living or the dead, is hardly in keeping with the notion of taking a cancer on oneself out of love and self-sacrifice. And yet the sentimental appeal of this idea is very great, just as great as is that of the love pact in "A Madonna of the Trenches" or the loves that cannot declare themselves in "The Gardener," or the dead children gathered into the magical country house in "They." Just as popular are the notorious emotions in "Mary Postgate" and "Swept and Garnished," where the themes of revenge and hatred are as brutal and simple as the falsity of the tale is elaborate and extreme.

It is arguable, indeed, that the themes of the later stories are more, not less, "popular" than those of the early ones. What could be more blatantly in keeping with pieces in the tabloid papers than the apparently recondite subject of "Unprofessional," with the suggestion that the sources of cancer may be related to astrology? But if the themes get even more popular, and if Kipling shows an even deeper understanding of the things that most absorb and preoccupy the minds and hearts of "ordinary people," the gap between the way his art works and the sort of stuff it is working on seems to grow ever wider.

And yet that "seems" may be misleading. The incongruity between the touchingly banal or embarrassingly virulent theme, and the way it is concocted and handled, may have much to do with the undoubted individuality of the aesthetic effect. If Kipling's dream virtuosities deprive his theme of truth, rather as "Dayspring Mishandled" deprives Chaucer of any "Chaucerianness," it compensates by giving us a memorable new

Kipling dimension, a phrase as imperishable as anything he wrote, in verse or prose. But it is true of him in general that he takes the common nature out of anything he treats, and fills the gap with his own kind of falsity/authenticity. Shakespeare and the Bible, in "Proofs of Holy Writ," suffer the same kind of total denaturing as the Soldiers Three. A Sussex house and village, in "An Habitation Enforced," loses every last trace of natural unforced contingent existence, and becomes as complete a simulacrum in Kipling's own image of the authentic, as if it were on a film set in a modern television production.

So intelligent and perspicuous a genius, and one with such a fund of worldly and practical curiosity, would certainly have intimations of what was happening, although a complete lack of self-consciousness is one of the most important specifications of this art's immediacy and vividness. (So is the pretense, never so wholeheartedly and successfully maintained in any other authorial context, that the writer is not a writer at all, has none of a writer's self-absorptions, blocks, hidden preoccupations.) Nonetheless his narrators are also dreamers, and the use of dream in sickness as a form of narrative is recurrent in his work, from "The Bridge Builders" to "Swept and Garnished." Some of the delusions, like Mary Postgate's possible ones, or that of the sick woman in "The Wish House," are left as much in the area of uncertainty as those of the governess in "The Turn of the Screw." And Kipling always shows subtlety in the use of delusions, just as he understands the hidden connections between compulsive sexual love and stress-induced disease, as in "The Wish House." Stress, in all his stories, is true beyond all his normal build-up of authentic non-reality.

For all their greater elaboration of technique, and their more subtly personal use of the theme of illness, the later stories are also just as old-fashioned, as essentially Victorian, as earlier ones. "The Wish House" and "The Gardener" are the same sort of exemplary tales as "A Conference of the Powers" and "The Miracle of Purun Bhagat." The former of those two exhibits as well Kipling's basic knowledge that to an artist all things are art, and that he himself has no greater title to authenticity than the novelist Cleever, who listens in respectful amazement to the subalterns' stories of campaign. As a writer he knows that no narrative is without art, and he incurs the indignation of the subaltern for implying this. "I beg your pardon," he said slowly and stiffly, "but I am telling this thing as it happened." In a very late variation of the same point Kipling imagines the Soldiers Three rounding on him and telling him he has got them all wrong. Every last detail about them is true only in terms of Kipling's inspired kinds of falsity, the falsity that "overbears unbelieving" by insisting that the truth has nothing to do with "literature." Kipling's French mentors, like Verlaine, are in the background here. Kim himself can be seen in one light as a fantasy of the author who is not an author, the little friend, also a small imp, who has unlimited access not only to the way the world is run but to its spiritual and unworldly side as well.

"Mrs. Bathurst" has a special interest in the development of Kipling's narrative art because of the way in which it avoids any of his usual assertions of a meaning, his special knowledge of the way things are, or his own ambivalent status as artist and magician. It is not in itself a specially ambitious work of art, although the way Kipling tells it has attracted a great deal of critical attention. Its point seems to be an evasion of that old apparition—truth like the sea-monster or naked lady, emerging unbelievably from the depths. The other stories that deal in the preternatural, or in possible delusions, have an either / or drawback: their effect depends on a hidden clarity and a hidden truth (the young soldier in "A Madonna of the Trenches" invents a reason for his breakdown while concealing the true one) and all the pointers in them have a knowing look. With "Mrs. Bathurst" this is not the case. There is no special pretension about it—no author could be less pretentious than Kipling is about his tales—and I certainly would not claim that he was deliberately trying out a new "smart" technique which he then failed to follow up. Nonetheless the tale seems in some sense to reverse the image of overwhelming falseness /authenticity which is the hallmark of Kipling manufacture. How does this come about?

In the first place the presentation is unusually perfunctory. Compare it in this respect with "Wireless" or "The House Surgeon." It seems to have been one—the only one carried through—out of a list of possible stories with a South African background which Kipling jotted down at the time. None of them sound very interesting or very promising. Neither does the "idea" of Mrs. Bathurst as Kipling gives it in *Something of Myself*—a sentence he had heard about a woman in New Zealand who would never scruple to set her foot on a scorpion or help a lame dog over a stile. To add to this, Pyecroft and Pritchett, the sailor and marine, and Hooper the railways inspector, are sketchy figures, lacking that elaboration of false personal being which Kipling gets into his other story characters, like the quartet of India civil servants in "At the End of the Passage." The story, in fact, seems to reverse all the normal Kipling tricks, even while it suggests them.

It also employs a tactic of receding narration which adds to the processes of anti-climax. Hooper is about to tell the narrator a bizarre railway incident, authenticated by the false teeth he has in his waistcoat pocket, when Pyecroft and Pritchett arrive, and are soon launched into reminiscence of their own about "Boy Niven," a young sailor of years back who had led his seniors on a wild-goose chase round an uninhabited island in Vancouver archipelago. "We believed," says Pyecroft, and the tale teller, now "Mr. Niven," a warrant officer, has made a success in life. By way of desertion we arrive at Mrs. Bathurst, who is filled in with a sudden access of Kiplingesque falsity: after a page or so of detail she seems to be taking her place in the gallery of Kipling's meticulous unbelievables. We also seem headed for one of his emphatic clichés, and one we have met before, that of the kind of woman who can inspire a passionate and disastrous love.

This impression is dissolved as the words continue, and as the image of Mrs. Bathurst herself dissolves as she walks down the platform in the cinematograph, "like a shadow jumpin' over a candle." (In "A Sahibs' War" the narrator sees the image of his dead Kurban Sahib "riding as it were upon my eyes.") Mrs. Bathurst becomes a narrative figure, with all the falsity of such a figure in Kipling, only to lose that status immediately. The image of her that remains, and it is a disturbing and touching one, is on the early cinematograph—"Home and Friends for a tickey" (a South African threepenny bit) leaving a train in London—"the passengers got out and the porters got the luggage—just like life," Pyecroft remarks. Mrs. Bathurst has been, as it were, saved from the fate of being a Kipling character, and remains only a compelling image, like that of Michael Furey in Joyce's "The Dead," who is a figure standing under a dripping tree. In that form she acquires immense potency, and not only for Vickery, who watches her avidly every showing on the screen, and then gets drunk with the shipmate he has dragged along with him to confirm her identity. Kipling intuited, as Joyce was doing, the way an emptiness in modern life was to feed on images, usually banal ready-made ones, mass-produced. Something in Mrs. Bathurst anticipates Greta Garbo. Both Joyce and Kipling, in their different ways, fill such images with the delicacy and power of art, so that in one sense the reader "believes," along with Gabriel Conroy and Vickery.

Yet Mrs. Bathurst is not a conundrum, or mystery story. Uncertainty is used only to enhance the image. In the stories where concentration pays off, or solutions are on offer, Kipling is either indulging emotional violence, as in "Mary Postgate" and "Swept and Garnished," or inching his way towards the cliché of a deep true compassionate meaning, as in "The Wish House" and "They." In either case the details of oddity are working towards an outcome. These can be climactic as they are obscure, as in "Swept and Garnished," where we are never told what Frau Ebermann looked at and saw, as the final horror in her delusion about Belgian children in her flat. As Angus Wilson explains, there was an allied propaganda story, one would have thought barely credible even at the time, that the Germans were systematically amputating the right arms of little Belgian boys so that they would never be able to serve against them. Kipling degrades art by both withholding and proffering this monstrous canard, and he does similar things in the South African stories that are more or less contemporary with "Mrs. Bathurst," such as "The Comprehension of Private Copper." In the undoubtedly powerful story, "A Sahibs' War," the son of the Boer church minister who takes the oath of

neutrality and then treacherously shoots the British, is an imbecile, and
the Sikh soldier narrator finds even his mother's love for him repulsive.

In these stories the operation of falsity / authenticity is reinforced by
inner knowledge, not directly divulged, but held outside the story for the
appreciation of those in the know. A rotten cause and hypocrite faith like
that of the Boers would naturally breed idiot children, abhorrent to all
true followers of the Raj, like the Sikh trooper, for whom the murdered
captain is his own child, and who is utterly desolated by his death. In stories like these undeclared falsity lurks behind, and in support of, the emphatic falsity in the Kipling scenario. And yet both seem necessary to this
tale's prime old-fashioned purpose: to make the reader feel, and feel
with, the Sikh narrator in his loss. And that purpose is abundantly
achieved.

Overkill of a kind is a Kipling hallmark. His daemon seem to have
the power of putting more in a tale than meets the eye. And this can either add to the dimension of its truth or falsity, or both together. The
success of "Mrs. Bathurst" comes from the way all the stories it contains
run away into nothing, leaving only the image. People love stories,
which seem to give shape and meaning to uncertainties and vanishings;
and the idea of "the story in it," which Kipling may have picked up from
James, is played with by the poetry of the tale, its suggestion of great
distances and small units—ships and boarding houses—with their con-
stricted lives, emotions and fantasies. As so often in Kipling's best work
there is an insistent weight of unmentioned event and destiny, as if in the
background of "Recessional." "Far called, our navies melt away, / On
dune and headland sinks the fire." Incongruous but harmonious with
this are what "They" calls "cross-sections of remote and incomprehensible lives through which we raced at right angles." The burden of falsity
is placed on these "lives" themselves, the characters whose version of
events and people is simple-minded or platitudinous, crudely fascinated, pathetically obsessed.

Thus the various stories in "Mrs. Bathurst" start up and flicker out,
"like a shadow jumping over a candle." The fantasy about his uncle's farm
told by Boy Niven, in which Pyecroft and Pritchett and their mates once
"believed," merges with the possible versions of what may have happened between Vickery and Mrs. Bathurst. Did he promise to marry her?
Did he do away with his own wife? Did he desert her, perhaps when she
was pregnant? Did she then do away with herself? What was the story that
he told the captain, which caused him to be sent on the assignment up
country from which he deserted? Delighting the characters who
obliquely refer to them, these lurid speculations hover over the pathetic
reality of the story, caught in its one touching image, an image which in-
voluntarily places and falsifies the "words of wisdom" uttered by the
characters themselves. These are Hooper's, in his slow comment on a
man in Vickery's seeming situation: "He goes crazy—or just saves

himself"; and Pyecroft's verdict on Vickery's being a family man: "'ave you ever found these little things make much difference? Because I haven't."

So "we all reflected together," to save the appearances, a process aided by the picnic party going past singing "The Honeysuckle and the Bee," a little song which invents a sufficiently happy story. But with subdued cunning Kipling's narrative returns to the story aborted right at the beginning, and joins it up with the other fragments. Hooper the railway man had found two tramps burned to a crisp by lightning, in a teak forest up the line, and one of them had some false teeth, "shining against the black," which he kept as a curio but never exhibits during the story. Two circumstances in this climactic event impress his auditors—and the reader. One is that there are two tramps, and one is squatting down and looking up at the other—"watchin' him"—a detail twice repeated. The other is that both are burned to charcoal, as if damned.

Belief in a story and belief in hell go together. The illustrator in the *Windsor Magazine*, in which the story first appeared, certainly seems to have believed, to the point of portraying the second tramp, looking up and watching, as an obvious female figure. C. A. Bodelsen, who in *Aspects of Kipling's Art* has most thoroughly investigated what its readers have made of the story, dismisses any notion that Kipling intended the second tramp to be Mrs. Bathurst. The story plays with its readers, parodying the marvelous power of a Kipling tale to "overbear unbelieving," the power which Kipling deploys with such relish in "Wireless"—which uses the Marconi transmission in the same way that "Mrs. Bathurst" uses early cinema—or "On the Edge of the Evening." Because "Wireless" devotes all its ingenuity to the proposition "Wouldn't it be fascinating if? . ." it has no dimension apart from its own brilliant use of the Kipling authenticity effect. The different achievement in "Mrs. Bathurst"—and a very unusual one for Kipling—is to have things both ways. The reader partakes of the delicious and primitive terror which the characters and the "I" of the story are, as it were, hugging to themselves. Everyone likes the idea of lost souls. But, beyond this, the story's true vision is of size and littleness, the pathos of space, the small candles of human kindness and affection in the increasingly impersonal, mechanical, mixed-up world. Something in "Mrs. Bathurst" takes its place with the poetry of "The Dead," with Keats's vision at the back of "The Eve of St. Agnes." There is far more true Keats in the tale than when Kipling uses his poetry in "Wireless." Perhaps the shadow jumping over a candle was suggested by Madeline's taper, whose "little smoke in pallid moonshine died."

And yet Kipling spoils it. Indeed it may be an important if unconvenanted part of his general aesthetic effect to spoil things. Not that he insinuates too much the notion of jest, of making for the reader an elaborate spoof of things. On the contrary, after the first paragraph, with its superb and vividly surreal setting of the scene—an opening characteristic of Kipling at his best—the story never quite picks up, as if the author's own interest had silently departed too early. This too seems an exaggeration of an impression not uncommon where the stories are concerned, especially the later ones: and at the same time Kipling's air of not taking his own anecdotes very seriously does not seem wholly deceptive. Hardness and flippancy are not simulated. All this produces a complex, nervy, all-too-human effect: the very opposite of Joyce's fluency and calm in "The Dead." "Mrs. Bathurst" seems determined to bring out and emphasise all the tiresomeness of Kipling's method (as one talks of a remarkable but tiresome personality) but the final impression it makes is quite different.

It is an important paradox for the art of the Kipling story. A true and impersonal sadness can exist behind the all-too-personal ebullience, as a lack of knowledge lies behind all the knowingness and all the pointedly completed anecdotes. Kipling's daemon, who is, naturally enough, a kind of super-Kipling, is not—as "Mrs. Bathurst" shows—the ultimate artist in these stories. By exploring its different modes of falsity the art shows the scale and point of truth. As we emerge, spellbound, it is both a natural and a proper response to feel of each tale: "I don't really believe a word of it." But "not to believe" is, with Kipling, a gripping as well as an enlightening experience, for it points us to that unexplained world which can lie behind his artful unrealities. The unreality in "A House Surgeon," for instance, is in some sense a guarantee of its basic and horrible truth—the truths about neurosis and depression—mixed up in a way which only Kipling could manage with the artful fashion in which he manipulates the story, its properties and denouement. The same is true in its own way with an early tale like "The Strange Ride of Morrowbie Jukes." It is an art which has to show off in order to reveal; and the antics of display are its form of reticence. Even in "Baa Baa Black Sheep" Kipling provides something that does not ring right—his own family background. No wonder he makes play, in "A Madonna of the Trenches," with the idea of a mind's concealment of its real trouble behind some more spectacular explanation.

As so often with good writing it comes down to personality, to our growing sense of it and response to it. In his book on *Prose Style*, Herbert Read objected to a description of dried blood on the parade ground cracking and curling up at the edges, "like dumb tongues." Did anyone actually see those tongues? he asks. He is right: no one could, for Kipling deals in every kind of positive falsity in order to get things negatively right according to the way his inner being works. He has no impersonal skills at all, no undisputed accuracies. Dick going blind in *The Light that Failed* tells much about Kipling's own experience and inner life, but when Faulkner makes the blind lieutenant in *Soldier's Pay* say: "When are they going to let me out?" he finds words for the condition that can be universally felt and realised. Kipling has first to create a false structure before that process can take place: a structure wonderful and characteristic in itself, and not less so for what can lie behind it.

Coming to Terms with Kipling: *Puck of Pook's Hill, Rewards and Fairies,* and the Shape of Kipling's Imagination

Peter Hinchcliffe*

For more than a generation critical studies of Rudyard Kipling have begun or ended with the admonition that surely it is now time for readers to come to terms with his work. Coming to terms in this context seems to imply that with the demise of the British Empire the imperialist content of Kipling's writing has been neutralised. After all, W.H. Auden assured us as long ago as 1939 that time had already pardoned Kipling and his views, although this may have been a premature judgement. A book like Jonah Raskin's *The Mythology of Imperialism* (1971), for all its special pleading and polemics, shows that Kipling's work can still act as tinder to a new generation's ideological sparks. He is not yet a safe man to read.

There is another sense in which we can speak of coming to terms with Kipling. Whatever our political response to reading Kipling may be, we might reasonably expect that, almost forty years after his death, some consensus would have been reached about the total shape of his work, but this has not happened either. There are two continuing and, I think, misleading trends in Kipling criticism. One is the attempt to construct a selective canon from the whole mass of his writing. The other is the tendency for critics of Kipling to write in complete isolation from each other, and often with the assumption that opinion about Kipling is inevitably polarized—inevitably, at least, for everyone except themselves.[1]

A selective canon might seem a practical necessity in discussing an author whose complete works run to nearly forty volumes. However, what marks the selectors is not the desire to reduce discussion to manageable form but an act of faith that if only the proper selective criteria are applied "the good Kipling" in the form of a few stories and poems of unalloyed purity will emerge from the dross. This phrase, "the good Kipling," has recently been adopted as the title of a book by Elliott L. Gilbert in which half a dozen of Kipling's stories are analyzed, not to claim that they are the six best, but to stake out the area of Kipling's work in which the good Kipling is to be found.[2] Many of the most interesting pieces of Kipling criticism build their case through selection, like Edmund

*From the *University of Toronto Quarterly* 45, no. 1 (1975): 75–90. Reprinted by permission of the University of Toronto Press.

Wilson's "The Kipling that Nobody Read" or T.S. Eliot's introductory essay to his *Choice of Kipling's Verse,* in which he attempts to distinguish Kipling's great "verse" from his indifferent "poetry," and this kind of selection can be found as early as Andrew Lang's reviews in the 1880s.[3] The oddity of such attempts is that the various good Kiplings bear so little resemblance to each other. Instead of consolidating critical opinion about Kipling, the selective canonists' work seems destined to perpetuate a fragmented view of him.

A perfect example of the other misleading tendency is to be found in the opening sentences of C.S. Lewis's "Kipling's World":

> Kipling is intensely loved and hated. Hardly any reader likes him a little. Those who admire him will defend him tooth and nail. . . . The other side reject him with something like personal hatred. . . . For the moment, I will only say that my sole qualification, if it *is* a qualification, for talking about him is that I do not fully belong to either side.[4]

But it is precisely this qualification that makes Lewis a more typical critic of Kipling than he thought himself. A lot of Kipling criticism is rancorous or defensive, but remarkably little of it shows the kind of polarization that Lewis accepts as the norm. Much more common is an attitude of "Yes, but—," an ambivalence that seizes Kipling's critics quite suddenly, as the hostile ones remember aspects of his writing that they must praise and his admirers remember things that they must condemn. The *locus classicus* of this ambivalence is Henry James's remark in 1892, just after he had served as best man at Kipling's wedding: "Kipling strikes me personally as the most complete man of genius (as distinct from fine intelligence) that I have ever known."[5] The praise and the reservation are both genuine, and they both carry equal weight.

If there is a common element to be found among Kipling's critics it would seem to be dismay that his writing does not fulfil their expectations just at the point where they were most confident that it would. One could rejoin that it is foolish of critics to expect an artist to fulfil all their preconceptions about his work, but so nearly universal is this experience of dismay in the face of Kipling's writing that it surely indicates something more than critical arrogance. Perhaps Kipling's imagination is so discontinuous that his readers can come to terms with only a few of its paradoxical facets at a time.

To talk about discontinuities and paradoxes here may sound like a paradox itself, because one of the most obvious aspects of Kipling's work is that it is consistent to the point of obsession. Once he had formulated an idea and embodied it in an image Kipling could not leave it alone. His characteristic themes and images came to him almost full-blown very early in his career, and he stuck with them for half a century. Yet at the same time that he recognizes this consistency, the reader of Kipling is continually struck by contradictions and discrepancies in his work. Some of these contradictions are superficial and can be accepted without much difficulty. For example, at the time of the South African War Kipling wrote a bitterly jingoist attack upon the "treachery" of Boer sympathisers in two tracts," The Science of Rebellion" and "The Sin of Witchcraft." How does one reconcile this with Kipling's deeply compassionate treatment of these same attitudes in stories like "A Burgher of the Free State" and "The Comprehension of Private Copper," written at about the same time? Perhaps it is sufficient to invoke the Lawrentian axiom: "Never trust the artist. Trust the tale."

But there is another kind of contradiction present throughout Kipling's work which can be neither explained nor rationalized. Many of Kipling's ideas and the images in which they are embodied are truly irrational, almost in the way that some numbers are irrational. They are the literary equivalent of surds, like the square root of minus one. Kipling's readers are constantly confronted by terms that are obviously of crucial importance to Kipling himself but which resist any attempt at analysis. What, for example, does Kipling really mean by the Law and the related notions of work and discipline that show up in so many guises throughout his writing? Why should the school of Law be the jungle? How can Kipling reconcile a view of the human personality that is almost solipsistic with his obsessive insistence that man functions in a human way only when he belongs to a group?[6]

Since the time of Andrew Lang critics have been disturbed by Kipling's contradictions. Here are two representative examples. W.H. Auden writes:

> How can Nature and Man, the Jungle and the City, be opposed to each other, as Kipling is clearly certain that they are? If one asks him "What is civilization?" he answers, "The People living under the Law, who were taught by their fathers to discipline their natural impulses and will teach their children to do the same" . . . in contrast to the barbarian who is at the mercy of his selfish appetites. But if one ask him "What is the Law and where does it come from?" he refers one back to Nature.[7]

C.S. Lewis encounters the same kind of difficulty when he considers Kipling's assumption that all work justifies itself:

> The more Kipling convinces us that no plea for justice or happiness must be allowed to interfere with the job, the more anxious we become for a reassurance that the work is really worthy of all the human sacrifices it demands. "The game," he says, "is more than the player of the game." But perhaps some games are and some aren't. "And the ship is more than the crew"—but one would like to know where the ship was going and why. . . . We want, in fact, a doctrine of Ends.[8]

Strictures like these are just and inescapable, but in one sense they are not sufficient to alter our response to Kipling's writing. When we come across the Law or the jungle or work in the context of his stories and poems they almost invariably seem real—although this is not the same as saying that they seem true or good. When Kipling uses terms like these he cannot depict it in any other way. Like a surd his perception is real, and it is not reducible to other terms.

These surds in Kipling's imagination are the cause of his critics' dismay. They are stumbling blocks, and they are the reason why so many of his commentators have fallen back upon building a selective canon or have assumed that anyone who does not share their viewpoint must be a partisan enemy. To the extent that they distract and dishearten his readers Kipling's surds are a fault. I think it is our awareness that ultimately his work does not add up to one coherent whole that prevents us from placing Kipling in the same company as his contemporaries Hardy, Conrad, and Henry James. But the surds are also part of Kipling's strength. It is when his writing is informed by one of these imaginative discontinuities that it is most intense and Kipling is most certain of what he is saying. I think he knew it, too:

> I would go without shirt or shoe,
> Friend, tobacco or bread,
> Sooner than lose for a minute the two
> Separate sides of my head! ["The Two-Sided Man"]

What I am suggesting, then, is that we find in Kipling one version of the situation in which contradictory ideas or attitudes in an author's work do not cancel each other out but instead operate as a creative paradox, giving at least some of his writings a heightened intensity that they would otherwise lack. This is not an original insight. In different degrees it is probably true of most late Victorian authors, but what makes Kipling's case unique is that his imagination is informed by a multiplicity of such paradoxes, not just one or two, and that Kipling's paradoxes seem to have no obvious connections with each other.[9]

In the remainder of this paper I want to examine several different aspects of *Puck of Pook's Hill* and *Rewards and Fairies* in order to demonstrate how one of Kipling's surds, his notion of history, affects the form of his narrative and our response to it. First I want to show that despite their apparently random chronological arrangement the stories in these two books are a coherent unity, much more than Kipling's other collections of stories. Next I want to illustrate the peculiar quality of Kipling's prophetic vision by comparing it with two works by Bernard Shaw and E.M. Forster. In the fourth section I consider some other paradoxical elements in the Puck stories, related to the paradox of history. Finally, I will try to show that these two books are not dead ends in Kipling's writing, as has often been supposed, but instead they are in the main line of his development. If this sounds as though I am setting up my own "good Kipling" I can only reply that I see it as an unavoidable risk. And indeed, despite what one might expect, this act of rehabilitation does not bring us any nearer to coming to terms with Kipling. After everything has been said he remains elusive.

Puck of Pook's Hill and *Rewards and Fairies* are the neglected Kipling books. Children, for whom they were ostensibly written, seem never to have liked them much, and most adults who still read Kipling ignore them in favour of the more obviously adult stories.[10] Yet Kipling himself thought of the Puck stories as one of the central parts of his total work, displaying the most painstaking craftmanship and designed to reach the widest possible audience:

> Since the tales had to be read by children, before people realized that they were meant for grown-ups; and since they had to be a sort of balance to, as well a seal upon, some aspects of my "Imperialistic" output in the past, I worked the material in three or four overlaid tints and textures, which might or might not reveal themselves according to the shifting light of sex, youth, and experience. It was like working lacquer and mother-o'-pearl, a natural combination, into the same scheme as niello and grisaille, and trying not to let the joins show.[11]

They are among the few stories that he had no hesitation in ascribing to his "Daemon" of inspiration, and the long account of their composition in his autobiography, *Something of Myself*, is almost the only exuberant passage in that dour and reticent book.

An author is not always the best judge of his own achievement, but I think that Kipling's opinion of his work is justified here. In terms of technique, at least, the stories in these two books, all written between 1905 and 1910, are the culmination of the work that Kipling wrote when he was at the height of his fame and influence and before the watershed of the Great War turned him to the brooding and elliptical manner of his last stories. They are slick in a good and almost literal sense, presenting the smoothest of surfaces to the reader, as Kipling's own description of them implies. They are also intentionally complex, and a full reading of the Puck stories ought to do what Kipling suggests and look for the shapes that lie beneath the "lacquered" surface.

The stories in the two volumes and their accompanying verses are arranged in an order that discourages any simple chronological approach. Kipling stated that the stories in *Puck of Pook's Hill* occurred to him in the order in which they were printed, although the ones in *Rewards and Fairies* were apparently rearranged after their composition.[12] At the end of *Puck of Pook's Hill* Puck sums up the action of the book in these words: "Weland gave the Sword! The Sword gave the Treasure, and the Treasure gave the Law. It's as natural as an oak growing" ("The Treasure and the Law"). Ultimately, Kipling himself was not satisfied with this formulation,[13] and if, as I believe, one ought to consider both books as forming one interconnected narrative, this sort of linear progression does seem to be an oversimplification. However, arranging the tables of contents of the two books in parallel columns reveals a nicely symmetrical pattern of complementary stories.

The two sets of stories are enclosed in a kind of square frame. Each volume begins with a legend which has no claims to historicity, and whose subject is the forging of an inescapable destiny. "Weland's Sword" is about a destiny of power, and "Cold Iron" about a destiny of necessity. At the end of each volume is a fable set in medieval England in which the respective destinies reach their culmination in the acceptance of law by the English people, and this transformation of destiny into law also involves the setting of limits. In "The Treasure and the Law" Kadmiel the Jew uses the power of the gold treasure to ensure that the terms of Magna Carta will apply equally to all Englishmen, so that Norman can no longer claim unlimited superiority over Saxon, nor Christian over Jew. In "The Tree of Justice" the Norman barons are made to accept the continuity of legal authority from one king to the next, and for their part the Saxons give up their dream of a revived Saxon kingdom in favour of a united England.

Within this frame there appear to be parallel developments in each book. Following the initial story comes a group of three or four stories which work out some of the immediate implications of the two destinies. So "Weland's Sword" is followed by the three Norman stories, in which the power of the sword is used to capture England from the Saxons, then to obtain gold from Africa. Finally the power of the gold is used to safeguard England from further invasion. The chronology of the opening stories in *Rewards and Fairies* is more dislocated, skipping as it does from Tudor England to the Napoleonic Wars, to the end of the Stone Age, but there is a thematic unity here, and each story displays one implication of accepting a destiny of necessity, whose slogan is, "What else could I have done?" "Gloriana," "The Wrong Thing," "Marklake Witches," and "The Knife and the Naked Chalk" all demonstrate the workings of accepted necessity in the realms of politics, art, medicine, and priesthood, respectively. Next in each volume come two corresponding sets of stories, the three stories in *Puck* told by Parnesius, the British-Roman centurion, and in *Rewards* the two stories told by Pharaoh Lee, the English-French-American smuggler. These stories, in my opinion, are the core of each book, and their subject is the dynamics of leadership and the proper relations between leaders and followers. These groups are followed by two pairs of stories which seem intended to demonstrate the virtues that Kipling felt to be peculiarly necessary to his conception of the roles of leaders and followers. "Hal o' the Draft" and "The Conversion of St Wilfrid" deal with different kinds of fidelity: to a place, to one's master, to one's gods. "Dymchurch Flit" and "Simple Simon" are about the different kinds of self-sacrifice that leaders and followers must exercise. And so we come back to the stories that close the frame, as the voluntary disciplines of fidelity and self-sacrifice are codified into law.

Yes, but—the symmetry is not perfect after all. One story has been omitted from this schematic account, "A Doctor of Medicine," set in the Civil Wars, which comes between "The Conversion of St Wilfrid" and "Simple Simon" near the end of *Rewards and Fairies.* "A Doctor of Medicine" was probably one of the first of the *Rewards* stories to be composed.[14] Its subject, the healing of disease as a metaphor for the reconciliation of conflicting factions in society, is one that Kipling became more and more attracted to in his later work; so is its use of astrology. Yet it obviously does not fit into the pattern that I have inferred. To consider the place of "A Doctor of Medicine" in the Puck stories requires the construction of a whole new scheme that would link the royalist parson and the puritan astrologer with the French and English physicians in "Marklake Witches," with Tobias Hirte and Talleyrand in "A Priest in Spite of Himself," and that would eventually move right beyond the Puck books to show how all these stories are linked to the other tales of healing that appear in Kipling's work from *Actions and Reactions* (1909) to the end of his life. Such a consideration becomes, in fact, another demonstration of how difficult it is to come to terms with all the facets of Kipling's imagination at once. The structure that seemed so obvious disappears and is replaced by another, equally coherent, as soon as we shift our point of view.

Again Kipling's own description provides a hint as to where our difficulty lies. Niello is a composition for filling lines in engraved metal, and grisaille is a technique for representing objects in relief on stained glass. Kipling, it would seem, is trying to depict events and characters as simultaneously above and beneath and on a surface, and some readers may feel that his approach is more complicated than his material warrants, that he is carried away by his own ingenuity. But having said this about the Puck stories we have not dismissed them or even diminished their place in the Kipling canon. There remains another "Yes, but—." *Puck of Pook's Hill* and *Rewards and Fairies* seem to me to be among the most urgent and visionary books that Kipling ever wrote.

In his essay "Kipling's Place in the History of Ideas" Noel Annan remarks almost casually that, "*Heartbreak House, Howards End,* and *Puck of Pook's Hill* are the attempts by a socialist, a liberal, and a conservative to discern England's destiny."[15] This is a bold and useful comparison. Much more than one might expect, Kipling, Shaw, and Forster are writing about the same social and physical world. Heartbreak House, situated in "the hilly country in the middle of the north edge of Sussex" (stage direction to Act I), is barely twenty-five miles from Kipling's Dudwell Valley, and most of the play's characters resemble those "sufferers from the disease of the century" that Kipling solemnly guys in "My Son's Wife" (*A Diversity of Creatures*). As a colonial civil servant, the younger Wilcox brother in *Howards End* invites comparison (deliberately unfavourable?)

with many of Kipling's characters. On the other hand, Margaret Schlegel's invocation of the place names of southern England threatened by "creeping London" is similar to Kipling's litanies of place names in the two poems "A Three-Part Song" *(Puck)* and "The Run of the Downs" *(Rewards)*. Resemblances like these are worth mentioning, but what really makes the comparison worth while is a consideration of the similarity of purpose and also the essential difference that lie beneath the surface of these works.

Shaw's play, Forster's novel, and Kipling's collection of stories and poems all contain a vision of England on the brink of catastrophe. Each author has his own version of how this catastrophe will come about, but common to all of them is a realization that it cannot be explained in social and political terms. Its cause is fundamentally religious: England as a nation has forsaken its gods, and it will be destroyed unless it regains faith in them. Kipling's gods are not Shaw's and Forster's, but the need to recognize gods is the same in all three, and this recognition is not a matter of assenting to doctrine. Imperialism, socialism, and even "personal relations" have no efficacy in these books. To be saved, Captain Shotover tells the people of Heartbreak House, they must learn "navigation"—their business as Englishmen. In *Howards End* the brave language of connecting the prose and the passion is without power. What saves Henry Wilcox and the Schlegel sisters is their surrender to Howards End itself, the house and the wych-elm and the meadow.

Heartbreak House, Howards End, and Kipling's Puck stories are all prophecies of the Great War (although *Heartbreak House,* finished during the War and withheld until 1919, has the advantage of prophecy with hindsight). Shaw's and Forster's prophecies are overt, but for them the prospect of European war is only one symptom of England's plight, not its definitive sign. The mounting Anglo-German antagonism in *Howards End* is part of the general muddle that afflicts the world of the characters rather than a clear and separate evil. The air raid at the end of *Heartbreak House* is not the culmination that the characters long for but only an episode. In *Puck* and *Rewards* prophecies of war are both less obvious and more central. The stories begin in pre-history with "The Knife and the Naked Chalk," and the whole sequence ends with the Napoleonic wars, a hundred years before the stories were written. Germans are never mentioned, unless one chooses to identify them with the Winged Hats attacking Hadrian's Wall. But Kipling was much more certain than Shaw and Forster that the great event of his lifetime would be an apocalyptic European war that would determine the whole future course of England and her Empire. He had been preparing himself for this for years, long before Germany became an obvious threat to Britain.[16] Despite their apparent remoteness from contemporary affairs, the Puck stories keep repeating a lesson of immediate relevance to Kipling's audience: reconcile your internal differences so that you can guard yourselves against invasion.

However, there is more than a difference of emphasis among these works. The essential difference between Kipling's two books and *Heartbreak House* and *Howards End* lies in the authors' attitudes to time. Both Shaw and Forster see time's true movement as exclusively linear; Kipling does not. The characters of *Heartbreak House* are nearly all incapable of perceiving the movement of time, and this is a symptom of their folly. Time brings disaster to those who cannot imagine its movement: "Nothing happened. . . . Nothing ever does happen. . . . Nothing will happen," intones Mazzini Dunn, but Captain Shotover's language is filled with images of a ship drifting to destruction while the crew lounges below decks, and in the play's preface Shaw repeatedly uses the metaphor of an unsuspected overdraft resulting in sudden bankruptcy. The movement of time in *Howards End* is more complex, and its dangers are more immediate and various than in *Heartbreak House.* There are, for example, the goblins of panic and emptiness advancing and retreating during Beethoven's Fifth Symphony, and "creeping London's" threat to engulf all the relics of the past. But Shaw and Forster can also imagine a time when folly shall have ceased, and their work derives some of its meaning from being a preparation for this state. In the last chapter of *Howards End* Margaret's hope is that all the dangers among which she lives are only eddies in time's real current:

> "Because a thing is going strong now, it need not go strong forever," she said. "This craze for motion has only set in during the last hundred years. It may be followed by a civilization that won't be a movement because it will rest on the earth. All the signs are against it now, but I can't help hoping, and very early in the morning in the garden I feel that our house is the future as well as the past."[17]

"Learn navigation," "a civilization that will rest on the earth," "a house that is the future as well as the past"—this sounds like Kipling's language, too. A third of the Puck stories use ships and sailing as metaphors for the saving of England, and Margaret's words are echoed in "Puck's Song" and "A Charm," the introductory verses to the two volumes, and in passages like the description of Little Linden's farmhouse in "Hal o' the Draft" *(Puck)*. But although Kipling might echo the words he does not mean the same things by them. His house can be the future as well as the past only because in his imagination past and future are really the same. History moves in a circle, presenting us with versions of the same situation that are new only in appearance. The ways in which the past is continuously present in these books, in changeless landscape, in characters like Hobden the hedger, and, most importantly, in recurring threats of invasion—all of these are more than examples for Kipling. They are almost identities: "Men and Things come round again, eternal as the seasons."[18] Kipling's view of history is not a philosophical or systematic one. Rather it arises from an intuition that folly is the permanent condition of mankind, and this axiom is all that Kipling needs to formulate his conviction. Kipling's moral world is always one of fools and their guardians, and heroic action consists in carrying the fools' burdens and trying to protect them from the consequences of their folly. There is no "reason" for the guardians to do this; it is accepted unreflectingly by Kipling's characters, and, I think, by Kipling himself as an inevitable duty.

At the same time, Kipling and his characters know that this heroism is ultimately futile. That nothing will save fools from themselves is the most constant of Kipling's refrains, from Pagett, MP of *Departmental Ditties*, through the *bandar-log*, the monkey people of the *Jungle Books*, to spokesmen for appeasement building "bonfires on the ice" at the end of Kipling's life ("The Bonfires," 1933). This is the necessary and contradictory other half of Kipling's view of history. Human folly cries out for retribution, so the movement of history must also be linear, carrying mankind swiftly and relentlessly to a day of judgement. Yet this judgement day, which is always threatening, never actually arrives (except in animal fables, like some of the *Jungle Book* stories or "The Mother Hive," *Actions and Reactions*). Even "The Winged Hats" *(Puck)*, a story of "men without hope," ends with the lifting of the siege and the re-garrisoning of Hadrian's Wall. It is as though Kipling felt that a definitive judgement passed upon the fools would deprive the guardians of their function, and this would render his imaginative world impossible. Here, then, is Kipling's surd, the logically contradictory but profoundly felt conviction that history is at the same time rushing to judgement yet endlessly repeating itself. It is a disquieting perception, and it points toward another difference of vision that divides Kipling from Shaw and Forster.

Like Heartbreak House and Howards End, Kipling's valley is a place of refuge, but it is a refuge for guardians, not fools, and with its houses and mill and forge it is a fortress and an armoury, sometimes literally so, as in the Norman and Tudor stories, and always so in metaphor. *Puck of Pook's Hill* and *Rewards and Fairies* recount stories of invasions repulsed and of conflicts reconciled. Here is encouragement, for in a world where history repeats itself men can re-enact the victorious defences of the past. However, this encouragement brings no hope with it. The threat of invasion will never pass, the fortress is really under siege even when the times appear most peaceful. Kipling was intensely proud of the visual effects he created in these two books, and indeed the glow of Edwardian afternoons has never been better done. But just beneath this surface is what one can only call a pastoral nightmare. "Is the Kipling world really monstrous?" asks C.S. Lewis. Does it hide at its centre "a terrible vagueness, a frivolity or scepticism?"[19] Yes, it is monstrous and sceptical, but I would not call it vague or frivolous, nor would Kipling himself. His own phrase for this central emptiness, repeated again and again throughout his work, comes from the Bible: "A horror of great darkness."

I have already identified five stories as the core of the two books. They are "A Centurion of the Thirtieth," "On the Great Wall," and "The Winged Hats" in *Puck of Pook's Hill,* narrated by Parnesius, and "Brother Square-Toes" and "A Priest in Spite of Himself" in *Rewards and Fairies,* narrated by Pharaoh Lee. These two groups form the only continuous narratives in the two volumes, for the other stories told by the same narrators, Puck and Sir Richard and Harry Dawe, are all separate episodes. They are also the most comprehensive of the stories, both geographically and thematically. The Roman stories carry us the full length of England, from the Isle of Wight to Hadrian's Wall, and the two stories told by Pharaoh Lee are set in England, America, and France. This is not a *tour de force* of exotic scenery-painting like the voyage to Africa in "Knights of the Joyous Venture." In these five stories Kipling is concerned to show England as the outpost of the Roman Empire and as the heart of her own, and to emphasize her geographical position in relation to her allies and enemies. These stories are concerned with the crises of civil breakdown and invasion, the conditions under which a nation accepts peace or resorts to war, and above all with how leaders exercise power and how their followers respond to it. The verses that accompany these stories reflect their themes more directly than most of the others in the two books. They include "Cities and Thrones and Powers" and "A Pict Song," two poems which convey in vivid metaphors Kipling's ideas about the movement of history and of the dangers of treachery and invasion. The tailpiece to "Brother Square-Toes" is the famous (or notorious) "If—," Kipling's best-known compendium of advice to the aspiring leader.

Outlined in this bald fashion these five stories sound like perfectly appropriate vehicles for Kipling's themes, and on one level they are. As has often been noted, Parnesius is the ideal type of all the subalterns in Kipling's other stories. Pharaoh Lee, half-English and half-French by descent and an American citizen by choice, is a living embodiment of Kipling's most enduring political dream: a triple alliance of Britain, France, and the United States against the barbaric and dangerous rest of the world.[20] Kipling's imagination is spatial to an unusual degree,[21] and the significance of places, both in themselves and in their relations to each other, is displayed here more clearly than in any of the other Puck stories. Places in Pharaoh's stories show "The things that truly last when men and times have passed" ("Philadelphia"). In the Roman stories Hadrian's Wall, at once a frontier boundary and a microcosm of the society it is defending, is the most emblematic and the most exciting of all Kipling's spatial images:

> Just when you think you are at the world's end, you see a smoke from
> East to West as far as the eye can turn, and then, under it, also as far as the
> eye can stretch, houses and temples, shops and theatres, barracks and
> granaries, trickling along like dice behind—always behind—one long,

low, rising and falling, and hiding and showing line of towers. And that is the Wall! ["On the Great Wall"]

However, this impressive clarity of outline becomes hazy as soon as we consider some of the implications of Kipling's treatment of the theme of leaders and followers. Kipling's leaders are Magnus Maximus, the General of Britain who led a revolt against the central Roman Empire in 383 AD, George Washington, and Napoleon, with Talleyrand included in the last story as an *éminence grise*. Just as Parnesius is the type of the ideal subaltern, so Maximus, Washington, and Napoleon are all presented as types of Kipling's ideal leader, the military administrator and lawgiver who radiates an almost tangible aura of personal greatness: "We understood that Earth bred few men like to this man," says Parnesius of Maximus ("On the Great Wall"); Pharaoh Lee calls the others the "three men in this world who are quite by themselves" ("A Priest in Spite of Himself"), and similar phrases abound in both sets of stories.

The followers never waver in their loyalty, but if we reflect upon the actual conduct of Kipling's leaders it raises some misgivings about the appropriateness of the language used to praise them. First, all the leaders are, in varying degrees, enemies of England (Maximus because he stripped Britain of her protective armies and left her open to invasion). They are also in some sense traitors to a structure of authority that makes at least a nominal claim upon their loyalties. When Maximus first appears in "A Centurion of the Thirtieth" he is still the General of Britain, appointed by the Emperor, and Napoleon in "A Priest in Spite of Himself" is still a Consul of the Republic. Kipling does not quite regard George Washington as a traitor, but the latter's role in the American Revolution is a source of discomfort. "I'm sorry we lost him out of Old England," says Puck in "A Priest in Spite of Himself." Washington is presented with sympathy and admiration, but he is shown not in triumphant action but in passive endurance, saddled with the thankless task of holding back American jingoes who are trying to push the infant United States into a French alliance and a fratricidal war with England. The other stories in *Puck* and *Rewards* contain several examples of self-denying leaders—the Norman baron De Aquila, Queen Elizabeth, Sir Francis Drake, and the narrator of "The Knife and the Naked Chalk"—but Maximus and Napoleon are slaves of an idea of imperial glory that is inextricably bound up with overreaching personal ambition. Moreover, the endeavours of all three leaders are doomed to failure. Maximus's downfall is proclaimed by the blood-stained letter announcing his death, and Napoleon's is prophesied in the poem "A St Helena Lullaby." George Washington's failure must be inferred, but Kipling can expect his grown-up readers to remember that the fatal alliance against England that Washington was able to postpone actually took place twenty years later.

The correlative of selfish or powerless leadership is that loyalty itself becomes self-contained. The followers maintain their embarrassingly fulsome language of praise, but their real allegiance is to a self-imposed obligation. "It concerns us to defend the Wall, no matter what Emperor dies, or makes die," says Parnesius after the downfall of Maximus ("The Winged Hats"). This, actually, is a sensible attitude for a subaltern to take, and it is reinforced by the two supplementary stories in *Puck*, "Hal o' the Draft" and "Dymchurch Flit," both of which are concerned with accommodating one's personal desires to the responsibility that is due to a wider community. However, the change of governing theme from power to necessity as we turn from *Puck* to *Rewards* also affects both leadership and loyalty. Pharaoh Lee maintains his loyalty to passive Washington by keeping the latter's secret from Talleyrand, even though its contents have been public knowledge for five years. In "The Conversion of St Wilfrid" the quixotic postponement of his baptism by Meon, the Saxon chieftain, exemplifies a loyalty that is disinterested almost to the point of abstraction.

Most discussions of *Puck of Pook's Hill* and *Rewards and Fairies* concentrate upon their depiction of the peace and beauty of Sussex and upon their overt messages of heroism and endurance, by-passing or ignoring the ironic undertones that I have noted. Perhaps irony is not the right word after all, since it implies a deliberately chosen point of view, and I doubt if Kipling made such a choice. If we can trust his own words, the two books were written intuitively:

> My Daemon was with me in . . . both Puck books, and good care I took to walk delicately, lest he should withdraw. I know that he did not, because when those books were finished they said so themselves with, almost, the water-hammer click of a tap turned off. . . . *Note here.* When your Daemon is in charge, do not try to think consciously. Drift, wait, and obey.[22]

One cannot be absolutely certain, but I think it likely that Kipling's contradictions in these books are not part of his consciously worked "overlaid tints and textures." Yet I believe that he meant what he said. Like the Great Wall that fascinated him, Kipling's art is always hiding and showing at the same time.

The unacknowledged contradictions of history and leadership present in these books and the way the stories themselves form patterns that just miss being symmetrical are more concentrated versions of themes and patterns that we can find all through the work that Kipling wrote between the South African War and the outbreak of the Great War. If we go back even farther, to Kipling's stories of the Indian Empire, we find that many of them also display an indifference to the ultimate implications of imperial history and cynicism about the motives and effective power of highly placed leaders, while at the same time they praise unreservedly the self-contained loyalty of subordinates to the task at hand. Kipling is nowhere more consistent than in the nature of his contradictions.

The Puck books can be seen as continuing and focussing some of Kipling's earliest concerns, but it is also obvious that he never wrote anything like them again. There is a drastic change of subject and style in the work that Kipling wrote after the War, yet the break was not quite complete. I have already shown how "A Doctor of Medicine" points forward to the themes of healing and astrology that figure so largely in Kipling's later work. Here is another way of looking at these two books which at least suggests how they lie in a line of prospective development that was cancelled by the War. In one of the few contemporary appraisals of Kipling's art that took the Puck stories seriously, Dixon Scott praised them, *Rewards and Fairies* especially, as Kipling's greatest achievement. He then went on to make a strangely prescient remark:

> His system-seeking genius can now openly take up its true task, the task it has hitherto attempted only intermittently, and begin the sustained practice of that colossal kind of craftsmanship for which it is so singularly suited. It will beat out for itself a new form of imaginative prose, as unclogged by characterization as his verse. The devices of drama it will use, no doubt, and some of the tricks of narration; but its true medium will be massed impersonal things . . . the general surge and litter of sensation. What his genius can do with material of this kind we have already in some sort seen. Driving into the darkness that beleaguers us, swirling and thrusting like a searchlight in a forest, it could bring out the essential structure of events and display the soaring pillars of contemporary achievement.[23]

We will look in vain through *Debits and Credits* or *Limits and Renewals* for anything that sounds like this, but Dixon Scott was not totally mistaken in his prophecy. There is one book which in subject and scope corresponds exactly to Scott's prescriptions, Kipling's two-volume history *The Irish Guards in the Great War,* published in 1923 and written as a memorial to his son John, the boy who was Dan in *Puck of Pook's Hill* and *Rewards and Fairies.* Power and necessity, leadership and loyalty are all there, with the Great Wall come again in nightmare form as the trenches of the Western Front. Yet it is an opaque work, deservedly neglected by all except specialists in regimental history, its personal vision buried so deeply as to be virtually inaccessible.

But this, perhaps, is the greatest of Kipling's surds. Both the Puck books and *The Irish Guards* imply a deliberately confusing mixture of public and private attitudes. The former, one of Kipling's most public works, a prophetic and exemplary history of England, is set literally in his own back garden and told to his own children. In the latter book Kipling has chosen the most impersonal and official of genres as the monument to his personal grief. This reversal of expectations is disturbing enough, but if *The Irish Guards* is in any sense the complement to and fulfilment of the

Puck stories we face a paradox of terrible sadness and privacy. It is considerations like these which lead me to think that trying to come to terms with Kipling may be a mistake. Letting him keep his distance seems to be a prerequisite for grasping any facet of his imagination at all. Kipling must be read and criticised, but he is not one of those writers who can be possessed.

Notes

1. A useful overview of Kipling criticism is provided by the three retrospective anthologies which have so far been published. Andrew Rutherford, ed., *Kipling's Mind and Art* (London: Oliver & Boyd 1964), contains five reprinted essays and six new ones; Elliott L. Gilbert, ed., *Kipling and the Critics* (New York: New York University Press 1965), reprints fifteen essays; Roger Lancelyn Green, ed., *Kipling: The Critical Heritage* (London: Routledge 1971), reprints over sixty items written between 1886 and 1936.

2. Elliott L. Gilbert, *The Good Kipling: Studies in the Short Story* (Athens, Ohio: Ohio University Press 1970).

3. See *Kipling: The Critical Heritage* 44–50.

4. C.S. Lewis, "Kipling's World," in *Kipling and the Critics* 99. Revised reprint from *They Asked for a Paper* (London: Bles 1962).

5. Letter to William James, 6 February 1892, cited in Charles Carrington, *Rudyard Kipling: His Life and Work* (London: Macmillan 1955) 193.

6. For this last point, see Alan Sandison, "Kipling: The Artist and the Empire," in *Kipling's Mind and Art* 163 and 165.

7. W.H. Auden, "The Poet of the Encirclement," *New Republic* 109 (25 October 1943) 580.

8. Lewis, "Kipling's World" 109.

9. Half a dozen of what I call surds in Kipling's imagination occur to me; there may well be more. The Law and work I have mentioned already. I propose to treat history in some detail later in this paper. To these I would add the whole image of Empire, a doctrine of grace and the relations of each person to the society of which he finds himself a part. The element common to all of them is that they are concerned with how an individual can relate himself in some instrumental way to a universe which he can only perceive as ultimately meaningless. Such a similarity is probably too low a common denominator to be useful in critical discussion, and points up the difficulty of obtaining a synoptic view of Kipling's work.

10. See Gillian Avery, "The Children's Writer," in John Gross, ed., *Rudyard Kipling: The Man, His Work and His World* (London: Weidenfield & Nicolson 1972) 114–5.

11. Rudyard Kipling, *Something of Myself* (London: Macmillan, Library Edition 1951) 190.

12. *Something of Myself* 188. For a listing of serial publication and special copyright editions of the contents of both books, see James McG. Stewart, *Rudyard Kipling: A Bibliographical Catalogue*, ed. A.W. Yeats (Toronto: Dalhousie University Press and University of Toronto Press 1959) 248–52 and 267–74.

13. "Somehow 'The Treasure and the Law' . . . always struck me as too heavy for its frame." *Something of Myself* 189.

14. "A Doctor of Medicine" was the second of the *Rewards and Fairies"* stories to be published serially. It appeared in October 1909, one month after the introductory tale, "Cold Iron." See Stewart, *Bibliographical Catalogue* 268–9.

15. Noel Annan, "Kipling's Place in the History of Ideas," *Victorian Studies* 3 (June 1969) 340. Reprinted in *Kipling's Mind and Art.*

16. The *OED* cites Kipling as its example for "Armageddon" used as a synonym for the coming European War (in "A Song of the English," 1893). Surprisingly, I.F. Clarke's *Voices Prophesying War* (London: Oxford University Press 1966) does not mention Kipling, even though his concerns follow exactly the progression that Clarke traces in contemporary English letters. Kipling foresaw England's enemy at first as Russia in the 1880s and early 1890s, then France in *A Fleet in Being* (1898), then, after the South African War, Germany. Explicit prophecies of a European War are to be found in "The Army of a Dream" (*Traffics and Discoveries*, 1904), "The Parable of Boy Jones" (*Land and Sea Tales*, 1920, but first published in 1910), and "The Edge of the Evening" (*Diversity of Creatures*, 1917, but first published in 1913). Warnings against invasion also become increasingly prominent in Kipling's verse after 1902.

17. E.M. Forster, *Howards End* (Harmondsworth: Penguin 1941) 316.

18. *Something of Myself* 223.

19. Lewis, "Kipling's World" 110.

20. See Carrington, *Rudyard Kipling* 445. Carrington's remarks are in the context of America's entry into the Great War, but Kipling's notion of an alliance with the United States dates from "The White Man's Burden" (1899). His post-war writing is much concerned with the idea of Britain and France forming a spiritual community.

21. Cf. the imagery of "The Brushwood Boy" (*The Day's Work*), Kipling's analysis of the spatial imagination in "Some Aspects of Travel" (*A Book of Words*), and this remark from *Something of Myself* 91: "I visualised it [the meaning of the British Empire], as I do most ideas, in the shape of a semicircle of buildings and temples projecting into a sea—of dreams."

22. *Something of Myself* 210

23. Dixon Scott, "The Meekness of Mr Rudyard Kipling," *Men of Letters* (London: Hodder & Stoughton 1916) 61–2. The original (1912) version of this essay is reprinted in the *Critical Heritage* volume, pp 308–17.

Kipling's "Mary Postgate": The Barbarians and the Critics

Peter E. Firchow[*]

When Edmund Wilson probed what he took to be Kipling's psyche in "The Kipling that Nobody Read," one of the essays in *The Wound and the Bow* (1941), it was primarily to the late work that he referred. The earlier work, that preceding the First Great War, so the implication ran, was the Kipling that everybody read, although even here Wilson's choice of the past tense in his title emphasized his suspicion that after 1910 Kipling ceased to attract new readers. By now that suspicion has become a virtual certainty and the Kipling that nobody read or, for that matter, reads, includes practically all of Kipling, early, middle, and late.

But if Kipling seems, from the point of view of the mass audience,

*From *Études Anglaises* 29, no. 1 (January–March 1976): 27–39. Reprinted by permission of Mme Jean Didier, Didier Érudition, Société Nouvelle Didier Erudition.

safely dead, that does not mean that serious attempts have not been undertaken to galvanize him back to life. Ironically (the expected loyalties of the Kipling Society aside), those attempts have come chiefly from a quarter which Kipling affected always to despise, namely from intellectuals and academics. T.S. Eliot's introductory essay to A *Choice of Kipling's Verse* (1941), with its open advocacy of Kipling as a great versifier if not a great poet, sent shocks of dismay through much of the Anglo-Saxon intellectual community. In the end this turned out to be a good thing, for it provoked in reply some of the best essays on this author that we possess, notably Wilson's, Orwell's, Trilling's, C.S. Lewis's and Ford's. And these essays in turn stimulated, though only after some delay, others which, more circumspectly than Eliot, came to Kipling's defense: W. Somerset Maugham's introduction to A *Choice of Kipling's Prose* (1952), whose title and opinions overtly echo Eliot's, or Randall Jarrell's "On Preparing to Read Kipling" which prefaces his anthology, *The Best Short Stories of Rudyard Kipling* (1961).

The most concerted and, in many ways, the most disconcerting effort, however, to rehabilitate Kipling has come from the universities. Though Kipling still remains the butt of easy academic jibes and a convenient target for anti-imperialist giant-killers, it is striking that in less casual contexts the academic response has been almost wholly positive. Open any one of the multitude of university-connected studies of Kipling which have appeared in the last twenty years and you will find Kipling in the guise of a sorely "misunderstood" writer who was neither racist nor imperialist, but merely a remarkable artist. Why this should be so is not entirely clear, though no doubt the inevitable action-reaction pattern of literary history may be partially to blame. And then, too, as Kingsley Amis once complained, there is a lamentable tendency in modern critical writing to give one's author a score of ten out of ten in every category. What is surprising is that there has been practically no reaction to *this* reaction, that there has been no academic devil's advocate.

In a small way, that is the role I wish to play here, to try to demonstrate that at least in respect to one of Kipling's short stories, "Mary Postgate," contemporary academic criticism has been generous to a fault. I choose this particular story because, as even Kipling's staunchest rehabilitators recognize, here is a weak spot in his artistic armor; and because here, therefore, the critical patchwork becomes most apparent.

Begun in March 1915, "Mary Postgate" is a story about a lonely, middle-aged servant-companion's loyalty and revenge: loyalty to her invalid mistress and her mistress' boisterous nephew Wynn, and revenge for the death in an accidental plane crash of that nephew and for the killing of a small child in a nearby village. The murderers are the German nation in general and a German airman in particular who, gravely wounded, drops into the garden while Mary is burning Wynn's effects. The story climaxes with Mary's gloating at the German's slow and painful death: "an increasing rapture laid hold of her. She ceased to think. She gave herself up to feel. Her long pleasure was broken by a sound that she had waited for in agony several times in her life. She leaned forward and listened, smiling. There could be no mistake. She closed her eyes and drank it in. Once it ceased abruptly. "Go on," she murmured, half aloud. "That isn't the end." When the end does come a moment later, she shivers from head to toe. " 'That's all right,' said she contentedly," and she trots off to indulge in a "luxurious hot bath before tea."[1]

What to make of this curiously cruel tale? Was it written by a man who could fairly be described, as Bonamy Dobrée described Kipling in 1929, as the symbol "not of hate, but a deep compassion; not indignant grandiosity and brute force, but humility and tenderness amounting to deep pity?"[2] Pity for whom? one wonders. Dobrée later elaborated his original analysis of Kipling into a full-length study, *Rudyard Kipling: Realist and Fabulist* (1967), but his subject is still the same humane, avuncular soul of nearly forty years earlier. Though he is aware of Kipling's deep-rooted conviction that the Germans, by their aggression and cruelty, had put themselves beyond the pale of the Law, Dobrée nevertheless asserts that " 'Mary Postgate' . . . is not a story embodying hatred of the Germans." Instead, it is merely a realistic tale, for after all, given Mary's feelings for Wynn, and her emotional state as she is burning Wynn's effects, "one may wonder whether, if people would look into themselves . . . they could with certainty say they would have acted otherwise?" Or to take another instance of this "shocking realism": Mary does not consider "that, after all, Wynn was equipped to do the same thing; and Kipling could have pointed out to her that the German was only obeying *his* Law." Or the final shocker: Mary's rejuvenation at the end of the story is due to the release of "her suppressed emotions toward Wynn."[3] In other words, it is strongly implied that "Mary Postgate" is not a story about German atrocities—that is merely the incidental background—but about an essentially individual conflict, culminating in the sudden release of years of repressed hostility.[4]

This kind of interpretation of the story is by no means new with Dobrée. Kipling's authorized biographer, C.E. Carrington, declares flatly that this story is "entirely personal, a tale about frustrated passion and vicarious revenge, not about any particular campaign. It is concerned with the quality of ruthlessness, an extension of the sardonic verse, 'the female of the species is more deadly than the male.' "[5] To be sure, Carrington avoids Dobrée's implicit identification between Wynn and the German airman, placing the stress wholly on Kipling's misogyny. The real villian of the piece, it seems, is not the German, not Mary Postgate, but "das ewig Weibliche." The opposing, yet parallel, view to this is W.W. Robson's contention that "Mary Postgate," while admittedly containing some bitterness—attributable to "poignant personal reasons"[6] —is neither an attack on Germans nor on women. "What those who condemn Kipling would say," Robson argues, almost certainly referring to Boris Ford, "is that the author is quite aware of the moral incoherence of Mary, but exploits her as a vent for the release of emotions which a sahib himself cannot admit that he feels; women, as contradictory and inferior beings, can be allowed the indulgence which the author himself desires. But this amounts to attributing to Kipling—the Kipling of this story—the outlook of young Wynn. It ignores the careful art of the story in avoiding any sentimentalization of Mary or Wynn or the relationship between them. Above all, it ignores the essential identity—symbolic, of course, not literal—between the dying airman and Wynn. (He too, like Wynn, has fallen from his airplane.)"[7] Leaving aside for the moment that Wynn has not fallen from his airplane but crashed *in* it, one wonders what Robson finds so shocking about equating Wynn's point of view with Kipling's. This is nearly as curious as Dobrée having Kipling hypothetically point out to Mary that the German has *his* Law, almost immediately after having demonstrated that for Kipling the Germans had no Law.

These two threads—the resentment of a bullied servant-companion and the innate sadism of the human female—of this interpretation are effectively joined in J.I.M. Stewart's essay on Kipling in *Eight Modern Writers*. Stewart, like Carrington and Dobrée, argues that "the horror and fear and hate in the story are occasioned by Mary, not by the wicked Germans." He then adds suggestively that this may not have been what Kipling thought he was doing. This interesting distinction between a conscious and an unconscious intention, one to which I shall revert later, may derive from Noel Annan's 1954 essay on Kipling, where Annan sees "Mary Postgate" as a great opportunity missed: a story in which art and irony (the unconscious?) are sacrificed to Kipling's rigid insistence on preaching that Germans are outside the Law (the conscious).[8]

J.M.S. Tompkins, the most generally praised interpreter of Kipling's shorter fiction, provides a reading of "Mary Postgate" which, while quite as sympathetic to Kipling as any of the foregoing, offers some novelties. Her reading stresses the "normal" rather than the "abnormal" relations of Mary to Wynn, and to the German airman. Mary's feelings towards Wynn, in her view, are not those of a resentful servant or a frustrated would-be lover; on the contrary, they are those of a grieving foster-mother. Mary's hatred of the German airman is not endorsed by Kipling, it is simply the predictable response of a woman who has been so tried by sorrow and horror that she lapses into temporary insanity. What we have here, Tompkins affirms, is a Kipling who means to demonstrate in drastic ways how cruelly the war can affect even the best of people.[9].

C.A. Bodelsen picks up this note and strikes it even louder. For him, "Mary Postgate" is "a very subtle story, where obviously a good deal must be read between the lines." In doing so, Bodelsen notes that the pleasure Mary takes in the dying German's agony carries sexual overtones and is therefore "sadism in the original sense of the word." But it is known that

Kipling does not approve of sadism. Can it therefore be "really believable that Kipling should have gone on record like that with what would be almost a glorification of perversion?" Obviously not, from which it follows logically that Mary's and Kipling's attitudes are not to be confused. Like Tompkins, Bodelsen concludes that, in the final analysis, "Mary Postgate" is a cautionary tale of how, impelled by the horror of German warfare, "a kindly and respectable English spinster finds herself turned into a torturer."[10]

These are the main interpretations of "Mary Postgate" put forward by scholars in the last two decades. Let me stress that none of these analyses exceeds a few pages in length and the majority take up only a page or so. Bodelsen's, for instance, is relegated to a lengthy footnote. Indeed, in at least one recent scholarly study of Kipling's stories, Elliot Gilbert's *The Good Kipling, Studies in the Short Story* (1971), discussion of "Mary Postgate" and of the related "hate" stories is omitted altogether. Despite avowals to the contrary, it seems the most effective way of dealing with the "bad Kipling" is to ignore his existence.

What to make of all this? Are Kipling's academic apologists justified in separating Mary from Rudyard, in denying allegations that Kipling is here vicariously but lovingly extracting the tooth that is owing him? The answer, I would respectfully submit, is no. No, because if for no other reason, there are ample grounds to suspect that all the available evidence has not been brought to bear on the case of "Mary Postgate."

It is true, as stated earlier, that Bonamy Dobrée does concede that Kipling was not specially fond of Germans. He quotes him as saying in a speech at Southport in June 1915 that "however the world pretends to divide itself, there are only two divisions in the world today—human beings and Germans"; and he quotes from *France at War* (1915) to the effect that "we are dealing with animals who have scientifically and philosophically removed themselves inconceivably outside civilisation."[11] But it is also true that Dobrée makes nothing whatever of these quotations, thereby suggesting that Kipling's sociopolitical opinions had nothing whatever to do with his art.

Kipling was a vigorous and notorious Hun-hater.[12] Notice, for example, how he describes the Germans in *The Eyes of Asia* (1918), from the point of view of a couple of Indian officers fighting with their regiments on the Western Front. "The nature of the enemy," one of them writes home, "is to commit shame upon women and children, and to defile the shrines of his own faith with his own dung. It is done by him as a drill. We believed till then they were some sort of caste apart from the rest. We did not know they were outcaste. Now it is established by the evidence of our senses. They attack on all fours running like apes. They are specially careful of their faces. When death is certain to them they offer gifts and repeat the number of their children. They are very good single shots from cover."[13] Are we really to understand here, in the manner of Tompkins' interpretation of "Mary Postgate," that this is a lamentable case of battle fatigue? Or, as Dobrée might have had it, that this is a shockingly realistic account of what it was like to be an Indian officer at the front? Or should we distinguish, in the style of Bodelsen, between the views of Subidar Major Bishen Singh Saktawat and those of Rudyard Kipling?

As early as 1902 Kipling had heaped scorn on a British policy which sought "to league anew / with the Goth and the shameless Hun!" (A name for the Germans which Kipling is generally thought to have invented). When the war finally came, he trotted his Huns out once more in "For All We Have and Are" (1914):

> For all we have and are,
> For all our children's fate,
> Stand up and take the war.
> The Hun is at the gate!

George Orwell in his essay on Kipling even goes so far as to argue that the famous phrase from "Recessional"—"lesser breeds without the Law"— refers not to the Chinese or the Indians, as is popularly thought, but to the Germans.[14] It is quite clear that Orwell is wrong in this assumption, but the very fact that he could put such a notion forward without provoking any kind of surprise, reveals how strongly Kipling and hatred of the Germans were associated in the public mind.

To be sure, all this evidence is extraneous. At best it can prove that Mary's hatred for the Germans was not alien to Kipling, and it can perhaps also reinforce the suspicion that Mary is, on one level at least, a mouthpiece for his hatred. But it can prove no more. What is not extraneous, however, and what can prove more is the poem, "The Beginnings," which Kipling appended to "Mary Postgate" and whose theme makes it a (conscious?) counterpart to Ernst Lissauer's infamous "Hassgesang gegen England" ("Hymm of Hate"):

> It was not part of their blood,
> It came to them very late
> With long arrears to make good,
> When the English began to hate.
>
> They were not easily moved,
> They were icy willing to wait
> Till every count should be proved
> Ere the English began to hate.
>
> Their voices were even and low,
> Their eyes were level and straight
> There was neither sign nor show,
> When the English began to hate.

It was not preached to the crowd,
It was not taught by the State.
No man spoke it aloud,
When the English began to hate.

It was not suddenly bred,
It will not swiftly abate,
Through the chill years ahead,
When time shall count from the date
That the English began to hate.

This poem seems clearly intended to serve as a kind of moral signpost for
the story. The stanza by stanza tracing of the development of England's
hatred for Germany matches the gradual intensification of Mary's emotional response. As with the English in the poem, Mary is originally patient and good-natured, outwardly unemotional but inwardly full of deep
and genuine feeling. These virtues have been tested and found true in
years of devoted service to Miss Fowler, to the Village Nursing Commit-
tee, and in caring for Wynn. Again as in the poem, Mary does not give
vent to noisy denunciations of the Germans, nor, for that matter, does she
hear any. Her hatred arises individually and spontaneously and in reaction to what she herself has seen and suffered—Wynn's and the little
girl's deaths—not to any propaganda, public or private. Mary, in short,
hates just as Kipling tells us the English do.

From this it seems safe to conclude that "Mary Postgate" is a story
designed to illustrate how the English, epitomized by the humble figure
of Mary Postgate, came to feel hatred for the Germans. "English" here includes not just Mary, not just middle-aged women, not just servants, but
all loyal English men and women, Kipling as well. But it does not mean,
necessarily, that Kipling likes or approves of this hatred per se; neither, of
course, does it mean the opposite. The ultimate responsibility, it is clear,
for this hatred and for the war which is its immediate cause, rests squarely
with the Germans. If they are allowed to die wretchedly, that is their fault
alone. It is in this limited sense that Dobrée is right in arguing for the realism of "Mary Postgate": Kipling *is* depicting a hatred which actually exists. But Dobrée is surely wrong to suggest that Kipling is to be separated
from that hatred. If Mary is English, then she is automatically privileged
to hate, and if she is privileged to hate, then she cannot, obviously, be
held responsible for the death of "It." Neither can Kipling.

As if all this were not clear enough, Kipling had already made a preliminary study of this subject in a somewhat earlier story, "Swept and
Garnished" (written in October 1914). The title alludes to the Germans'
reputation for fanatical cleanliness, a mania which does not extend, in
Kipling's view, to their consciences. The setting for most of the story is
the immaculately neat apartment of a slightly indisposed Frau
Ebermann. The tone is set by her opening reaction to the news that the

German army has won another victory, capturing multitudes of prisoners and guns. "Frau Ebermann purred", Kipling informs us, "one might almost say grunted, contentedly." (477)[15]

This woman is haunted by the ghosts of five Belgian children, all victims of German atrocities. There is some coyness about these ghosts on the part of the omniscient narrator: are they simply figments of her fever, that is, her diseased conscience? Or are they real? Though this ambiguity is never resolved, it becomes amply clear that, real or symbolic, these five children are only a tiny percentage of the "hundreds and hundreds and thousands and thousands" (484) of dead Belgian children who are making the circuit of Berlin homes to prove to these morally unclean people that everything cannot be swept and garnished. At the end of the story, they propose to make a little excursion to the Emperor's palace. Murder will out, as Chaucer concluded long ago in a tale not wholly dissimilar.

Though none of the critics have made the connection, it seems fairly clear that "Mary Postgate" is a reprise of "Swept and Garnished." Mary's removal and destruction of Wynn's things are also acts of cleanliness, but of moral, not merely physical cleanliness. Mary's sweeping and garnishing are spontaneous and emotional, whereas Frau Ebermann's are merely the products of rigid habit. In the English home, Miss Fowler is a genuine cripple who needs a helper, while Frau Ebermann is only a momentarily bed-ridden tyrant. Their reactions to the suffering of their nations' enemies, superficially similar, are at bottom radically different. Mary acts resolutely and with an easy conscience: she dispenses justice, the only kind of justice a barbarian can understand. She is against the airman and for the dead child. Frau Ebermann, on the other hand, is testy, irresolute, cowardly. Her conscience is filthy, she grunts contentedly at barbarous victories, she loves the soldier above all foster-motherly feeling. Not surprisingly therefore, Mary grows youthful at the end of her experience; Frau Ebermann ages.

There is a resemblance in technique between the two stories as well, namely an unresolved hint that the events may be taking place only in the minds of the central characters. This is one of Kipling's favourite narrative devices which, as we have seen, functions so prominently in "Swept and Garnished" that it might almost be called a ghost story. In "Mary Postgate" there is the same ambiguity, but so much less obvious that it has been usually disregarded. J.I.M. Stewart, one of the few who does touch on it, argues that "conceivably against Kipling's conscious intention, the German is not quite real—there is no final thought that the police or military must be called, the body disposed of."[16] According to Stewart, it follows from this ambivalence that Wynn is perhaps to be identified with the German airman.

Interesting as Stewart's hypothesis is, there are some grave flaws in it. While it is certainly odd that neither the police nor the military are notified of the German airman, it is surely quite as odd that Mary does not mention him to Miss Fowler either, or for that matter does not tell her about the explosion in the village and the dead child. Surely there is no doubt about the reality of the dead child? There is, in fact, a quite simple explanation for Mary's apparently curious behavior; she is merely following Dr. Hennis' and Nurse Eden's instructions "not to say anything—yet at least" (506), presumably to prevent a panic in the village. What there is a definite doubt about, however, is the cause of the child's death. Mary's explanation of a bomb is her explanation exclusively, confirmed neither by Nurse Eden nor by Dr. Hennis, and supported only by her suspicion that she heard the sound of propellers as she was walking past Vegg's Heath, Wynn's habitual landing field. In fact, Mary's explanation is contradicted outright by Dr. Hennis somewhat later when he tells her that "the accident [sic] at the 'Royal Oak' was due to Gerritt's stable tumbling down. It's been dangerous for a long time." (506) Mary remains skeptical and so presumably should the reader, but nevertheless Hennis cannot be simply disregarded, for if Hennis is right, it follows that the German airman is either a figment of Mary's imagination or else not guilty of the child's death. Miss Tompkins' assertion that Hennis is intent on hushing up the truth is by no means self-evident in the context of the story; Nurse Eden shares Hennis' view and, for a time, even Mary is half-way persuaded. Besides, what conceivable personal interest could Hennis be serving by trying to cover up the truth? Are we to suppose that Hennis and Nurse Eden are in fact German spies? Hennis may be and probably is wrong, but his explanation cannot be simply dismissed out of hand.

Kipling deliberately cloaks the entire incident in ambiguity. No one at the actual scene either sees or hears a German plane, nor any other plane for that matter. To be sure, as a point of historical fact, air attacks were sometimes made with the engines shut off, but it is nevertheless suspicious that an entire village should have been thus left ignorant of their presence.

What is the purpose of all this ambiguity? To suggest that German atrocities against children and civilians are the hallucinations of middle-aged spinsters? Surely not, since such atrocities form the substance of the earlier story "Swept and Garnished," and since German bombing raids, beginning in January 1915, were obviously far too real to be ignored. Why then? To suggest that Wynn, like the German, might have killed children in the line of duty? No again, since not only is this possibility expressly denied in the story (Wynn is a "gentleman," the German is an "It"), but the British were at this time only using aircraft in combatant areas. Was it then to express, as Stewart and others intimate, an even greater abhorrence for women than for Germans? Possibly, since Kipling's hatred for women ran notoriously deep and surfaced repeatedly in places like "Baa Baa, Black Sheep" and *The Light that Failed*. Nevertheless, this hypothesis is belied by the appendage of "The Beginnings" with its supra-sexual hatred and by the fact that the description of the German airman evokes—with his head as pale as a baby's—the dead child as much as his uniform does Wynn.[17] Even more important, it is also belied by the fact that on Mary's return from the village, Miss Fowler tells of two planes having passed overhead half an hour earlier. The attack was real enough, apparently, and not a figment of an hysterical spinster's imagination—though even at this point a lingering doubt still remains. Since their nationality is not specified, there is a possibility that the planes might have been British. Wynn's base, after all, is obviously within easy flying distance. This possibility is admittedly rather remote, especially in view of "The Edge of the Evening" (also in *Diversity of Creatures*), another story in which German airmen appear unexpectedly and are summarily dispatched. But what then is the cause of this elaborate display of Bismarckian red herring?

Some part of the reason lies, I suspect, in Kipling's desire to emphasize the spiritual and not merely the physical damage of this particular war. This would account for the focus, in "Swept and Garnished" as well as in "Mary Postgate," on women and domestic surroundings. Even here, Kipling seems to be saying in the former case, can we see the root of the evil; and even unto here, in the other, does that evil penetrate. If Kipling had been merely an Ian Hay sort of writer, Wynn would have been the hero of his story, never an old maid like Mary. The very fact of Mary's drab appearance and existence suggests Kipling's conviction that England is engaged in a war in which the feelings and doings of ordinary people matter as they never had before. And for this the Germans are to blame: for they kill not the armed warrior, but the child and the civilian.

Something of this is suggested by the juxtaposition of Mary's firing Wynn's personal effects—his books, his toys, and other memorabilia—in the "destructor" while watching the German die. Indeed, the German's death and the burning down of Wynn's funeral pyre ("sprinkled with sacrificial oil") occur simultaneously. But this emphatically does not mean that Wynn and the German are to be identified. On the contrary, it means that Wynn's death has, to some small degree at least, been paid for, even if only in the imagination. An eye for an eye, and a tooth for a tooth: that is the Law. And that is why the airman resembles not merely Wynn but also the dead child, that is why, in "Swept and Garnished," the children are waiting in Berlin until "our people" get there. Before the new-made angels can enter paradise, the new-made devils must be sentenced to hell. In Kipling's world, the wounds of grief can only be washed clean in the blood of one's enemy.

There are hints elsewhere that the story is to be read on this level of spiritual allegory. Wynn is perhaps to be viewed as a sacrificial Christ figure whose name presages ultimate victory; and Nurse Eden's name suggests the prelapsarian condition of rural England before the German Satan quite literally fell into it (and the child Edna's name is also, significantly, a near anagram for "Eden"). Even more pointedly, the airman falls into a *garden*, where he pleads for a mercy he himself is not prepared to give, and where instead of yielding to his wiles and seeming innocence, the virginal "Laty" Mary gives him death.

In the context of the story, Mary is undoubtedly good, no matter what later ages and critics have thought of her. It is only very superficially that Mary demonstrates the "truth" of the female of the species being deadlier than the male: she puts paid to a German, whereas Wynn never did. To argue such a position seriously, however, would necessarily entail arguing that Mary's inaction is more reprehensible than the German's action; for despite being an "It," the German is still a man. Moreover, Mary's relation to Wynn is wholly different from that of the "Aunty" figure to her charge in either "Baa Baa, Black Sheep" or *The Light that Failed,* the two *loci classici* of Kipling's alleged hatred of women. Mary genuinely loves Wynn—the match that lights his pyre also burns "her heart to ashes" (436)—and she patiently submits to a great variety of indignities for his sake. If she resembles anyone in those two stories, it is the kind and gentle mother figure.

But why then choose a woman, and specifically a woman like Mary Postgate, and show her behaving in ways which Kipling must have realized might be thought of as unwomanlike, even when directed at Germans? The answer to this rather important question is to be found, I think, in Mary's concluding ruminations as she waits for the fire to burn out and for the German to die. "A man, at such a crisis", she thinks, "would be what Wynn called a 'sportsman'; would leave everything to fetch help, and would certainly bring It into the house." (440) But she, because she is a woman and not "a sportsman," does not (and, suggestively, the books she is burning—Henty, Marryat *et al,* are full of the "sportsman's" ethic). This should not be taken to mean, however, that Mary is, in Kipling's view, acting reprehensibly. On the contrary, she— along with her fellow countrymen in "The Beginnings"— has come to realize, as Wynn could not, that it is impossible to be sportsmanlike with an enemy who specializes in hideously unsportsmanlike conduct. Hence the huge revolver and its dum-dum bullets which, according to Wynn, "were forbidden by the rules of war to be used against civilized enemies" (437). But then the Germans are *not* civilized; they are, as Kipling so unambiguously put it, "inconceivably outside civilization." The Law of the Jungle, as *The Jungle Books* testify, applies only to such animals as possess a Law.

There is an analogy here to Maupassant's famous story, "Lit 29," which is worth exploring, if only briefly, because it makes a similar distinction between a man's and a woman's duty in fighting against a hated enemy. Maupassant's Captain Epivent, like Wynn, is a sportsman who fights fairly in the field; and his mistress Irma, though in all other respects radically different from Mary, fights unfairly and to greater effect at home. Infected with syphilis by a Prussian officer during the war of 1870, she continues consciously to lure the lustful enemy into her bed, there to put him *hors de combat*. Her apparent shame is in reality a great virtue; her immorality one of France's greatest glories. So too with Mary, although in a rather less lurid fashion. "But it was a fact," Mary thinks to herself. "A woman who had missed these things [a husband and family] could still be useful—more useful than a man in many respects." (440) Women, while socially and perhaps biologically disqualified from actual participation in battle, can and must do their duty in other, less glamorous ways. They also serve, to sum it all up, who only stand—or lie—and hate.

"Mary Postgate," one can agree in conclusion, is a story that has been misunderstood, perhaps chiefly because of an unwillingness on the part of the dons to face up squarely to Kipling's unsightly moral underbelly. Old Testament hatred and vengefulness are not popular literary commodities nowadays and the attempt to play down their presence in Kipling is understandable. Still, these qualities were undeniably very much a part of his stock in trade, as "Mary Postgate," but not "Mary Postgate" alone, can testify. To deny that is to turn a bull into an ox. Like most writers who have achieved great and perhaps excessive popularity in their own lifetimes, Kipling is very much fixed in the prejudices of a particular time and place. He must be understood within those limits, or not at all.

When "Mary Postgate" was published, its shrill hatred produced no disapproval, or even surprise. Better men than Kipling had been "guilty" of such intemperance. Winston Churchill, for example, fulminated repeatedly against German monsters and "baby-killers." Even the distinguished classical scholar, Gilbert Murray, viewed calmly in his pamphlet, *Thoughts on the War* (1914), the prospect of what would hopefully happen to a German student he had known at Oxford. Paul Maass, Murray observes paternally, had sent him not long ago a photograph of his first baby, Ulf, and Murray and Maass had exchanged jokes about his wise appearance, his knowledge of Greek, and so on. "And now," Murray continues, "Maass is with his regiment, and we shall do our best to kill him, and after that to starve Ulf and Ulf's mother."[18] Are we then to conclude from these remarks that Churchill or Murray or even Kipling would have enjoyed watching the actual, step-by-step demise of some wounded German? Surely not. The abstract desire for the death of a hated enemy, even an elaborately executed daydream on this subject like "Mary Postgate," is quite distinct from the real thing. Siegfried Sassoon, who had rather more opportunity to witness such events, realized this fully. In the semi-fictional account of his war-time experience, *Memoirs of an Infantry Officer* (1930), he describes how virulently his civilian friends and relations hated the Germans, whereas he himself, who was daily exposed to their enmity, bore them no grudge. His Aunt Evelyn, for instance, felt that it was her patriotic duty to agree with her vicar's axiom that "every man who killed a German was performing a Christian Act." Even so, Sassoon goes on to say, alluding more or less obviously to Kipling's story, "if Aunt Evelyn had found a wounded Prussian when she was on her way to the post office, she would undoubtedly have behaved with her natural humanity (combined with enthusiasm for administering first aid)."[19] That Mary Postgate does not do so is less a function of her own cruelty than of Kipling's ignorance. As C.E. Montague was to observe in *Disenchantment* (1922), "war hath no fury like a non-combatant."[20]

Notes

1. Rudyard Kipling, *A Diversity of Creatures*, Vol. XXVI of *The Writings in Prose and Verse* (New York: Scribners, 1917), pp. 512–513. All further references to this volume will be included in the text, by page number enclosed in parentheses.

2. Bonamy Dobrée, *The Lamp and the Lute* (London, 1964 [1929]), as reprinted in *Kipling and the Critics* (New York: New York University Press, 1965), p. 53. An earlier version of the same essay appeared originally as "Rudyard Kipling", in *The Monthly Criterion*, VI (December 1927, 499–515, and has been reprinted in *Kipling: The Critical Heritage*, ed. R. L. Green, (London: Routledge & Kegan Paul, 1971).

3. Bonamy Dobrée, *Rudyard Kipling, Realist and Fabulist* (London: Oxford University Press, 1967), pp. 131–133.

4. The strongest case yet put forward for "Mary Postgate" as a philanthropic document is Nevil Coghill's 1965 essay in the *Kipling Journal*. "To me 'Mary Postgate' is a masterpiece of utter beauty and sympathy," Coghill proclaims, adding a few sentences later that "it is the case one step further than 'Father, forgive them; they know not what they do.' It is the step that we ought to imagine the dying German might have taken, had he known as much about Mary Postgate as we do." 32 (December 1965), 69.

5. C. E. Carrington, *The Life of Rudyard Kipling* (Garden City, N.Y.: Doubleday, 1955), p. 334.

6. An allusion to the death of Kipling's son at the front in late September or early October 1915, which, since the story dates from March of that year, can hardly be accurate.

7. W. W. Robson, "Kipling's Later Stories," in *Kipling's Mind and Art*, ed. Andrew Rutherford (Stanford: Stanford University Press, 1964), pp. 273–174.

8. J. I. M. Stewart, *Eight Modern Writers* (Oxford: Oxford University Press, 1963), p. 277. His later *Rudyard Kipling*, (London: Gollancz, 1966), adds nothing to this interpretation. Probably Stewart also means to hint at what he takes to be the ultimate source of Kipling's misogyny: latent homosexuality.

9. J. M. S. Tompkins, *The Art of Rudyard Kipling* (London: Methuen, 1959), pp. 135–137.

10. C. A. Bodelsen, *Aspects of Kipling's Art* (Manchester: University Press, 1964), p. 102 n.

11. Dobrée, *Kipling*, p. 131.

12. In Max Beerbohm's famous parody, "P. C., X, 36," Santa Claus is arrested for, among other reasons, being a German. The only essay wholly devoted to the subject of Kipling's attitude toward Germany is Basil M. Bazley's "Kipling's Opinion of the Germans," *The Kipling Journal*, 12 (July 1945), 3–5. Bazley begins by asserting that Kipling's opinion was thoroughly consistent: a "dislike—hatred is perhaps not too strong a word—of everything German" which was "of no recent growth."

13. Rudyard Kipling, *The Eyes of Asia* (Garden City, N. Y.: Doubleday, 1918), pp. 7–8.

14. George Orwell, *A Collection of Essays* (Garden City, N. Y.: Doubleday, 1954), p. 124.

15. The German airman, it might be recalled, attracts Mary's attention by his animalistic grunts. This swinish aspect of the Germans may be further suggested here by the name "Ebermann." ("Eber" is the German word for boar.) Perhaps we are also intended to pick up an allusion to Matthew 12: 34, "O generation of vipers, how can ye, being evil, speak good things?" since the title of the story, after all, is taken from Matthew 12: 44, "Then he [the unclean spirit who is cast out] saith, I will return into my house from whence I came out; and when he is come, he findeth it empty, swept and garnished." The real point of this, as far as the story is concerned, emerges only in the following verse: "Then goeth he, and taketh with himself seven other spirits more wicked than himself, and they enter in and dwell there: and that last *state* of that man is worse than the first. Even so shall it be also unto this wicked generation." For the five good Belgian spirits, it seems, there are seven evil ones dwelling in Frau Ebermann.

16. Stewart, *Eight*, p. 277.

17. As a critical curiosity, one might mention here Malcolm Page's argument that the airman may not be a German at all. Noting that, aside from a few words of broken English, the airman speaks nothing but French, Page concludes that he may very well *be* French. "Otherwise," Page argues, "we must construct tortuous explanations: that a German speaks two languages, and does not know whether he has crashed in England or France." Kipling's point in all this, according to Page, is to "underline his picture of the consequences of war." ("The Nationality of the Airman in 'Mary Postgate.'" *The Kipling Journal*, 37 (June 1970), 15. An article still remains to be written which would maintain, on the basis of Mary's demonstrated, though faulty, knowledge of German, that she is a spy.

18. Gilbert Murray, *Thoughts on the War* (Oxford: Clarendon Press, 1914), p. 9.

19. Siegfried Sassoon, *Memoirs of an Infantry Officer* (New York: Collier, 1969), p. 103.

20. C. E. Montague, *Disenchantment* (New York: Brentano's, 1922), p. 279.

Some Links between the Stories in Kipling's *Debits and Credits*

Lisa A. F. Lewis[*]

In 1897, Kipling declared that his works could be read in more than one sense, "giving a new pattern in a shift of light."[1] By 1926, he had greatly developed this technique; there is a complex design hidden in the book *Debits and Credits*, conveyed by themes and images which recur in different poems and stories. Read as a single work, the collection illuminates his views of death, sex, law and religion, and of his own literary career, as he looked back over his life and forward to his end.

He introduced multiple meanings to his children's books, written for ever older age-groups as his own children grew up. *Stalky and Co.* (1899) he described as "tracts or parables on the education of the young."[2] In *Rewards and Fairies* (1910), the tales are "in three or four overlaid tints and

[*]Reprinted from *English Literature in Transition 1880–1920* 29, no. 2 (1986): 74–85, by permission.

textures, which might or might not reveal themselves according to the shifting light of sex, youth and experience."[3]

Some attempt at a unifying message appears in the next collection of adult short stories, *A Diversity of Creatures* (1917). In putting the book together, he seems to have noticed the neurosis in the prewar tales and the change of attitudes once war had broken out; poems such as "Rebirth" and "The Children" emphasize this contrast. In the last story, Mary Postgate, victim of peace, finds release in a dreadful act of war. This paper argues that in *Debits and Credits*, the next major collection, most of the stories were deliberately made to produce a whole greater than their sum. Links do not exist only within *Debits and Credits*. They can be found with stories in other collections, as the Masonic characters appear in "Fairy-Kist" and Death and St. Peter in "Uncovenanted Mercies" in the later book *Limits and Renewals*. In *Debits and Credits*, however, there exists a Jamesian "Figure in the Carpet," revealing different aspects of itself to different age groups, to men or to women, to Masons or non-Masons, by cross-reference between the tales.

One would expect such a group of interconnected stories to have been written more or less together. In the manuscripts of *Debits and Credits* at Durham University,[4] several show signs of redrafting, often more than once. "The Enemies to each Other," for instance, is only a fragment, marked "Once called 'How the Peacock Kept his Tail.'" Professor Carrington's notes from Mrs. Kipling's diaries[5] give dates of work on all the others. Of the fourteen stories in the collection, nine were definitely written or revised within the two years 1923 to 1925. Two more, though written earlier, probably received a final revision. "Sea Constables" and "In the Interests of the Brethren" were published in 1915 and 1918 and cannot be considered in this group, though they may have suggested themes and images to be used later. The exact date of "On the Gate" is unclear. It may have started as a story about St. Peter, begun in April 1916; according to Rider Haggard, Mrs. Kipling persuaded her husband not to publish it.[6] In 1920, he reverted to St. Peter in "The Department of Death"; the (incomplete) draft at Durham is so headed. Parts of it appeared as "On the Gate" when the book came out in 1926 (all the other stories were first published in magazines). "The Janeites" was written in March 1922. In October 1923 Mrs. Kipling records a surge in his inspiration, leading to a major overhaul of his existing material. "A Friend of the Family" was revised on 2 November and by 13 November four stories were ready for his agent: "The Enemies to each Other," "The United Idolators," "The Janeites" and "A Friend of the Family." On 10 November he wrote "The Prophet and the Country." This, I suggest, was the first story written expressly to fit the design. The year 1924 was to produce four vintage tales: "A Madonna of the Trenches," "The Wish House," "The Bull that Thought" and "The Eye of Allah." By December, with two stories still to write, he was already putting the book together. "The Gardener," last story in the book, was written in March 1925, and in August he wrote a Stalky story—presumably "The Propagation of Knowledge" —after meeting an old school friend called Griffiths, whose Welsh name suggests the original of "Taffy Howells." Most of the poems are not dated; they comment on, or add to, both individual stories and major themes in the book.

What was happening to Kipling during this time? There was the War; he visited the Navy and the trenches on the Flanders front. In 1915, the year of "Sea Constables," his son was killed. After the Armistice, he wrote *The Irish Guards in the Great War,* which involved meeting a lot of "the living and returned young,"[7] and gave him the background for his new set of soldier tales. In the latter half of 1922 he was extremely ill and believed for a time that he had cancer. Then in 1924, the year of those four great stories, his daughter got married, and the two older Kiplings were left alone together. His son's death, his own illness, and his daughter's marriage: these, I believe, were the most important influences on his work at this time. Background material came from visits to Spain, France, Italy and the Belgian war cemeteries. He was involved in the founding of a Masonic Lodge at St. Omer.[8]

That deeply perceptive Kipling critic, Dr. Tompkins, pointed out how "in the collections of his middle and later life, Kipling seems to have intended the first and last tales to serve as the pillars of an archway . . . framing the section of life we see between them."[9] If there is a design in this book, it is in the first and last stories that one would expect to find it. Surprisingly, Tompkins found "no substantial links" between "The Enemies to each Other" and "The Gardener." The links are substantial indeed.

One is about The Garden of Eden, the other called "The Gardener." In connection with "The Enemies to each Other," Kipling offers apologies to the shade of Mirza Mirkhond, as well he might; the first three pages are, with a few alterations, a condensed version of a passage in the Persian writer's work, *The Garden of Purity.* There is a translation of this by E. Rehatsek in the library at Bateman's. In his preface, Rehatsek says that "Rauzat" literally means a garden, but "usage has in all Muhammedan countries, as well as in India, assigned to it the significance of a *mausoleum* surrounded by a garden or park. The work 'Safa' is a plural, meaning pure, holy and by extension illustrious."[10] The title *Rauzat-us-Safa,* he adds, can mean either "The Garden of Purity" or "Mausoleum of Illustrious Men." The second meaning describes the cemetery at Hagenzeele Third in which Helen Turrell meets the Christ figure and supposes him to be the gardener. "Hag" is German for enclosure, and "Seele" for soul.[11] The first tale is about the Creation; the last ends with the Resurrection. One starts with a man alone, Adam before the creation of Eve; the other ends with a woman alone, the bereaved mother Helen. Helen and her lover have been enemies, since he seduced and then left her; he was both her curse and her blessing, since without him she would never have had her son, Michael. After the Fall, Adam and Eve feel shame and cover themselves; Helen's whole life is a masquerade to conceal her shame.

"The Enemies" is little regarded, but "The Gardener" has a high reputation. Reprinted in anthologies, the latter seems curiously flat. Its effect is not the same when wrenched from its setting and put down among tales of different dates. Jewellery is used as a metaphor for literature in "The Enemies," where storytellers are called "the stringers of the pearls of words," while King in "Propagation" sneers, "the pearls of English Literature existed only to be wrenched from their settings and cast before young swine rooting for marks." There seems a hint here of Kipling's intention; one can see the tales as pearls, the book as the necklace or setting. In "The Bull that Thought," a series of metaphors echo other stories: the wonderful champagne is described as "composed of the whispers of angels' wings" (recalling the angels in "On the Gate"), "the breath of Eden" (recalling "The Enemies to each Other"), and "the foam and pulse of Youth renewed" (recalling the waves when Beetle swims off the Pebble Ridge). In "The Wish House," just before Grace Ashcroft begins her confidence, "A couple of jays squealed and skirmished through the undraped apple-trees in the garden." The word "undraped"—a very fancy description for a tree without its leaves—calls attention both to the "undraped" truth we are to hear, and to the apple-trees, reminding us of the Garden of Eden. Grace, like Eve, feared a change in her lover's heart, and when it came she too tried forbidden magic.

Two important images recur throughout the book. The metaphor of locked and unlocked gates or doors develops from the earlier-written stories to the later ones, revealing a connection with the secrets of the heart. "The barriers of the Garden of the Tree were made fast" behind Adam and Eve. In the manuscript of "In The Interests" there is a passage in which Kipling praises Mrs. Burges and prophesies that Brother Burges will call to her after his death and she will come to open a gate for him. This may have been cut as coming too near a Masonic secret. In "On the Gate," a widow pushes her son into heaven, clutched in "that terrible mother-grip no Power has yet been able to unlock"; St. Peter controls the keys of Heaven's gate. In the poem "Gipsy Vans," respectable citizens are warned: "Lock your heart with a double lock / And throw the key away"—and then mocked for doing so. This poem precedes "A Madonna of the Trenches," one of the later and more complex tales, in which a secret is told behind a locked door about the suicide of a man "wedged up" in a dug-out with two charcoal stoves and his dead love's ghost. The two elderly ladies in "The Wish House" "closed the kitchen door" before Grace tells her secret love, and how she wished her wish through the letter-box in the closed door of the empty house. In "The Gardener,"

"Helen was as open as the day," an ironic statement which is denied in the poem "The Burden":

> *"One day of all my years—*
> *One hour of that one day—*
> *His Angel saw my tears*
> *And rolled the Stone away!"*

revealing the secret that her nephew was really her son.

The secrets of the heart do not always concern women. In "The Bull that Thought," the champagne "unlocks the heart" of M. Voiron and leads him to talk of Apis, who as a calf was shut into the farm where "One gate shuts all." At the end, the gates of the bullring "opened to the man and the bull together," saving Apis' life. Again, in "The Prophet and the Country" Kipling says "those Gates, I thought, were forever shut," referring to his night-walking Daemon; on the next page, he says that he was "under the influence of night and my Daemon." In the manuscript, he three times mentions that his Demon returned that night, to his fervent delight. In "The Eye of Allah," the abbey is locked before the scientific (but impious) secret is told. "Who is any son of Adam," asks Roger Bacon, guest at the Abbot's table, "that his one say-so should close a door towards truth?" The heart's secret may refer to women or cattle, literature or science.

The second metaphor, drapery or clothing, comes to stand for the facade which hides our primitive nature from the world. Adam and Eve are "delivered to shame and nudity and abjection." The Janeites live under camouflage screens; when the screens are ripped open, they are destroyed, all except for the simple giant Humberstall, who is left naked but for his boots, and dresses himself from their dead bodies. In "On the Gate," Normal Civil Death cares only for black draperies and "the whole millinery of undertaking," while the Imp who is turning into an angel has feathers on his wings, but to show this he must rip off his Holbein uniform.

These three passages may have suggested the use of the image in the later stories. While clothing can be a necessary defense, "We" who "dress up to Our ears" are not necessarily happier than the naked savages of "We and They" and "Gow's Watch Act IV Sc. 4." The covering may hide a mortal wound: death, the shedding of the body by the spirit, is a linking theme. "The Prophet and the Country" shows Tarworth sweltering in his yellow raincoat. This story has death for a secondary theme; his new life began with his wife's funeral. At the end, a motor-hearse appears in the dawn, covered by a pail which has slipped a little, showing the coffin beneath, and Tarworth says "'Say, Neighbour . . . There's somethin' very soothin' in the Concept of Death after all.'" In death he will be able to shed his obsessions. 'Arry in "The Wish House" looked "'S'runk an' wizen; 'is clothes 'angin' on 'im like bags'" after his accident. Rahere, in the poem following, sees a leper by a gallows, "cloaked from chin to ankle" to hide his deformities. In "In the Interests of the Brethren," Kipling had told how a dress-designer turned soldier said: "Satan himself can't save a woman who wears thirty-shilling corsets under a thirty-guinea costume." He picks this up in "A Madonna of the Trenches," where Bella Armine was compared to "somethin' movin' slow, in armour" (corsets did resemble armour in those days). This stands for the principles beneath her respectable surface. Under them, "She'd 'ad a bit of gatherin' in 'er breast"—the cancer that killed her. In "Propagation," the boys who have no sores to hide, bathe "as naked as God had made them, and as happy as He intended them to be." In "The Gardener," only her son's death allows Helen to drop, for one hour, the burden of her masquerade. There is no mention of her clothes, any more than of the secret locked in her heart, within the tale; the metaphors are implicit.

An important theme which also connects with these metaphors is that of sexual love. Kipling's view of sex is summed up at the end of "The Enemies to each Other," when Adam and Eve kneel together before an Altar on which is written the words of the Expulsion Order: "*Get ye down, the one of you an enemy unto the other.*" And it was answered, "Enough! It shall stand in the place of both Our Curse and Our Blessing." It was Eblis (Satan) who tempted Adam to ask for a wife, but though the pair quarrel bitterly, they can laugh together and agree, "upon no composition would I have it otherwise."

Grace Ashcroft tells of her love for the man who has left her. By the magic of the Wish House, she used her bad leg to keep him alive and well, "drawin' all manner o' dyed stockin's" over the sore until it "turned" to cancer. This selfless idea makes her tragedy bearable—she has turned a curse for herself into a blessing for 'Arry. In "The Prophet and the Country" there is no such sexual goodwill; Tarworth's sex relationships have gone very wrong. In two of the photographs which are central to his story, we see a woman first as man's enemy, then as man's victim. "Close buttoned" in his raincoat, the caravan door "pushed home," he tells how, ten days after his wife's funeral, he was "the freest—the happiest—man in the United States," while he continually abuses "the American Woman" for her "Presumption." Impotent as a film maker, he seems also to have been impotent as a husband for he constantly talks of "Virginity" and in one very suggestive passage keeps chewing on an unlit cigar. Too rigid a system, sexual, legal and religious, has unmanned him; his women have abused their power, which in his case is an unmixed curse.

"A Madonna of the Trenches" shows the shock effect on a young soldier of his elders' sexuality. Behind the sheltering curtain, he reveals how he saw the ghost of Bella, his favorite aunt, now dead of cancer, appear to him and his father-figure. In the squalid setting of the trenches, Bella's spirit was united with her lover in a scene which, stripped of all conventional decoration, still powerfully conveys the force of their love. Together they went into a dug-out, taking two charcoal braziers, and the live man wedged up the door from the inside to be taken out next day a frozen corpse. They had not consummated their love. Since it is told from young Clem's point of view, the story cannot comment on this; Kipling's verse-and-story form allows him to show in "Gipsy Vans" another view of the case, while "Gow's Watch Act V Sc. 3" parallels the Oedipal theme, using daughter / father-figure rather than son / mother and father-figures. Clem, left alone by the dug-out, had broken down, and later rejects his girlfriend, swearing that "Not till I see that look on a face . . . that look . . ." will he marry. This is probably a blessing for them; they may yet achieve a more mature relationship, with each other or with different partners. Clem's story told, he is draped in "some flamboyant" (Masonic) "robe" before Bella's widower enters, who must not know the secret.

In "The Gardener," Michael is unmarried, and it is his mother Helen who dominates the story—perhaps she will tow him into Heaven like the mother in "On the Gate." Her lover is never identified; we are only told the lie by which she accounted for her baby. Several critics have tried to guess who the father might have been.[12] All the clues seem ambiguous. My own belief is that he has been omitted because he simply is not important in the story; if he were made a real person, we might expect him to share Helen's grief, but that is not going to happen. The final poem makes clear that she is Mary Magdalene, as described in Kingsley's *Hypatia* (mentioned in "The United Idolators"): "Though God had forgiven her, she could not forgive herself. She fled forth into the desert, and there, naked and barefoot, clothed only with her hair, and feeding on the herb of the field, she stayed fasting and praying till her dying day, never seeing the face of man, but visited and comforted by angels and archangels."[13] This seems to me to complete the circle begun with Adam.

The law, always one of Kipling's interests, is another theme in the book, linked with motifs of labels, numbers, and official documents. The United Idolators riot, but they re subject to school rules, which the Head and Pot can vary when necessary. Their destructive outbreak is healthy—much more so than the repressive morality of Brownell the temporary master, whose subconscious hardly bears thinking about. Nevertheless, riot must be punished with a record number of beatings so that the law may be observed. In "The Janeites," 'Ammick and Mosse had been lawyer and detective, and tended to run their battery on legal lines. When Humberstall chalked the guns with Janeite labels, as he had no right to do, the subsequent inquiry was meant less to produce justice than to appease the angry sergeant-major. The inner heart of this story is the cult of Jane Austen, whose books tell of a drawing-room world all rules and conventions, and how its memory held the battery together when comfort and civilization are far away. "A Friend of the Family" shows how the law failed Bert Vigors, who did not employ a lawyer before the tribunal and so could not evade conscription, though he had a better case than the Margetts boys, who did. Hickmot, or Hickmer, the uncivilized shepherd from the Australian outback whose very name (label) is uncertain, avenged Bert's death by his illegal "bombing raid," which was officially accepted as a real one. So justice was done.

In "On the Gate," Normal Civil Death is obsessed with outward trappings: black-edged stationery, faked reports of edifying deathbeds, official archives, and his own degrees and titles. Real power lies with Death and St. Peter who, being above the law, can recruit a reformed Imp or issue passes to Heaven to "Officer and Party" in defiance of the regulations.

"The Prophet and the Country" is about a bad law and its consequences, and in the opening paragraphs a label is stuck on the narrator's car to show that his licence is valid. Later we hear that when Tarworth left America he also changed his name. There is no sign that he wants to get drunk; what he wanted was to make his film against Prohibition. He was scandalized when he saw Americans drunk and behaving foolishly. His neurosis does not prevent him from having a point, but in directly attacking his people's law he lost his place among them, and so fled into exile.

In "Madonna," young Clem is being sued for breach of promise; he broke his engagement because he could not keep its spirit, more important than the law. "Propagation" shows how King, by allowing himself to be distracted from the syllabus and using improper language, manages to teach the boys a great deal about the use of English, while they themselves discover how to beat the system to get the marks they need to pass into the Army. When Michael Turrell has died for his country, his "civil status" is "regular" at last; his silver identity-disc is returned to his mother and he is allotted a numbered grave, which will in due course receive a properly labelled cross.

The Eden myth as told in "The Enemies to each Other" combines Judaism, Christianity and Islam. Kipling believed in God, but did not accept the whole of the Christian (or any other) faith. The religious theme in the book is often linked with artistic creation, as Mirza Mirkhond reconciled the Koran with the Old Testament and traditional tales by making a good story of them. Alternative versions of the myth find an echo in "The United Idolators," where the schoolboys are compared to early Christians fighting over points of doctrine; Kipling's suggestion that Adam's real sin lay in wanting a wife is borrowed from these early Christians.[14] The mirrors on the Altars in which Adam and Eve worship themselves may refer to Sun God and Mother Earth cults, as well as the wilder forms of male arrogance and women's lib.

In "On the Gate," Kipling has mixed his religions with a reckless hand. The first sentence quotes from the Smaragdine Table of Hermes Trismegisthus, in a work falsely attributed to St. Albertus Magnus. This is alchemists' lore.[15] The Islamic Angel of Death works with St. Peter, and heaven's pickets include Mary Magdalene; Judas Iscariot; St. Ignatius

Loyola, founder of the Jesuits; Joan of Arc; John Calvin; the artists John Bunyan and Shakespeare; and the freethinking Victorian moralist Charles Bradlaugh, said to have challenged God to a fight.[16]

The God who "came late" to punish Grace Ashcroft is a Love God, against whom she sinned by cruelty to her earlier loves. Through the legend of the Wish House she outwitted his power. ("What is a God beside Woman?" says the poem.) Tarworth in "The Prophet and the Country" is a Fundamentalist, and our attention is drawn to this by his mention of other people's faiths. His womenfolk have set up a mirror on their Altar. They take the Bible literally and try to suppress all sin, even the minor sin of drunkenness. He tries to warn his people that this is going too far, but because of his personality defects and his lack of artistic talent he is mocked and his film is still-born.

Apis, the bull that thought, is named for an Egyptian bull-god in the Memphis cult of death. His tale is set in Catholic France and Spain; Christophe the herdsman believed in holy water, especially when stolen, though when he sprinkled it on Apis it had no effect. When the latter cleaned his horns, "it was as though he were interrogating the Devils themselves upon their secrets." Apis is constantly referred to as an artist; he is a primitive force, permitted within bounds in the ordered Catholic world, but only his genius saved him from death in the bullring. "The Eye of Allah" is set in a Catholic monastery of the thirteenth century. The rule is lax and they live comfortably, with mistresses, banquets served in silver and crystal, and furlined boots to keep out the cold. John Otho, the artist who is not really a monk though he wears the tonsure, visits Spain, and has a Jewish wife. Holy Church tolerates all this (or turns a blind eye to it) but not dissection or optical instruments—piety is more important than scientific truth. The artist, however, can show the symptoms of disease and draw bacteria with impunity. Art is beyond creeds; the artist is in touch with eternal truths which conventional religion may have temporarily forgotten.

On Michael Turrell's grave, at the very end of the book, the Christ / Gardener will plant flowers and sow grass. "A merciless sea of black crosses . . . a waist-high wilderness as of weeds stricken dead" will become a Garden of Purity, a Mausoleum of Illustrious Men, fit subject for poetry and legend.

Kipling must have been considering his own literary career, and whether his work would survive among future generations. He was under pressure to authorize the founding of the Kipling Society. In "The Janeites," it is remarked that Jane Austen was "fruitful in the 'ighest sense of the word"—one wonders if he was remembering his son's death and trying to console himself that his name might still live through his work. By writing of "mere flutes that breathe at eve" he may endure, as Horace did, "while Empires fall / And Gods for Gods make room." This question of literary survival comes up all through the book. Many of the texts referred to are uncertain. *The Garden of Purity* was translated, with conse-quent problems of accuracy versus style, which Kipling mocks unmerci-fully. The Bible, too, was translated into Latin and then into English, not always accurately; but Fundamentalists treat its every word as sacred. Horace's Odes were recovered through Byzantium and the Moslem world, from manuscripts which may or may not be accurate; Kipling in-vents Odes from a non-existent *Book V.* In "The Eye of Allah," the herbal of Pseudo-Apuleius is believed to be the work of Apuleius himself; its text, too, may be corrupt. Shakespeare's texts are disputed, and the "Ba-conian heresy" is still with us. In the long term, it is demonstrated, liter-ary survival is a chancy business.

By the time he wrote "Propagation," Kipling seems to have felt that it would not matter if his work survived as did the Tom O'Bedlam song, sung by vagrants, recorded by a collector of literary trifles, to inspire a young poet who would never know the author's name. To be enshrined in En-glish literature and used to plague sleepy schoolboys, to be remembered for one's lack of grooming (King quotes Macaulay's description of Johnson) or drinking habits (see Beetle on Addison)—was this really a better fate? In 1926, he said: "a pleasant tale for the young under the title of *Gulliver's Travels* . . . and a faint recollection of some baby-talk in some love-letters, is as much as the world has chosen to retain of Jonathan Swift, Master of Irony. . . . The utmost a writer can hope is that there may survive of his work a fraction good enough to be drawn upon later. . . ." Earlier in the same speech, he said of fiction that the world "will extract from it just so much of truth or pleasure as it requires for the moment. In time a little more, or much less, of the residue may be carried forward to the general account."[17]

This must be the thinking behind the title, *Debits and Credits.* It sounds like a catch-all phrase, capable of including almost any story, but like many of his later titles it is more subtle than at first appears. The con-cept of a balance is central to his philosophy. Sex, law, religion are things we can neither endure nor do without; even death is necessary to us. Men and women have opposing interests; sometimes one gains, sometimes the other; each has profits to set against their losses. Different forms of law or religion do their accounting in different ways. There are no perfect sys-tems; we must weigh up the debits and credits of each, for each is a curse as well as a blessing. To work, each must allow some exceptions, some lati-tude: "Yet doth He does devise means. . . ." Though certain moral princi-ples are vital and must be respected, "It's the Spirit, not the Letter, that giveth life," quotes Brother Burges. As for death, it is terrible, but also a merciful release; Azrael is an angel, and St. Peter's friend. The plots of Eblis against mankind are allowed for in God's plan: "This, too, lay in the foreknowledge of The Endless." The Garden of Eden is not quite lost, for herbs grow on the battlefield in "A Friend of the Family," the Christ figure plants out the graves in "The Gardener," and in the poem "The Supports" "*Mere unconquerable grass*" grows

> "*Where the fuming crater was, to heal and hide it under,*
> *He shall not—He shall not—*
> *Shall not lay on us the yoke of too long Fear and Wonder!*

This poem lies at the heart of the Kipling ethic.

He had long ago learned to conceal his moral in an amusing tale; the preaching tone of *Land and Sea Tales* (most of them first published in magazines of the 1890s) gave way to the hilarity of *Stalky and Co.* By 1926, the original readers of *Stalky* were grown up. He was addressing a new generation of adults, to whom the word "Victorian" was a pejorative, and he himself one of the guilty generation that caused the war, an "old was-ser" whose ideas were quite outdated. Therefore he hid them. As Truth says to Fiction in "A Legend of Truth": "*They need us both, but you far more than me!*"

There may have been a second reason. I believe that there is much of Freemasonry in his balance theory. Professor Enamul Karim finds it in *Kim*, where he calls it "the Masonic Middle Way."[18] It is possible that, while still believing in Masonic principles, Kipling was dissatisfied with the way his fellow-Masons put them into practice; he was not a regular attendant at any Lodge, though he was an honorary member of two.[19] If he also wanted to influence Masonic readers, he had to tread warily; already he risked offending them by setting four stories inside a Masonic Lodge.

While primarily intending to work on our subconscious minds, Kipling may have slipped in a clue to his design for those readers curious enough to track down his references. It would be like his impish sense of humor to lay such a clue where one would least expect to find it. We read "Propagation" as a delightful romp, just another Stalky story put in for light relief; a closer look shows it full of matter. The last story written, its surface theme is the study of literature. Background reading for this took me to Nathaniel Holmes' *The Authorship of Shakespeare* (1875), an important prop in the story. In that book is a set of tables, showing the repetition of certain words in different plays. These are trivial, and their application unclear, but they gave me the idea of making tables of repeated images and themes in *Debits and Credits*, with the results I have shown.

Why is the design so little noticed? Much of the blame must lie with "The Enemies." Dr. Tompkins came near it when she wrote: "Kipling's later tales hook into each other in all directions; if one is lifted up for inspection, several others come up attached to it."[20] (She also said that it was *Debits and Credits* that first roused her interest in the adult stories.[21]) Her point about the first and last tales as an "archway" would have given her the key, but working as she did with the whole *oeuvre*, she never in her book gave "The Enemies" a detailed analysis; it is not a good enough story to rate her attention. It is much neglected—most readers prefer to skip ahead to such favorites as "The Bull that Thought" and "The Eye of Allah." The pseudo-Oriental style is irritating. Mirza Mirkhond is little known and his work hard to come by, the reference merely baffling. Professor Carrington wonders why the story was ever published.[22] If it was an old draft revamped to fit the meaning of the book, then it seems the mystery is solved. An Adam story was needed to balance the Resurrection theme at the end of "The Gardener." Ignore it, and the archway is not seen; the design fails to emerge.

It is possible that these unifying themes and metaphors come from a subconscious process, the work of his Daemon. Nabokov once described this sort of thing as "those strange subconscious clues which are discoverable only in the works of authentic genius."[23] Yet I find it hard to believe that at this stage in his career, with all his experience, Kipling did not know exactly what he was doing. In the summer of 1923, he wrote to Rider Haggard about the latter's new manuscript: "It represented the whole sum and substance of your conviction along certain lines . . . to those to whom it is a message or a confirmation it will mean more than the rest of your work. . . ."[24] May Kipling not have been inspired, that October, to try the same thing himself?

Notes

1. Rudyard Kipling, Foreword to Outward Bound Edition of his Works (NY, 1897; rptd in *Two Forewords*, NY: Doubleday, Doran, 1935), p. 26.

2. Rudyard Kipling, *Something of Myself* (Lond: Macmillan, 1937), pp. 134–36.

3. *Something of Myself*, p. 190.

4. Presented to Durham University by Mrs. Kipling in 1937, after her husband's death, on certain conditions. They may not be used for collation, which is why I do not quote from them.

5. Kipling's daughter allowed C.E. Carrington to see her mother's diary while writing his biography, *Rudyard Kipling* (Lond: Macmillan, 1955). The diary was then destroyed. A copy of the notes is in the Kipling Society's Library; these, too, cannot be quoted directly.

6. Cohen, ed. *Rudyard Kipling to Rider Haggard* (Lond: Hutchinson, 1965), p. 101.

7. From "The Gardener." Quotations from *Debits and Credits* are taken from the Library edn (Lond: Macmillan, 1949).

8. Wimpole papers, cat. no. 21 / 24, University of Sussex Library.

9. J.M.S. Tompkins, *The Art of Rudyard Kipling* (Lond, 1959; University paperbacks, 1965), pp. 158–59.

10. Mirza Mirkhwand [sic], *The Garden of Purity*, trans by E. Rehatsek (Bombay: Oriental Translation Fund, Royal Asiatic Society, New Series I, 1891), I, p. 11. Kipling spells it Mirkhond.

11. I owe this point to Mrs. Margaret Newsom, Librarian, Kipling Society.

12. Carrington, *Kipling Journal*, No. 186 (1973), 17. Deas, quoted *Kipling Journal*, No. 205 (1978), 4; Newsom, *Kipling Journal*, No. 205 (1978), 8.

13. Charles Kingsley, *Hypatia* (Lond, 1853; Everyman edn), p. 344.

14. Edward Gibbon, *The Decline and Fall of the Roman Empire* (Lond, 1776; Dent's Everyman edn, 1956), I, p. 466.

15. M. Redgrove, *Alchemy Ancient and Modern* (Lond, 1911; EP Publishing edn, 1973), pp. 39–41. Also Roger Bacon, *The Mirror of Alchimy* (ca. 1265; English translation Lond, 1597).

16. G.C. Beresford, *Schooldays with Kipling* (Lond: Gollancz, 1936), p. 257; says they discussed this in the dormitory at school.

17. "Fiction," address by Kipling to the Royal Society of Literature (July 1926); collected in *A Book of Words* (Lond: Macmillan 1928), pp. 284–85, 283.

18. Emanul Karim, *Kipling Journal*, No. 217 (1981), p. 26.

19. Brother Harry Carr, trans. *Quatuor Coronati Lodge*, LXXVII (1964), 233,236.

20. Tompkins, p. 167.

21. Tompkins, pp. ix–x (not in hardback edn of 1959).

22. Carrington, *Rudyard Kipling*, p. 468.

23. Vladimir Nabokov, *Nikolai Gogol* (1944; Lond: Weidenfeld & Nicolson, 1973), p. 91.

24. Cohen, pp. 124–25.

Kipling's Unfinished Memoir

Something of Myself: A Reading of Kipling's Autobiography Harry Ricketts

Despite the remarkable resurgence of interest in Kipling's work in the last twenty-five years, his posthumously published autobiography, *Something of Myself: for My Friends Known and Unknown,* has yet to receive the attention it deserves. It has, of course, been extensively quarried by Kipling's biographers, and critics have used certain key passages (particularly from chapters 7 and 8) as the starting point for the reappraisal of the later stories, but it is true to say that no one has yet tried to discuss *Something of Myself* as a work in its own right, as something more than an adjunct to the short stories and poems.

So how should one "read" *Something of Myself*? I suggest that it should be read in the same way, with the same kind of alertness, as we have now learnt to read the later, more complex stories. As a prelude to doing this, I should like to mention that the best general guide to Kipling's later work remains C.A. Bodelsen's book *Aspects of Kipling's Art,* particularly chapter 6 which he calls "Kipling's Late Manner." I arrived at my own reading of *Something of Myself* independently of Bodelsen (who has little to say about it, although he is interesting about the first chapter), but rereading his book, I realised that I had unconsciously absorbed a good deal of his approach and some of his terminology, such as Kipling's use of what he terms "pointers" to suggest unexpected "layers" of meaning. Two short, general quotations from Bodelsen's book will serve as a convenient introduction to what I have to say:

> There is a veritable cult of indirectness and concealment. The clues to the subsidiary layers of meaning are nearly always buried in passages that, on a cursory reading, appear to be about something quite different.

> The technical devices characteristic of Kipling's late manner are nearly always clues to hidden meanings.[1]

From *Prose Studies* 4, no. 2 (September 1981): 153–68. Reprinted by permission of Frank Cass & Co., Gainsborough House, Gainsborough Road, London.

I should perhaps add (as Bodelsen does) that although clues to hidden meanings are extremely prominent in the later Kipling, neither his late stories nor *Something of Myself* is merely an ingenious crossword puzzle. Certainly, he does set puzzles for the reader, but this is a deliberate strategy intended to make the reader respond to the deeper layers of the material. In what follows I cannot pretend to offer an exhaustive study of *Something of Myself*. A more comprehensive account would relate it firmly to Autobiography as a genre and try to assess its undoubted interest for the literary historian. I shall instead be concentrating on what I take to be the most important layers of the work. These layers are, of course, all interdependent, but in order to present a clear line of argument I shall separate them out and discuss them individually under numbered sections.

I

I shall begin my reading of *Something of Myself* with the well-known account that Kipling gives in chapter 7 of how and why he layered the stories in *Rewards and Fairies*:

> Since the tales had to be read by children, before people realised that they were meant for grown-ups; and since they had to be a sort of balance to, as well as a seal upon, some aspects of my "Imperialistic" output in the past, I worked the material in three or four overlaid tints and textures, which might or might not reveal themselves according to the shifting light of sex, youth, and experience. It was like working lacquer and mother-o'-pearl, a natural combination, into the same scheme as niello and grisaille, and trying not to let the joins show.[2]

Rapidly written as *Something of Myself* was (between August and December 1935 and, according to Carrington, unrevised) it too is "worked" in different layers and reveals itself on different levels. The first and most obvious layer is that of the chronological account of the author's life. This surface layer, beginning true to type with the stock phrase "My first impression is," moves from Kipling's earliest memories in India up to his description of receiving the Nobel Prize. This account, therefore, only covers the first forty or so years of his life, although there are many passing references to later events, even up to the time of writing. The last chapter, "Working-tools," is (at least on the surface) concerned more specifically with his craft. Although *Something of Myself* was unrevised (which would help to explain some of its many factual errors), there seems to be no real evidence to suggest that Kipling ever intended to continue the chronological account beyond 1907 and so I shall assume that the text as it stands is substantially as Kipling intended it to be.

What strikes one most forcibly reading *Something of Myself* as a chronological account of Kipling's life are the familiar characteristics of immediacy and reticence. People and places, conversations and atmospheres are brought home to us in a series of masterly vignettes in which (as in the stories) every word is made to "tell, carry, weigh, taste and, if need were, smell" (221). For instance, the fifth act of a miniature drama on a London street is recalled with all the "economy of implication" of the stories of that period (c1889), so that we make the connection between the suicide's action and Kipling's own state of mind, although such a connection is never directly made:

> Once I faced the reflection of my own face in the jet-black mirror of the window-panes for five days. When the fog thinned, I looked out and saw a man standing opposite the pub where the barmaid lived. Of a sudden his breast turned dull red like a robin's, and he crumpled, having cut his throat. In a few minutes—seconds it seemed—a hand-ambulance arrived and took up the body. A pot-boy with a bucket of steaming water sluiced the blood off into the gutter, and what little crowd had collected went its way. (123–4)

After receiving an honorary degree from McGill (his first, as he mentions with some pride), Kipling engagingly describes how the students dumped him in "a fragile horse-vehicle" and one of them told him he had made a "dam' dull speech." "In '15 I met some of those boys digging trenches in France" (216), adds Kipling with the kind of characteristic jolt that he had used so effectively in the Stalky stories. But if the results of his early experiments "in the weights, colours, perfumes, and attributes of words in relation to other words" (112) are everywhere apparent in his autobiography, so too, it must be admitted, are the more irritating mannerisms of his work: the knowing, insiderish tone, the addiction to capital letters and the penchant for pseudo-Biblical phrasing. And then there is his reticence.

In *The Art of Rudyard Kipling* Miss J.M.S. Tompkins asserts of *Something of Myself* that

> In his seventieth year Kipling was writing the kind of personal statement that was approved in his twentieth, and it was "not out of character" for him to do so.[3]

This is true, but it is also true that all his life Kipling maintained a reticence about personal matters that was unusual even in a man of his particular upbringing, class and experience. His reticence, in fact, borders on an obsession, which leaves its mark all over his autobiography. It is there in the apparently nonchalant understatement of the extracts which I have already quoted, and also in the very title which, since it is directly relevant to Kipling's reticence, I shall discuss here.

The title not only serves to set a distance between *Something of Myself* and his other work ("and now something of *myself*"), but also warns the reader not to expect the full story ("*something* of myself"). Perhaps one can detect in the different possible emphases of the phrase a certain teasing of his readers' (very natural) curiosity about him; perhaps too the implication that "something" is all that one *ought* to tell, and even all that one *can* tell (about oneself and other people). Like his contemporaries, Conrad and Henry James, Kipling was preoccupied from very early in his fiction with the problem of "how to know," and his development of the story as puzzle needs to be seen in part at least as a response to that problem. ("Mrs. Bathurst" from *Traffics and Discoveries*, a story about a story developed from fragments of information which finally refuse to cohere is perhaps his best-known example.) He does, of course, like most writers, talk about thinking "in another man's skin" (224), but he is only too well aware of how wrong one can be in one's understanding of others or oneself. This is the point of an early tale called "The Last of the Stories" in which "I" meets Mulvaney, Learoyd and Ortheris in the "Limbo of Lost Endeavour, where the souls of all the Characters go" and they tell him that he simply did not "understand."[4] Underneath Kipling's apparently confident, in-the-know manner lies a basic uncertainty about what one does know and can know, and what one can tell. There is even at one moment in *Something of Myself* a strong suggestion that to *try* to know oneself may be a mistake, at least when one is young. Speaking of his early writing years in India, Kipling links his favourite "card" image (cf Section II below) with another favourite image, that of the young colt which must be broken to its work. (This "colt" image, recurrent in the early stories, occurs four times in *Something of Myself*.) The two images are brought together in chapter 3:

> But mark how discreetly the cards were being dealt me. Up till '87 my performances had been veiled in the decent obscurity of the far end of an outlying province, among a specialised community who did not interest any but themselves. I was like a young horse entered for small, up-country events where I could get used to noise and crowds, fall about till I found my feet, and learn to keep my head with the hoofs drumming behind me. Better than all, the pace of my office-work was "too good to inquire," and its nature—that I should realise all sorts and conditions of men and make others realise them—gave me no time to "realise" myself. (108)

Kipling clearly came to feel that it would have been positively dangerous and wrong for him as a young writer to have tried to "realise" himself and what he was doing. So another twist to the title is to raise the question of how much one should know about oneself. The title also, I think, contains one final suggestion and this is that while Kipling is ostensibly going to be telling (some at least of) the story of his life, he is simultaneously going to be writing about other important concerns ("something of myself, but also something about . . ."). In other words, we should read the title itself as a kind of "pointer," obliquely alerting us to the existence of submerged layers in the narrative.

Returning more specifically to the reticence of *Something of Myself*, it is not surprising to find that Kipling has nothing to say about certain sides of his life—his sex life, for instance. Like many Victorians (and, of course, in many respects Kipling was very much a Victorian), he simply thought that there were more important things to write about, certainly in one's autobiography. This said, *Something of Myself* does contain some remarkable omissions, of which the scrupulous refusal to make even the most indirect reference to Wolcott Balestier is a striking example. In fact, to learn anything of Kipling's tangled and often perplexing relationship with the whole Balestier family, we are forced to turn to his biographers. With the help of Carrington and Wilson, we find that despite the shortness of their acquaintance, Wolcott Balestier was almost certainly the most intimate friend that Kipling ever had. (He was, of course, co-author with Kipling of *The Naulahka*.) We also learn that it was immediately upon receipt of the news of his death that Kipling hurried back to England to marry Carrie, Wolcott's sister. It seems clear without indulging in too much guesswork that Kipling's feelings for the sister were closely related to his friendship for the brother. Again, there is no reference to his later feud with Carrie's other brother, Beatty (unless we see an oblique allusion to it in chapter 5 in the remark that he found "the atmosphere" in America "to some extent hostile" [160]). Yet, this episode is clearly of vital importance if we are to understand not only why Kipling decided to return to England in 1896, but also why he became so increasingly distrustful of the United States. (This distrust is continually emphasised in his autobiography and forms the fourth layer which I shall be discussing.) The extreme embarrassment and humiliation resulting from the publicity of the lawsuit which Kipling brought against Beatty (for, as he claimed, threatening to murder him) must have left the deepest impression on so private a man, and seems clearly related to his repeated accusation that America knew nothing of what he calls "law-abidingness" (150).

Miss Tompkins suggests that, in line with nineteenth-century autobiographical convention, the reticence in *Something of Myself* begins with public recognition, but in Kipling's case it may have had as much to do with his marriage which, of course, followed not long after what he ironically calls his "notoriety" (114). And certainly most of the notable omissions do involve his family: his wife is rarely alluded to and there is no mention of the deaths of his favourite daughter, Josephine or his only son, John. But even if we do take these silences to be at least partly a result of nineteenth-century practice, they are in themselves curiously informative, and to look more closely at Kipling's reticence and suppressions is to begin to attune oneself to how *Something of Myself* should be read. For example, I said just now (as do all Kipling's biographers and commentators) that he makes no mention of his son's death, and an initial reading supports this. Obliquely, however, he does allude to it in the sentence which describes John's birth:

> The Aunt and the Uncle had said to us: "Let the child that is coming to you be born in our house," and had effaced themselves till my son John arrived on a warm August night of '97, under what seemed every good omen. (164)

When you remember that John Kipling was blown up in 1915 at the age of eighteen and his body never recovered, that innocent-sounding phrase "under what seemed every good omen" takes on an irony that is all the more poignant for its restraint, its tight-lipped reticence. And not only that: if you take this cryptic disclosure together with the sentence that follows it—"Meantime, we had rented by direct intervention of Fate that third house opposite the church on the green" (164)—Kipling seems to be implying something very specific about Fate and its influence on his life. Kipling's attitude to Fate is the second 'layer' which I intend to consider.

II

In *Something of Myself,* as in so much of his work, Kipling is deeply preoccupied with Fate, both on a personal and on a national level. The very first paragraph announces this:

> Looking back from this my seventieth year, it seems to me that every card in my working life has been dealt me in such a manner that I had but to play it as it came. Therefore, ascribing all good fortune to Allah the Dispenser of Events, I begin. (55)

The image of Fate dealing him cards which he had only to play is repeated either literally (three times) or in variations like "'Lord ha' mercy on me, this is none of I'" and "'What else could I have done?'" (more than a dozen times in all). Knowing Kipling's practice, this repetition (a kind of "pointer") is not likely to be unintentional. Obviously, he feels he has had a specially favoured life (certainly as far as the working side of it went), but as *Something of Myself* also makes clear, if more indirectly, he is equally aware of how destructive Fate can be and has been. Fate is generous to some, but its favours are always uncertain and it will inevitably punish those who through carelessness or pride take its patronage for granted. In other words, if "all good fortune" is to be ascribed to Allah, *we* bring our own bad fortune on ourselves.

This darker side to Fate is mostly latent in the first half of the autobiography (up to Kipling's marriage), but it comes to the surface in chapter 5 in a telling sentence about the preparations for his honeymoon trip round the world: "It was all arranged beyond any chance of failure" (139). A page and a half later, he and his wife are in Japan, she is preg-

nant, his bank has gone bust, and they are forced to retreat to her parents'
home in Vermont on the strength of a refund on their tickets. ("These
things are all luck and – here's your refund." [141]) They settle in Vermont and when Josephine is born there in Bliss Cottage, the day before
Kipling's birthday and two days before his wife's, they congratulate her
"on her sense of the fitness of things" (146). As with the phrase "under
what seemed every good omen" in the account of John's birth, these
parentally complacent congratulations about Josephine's "sense of the
fitness of things" become almost despairingly ironic when one recalls
that she was to die of pneumonia only six years later. The double-
edgedness with which Kipling describes the birth of his first two children
(that of his third child, Elsie, who survived him is significantly never
mentioned) suggests that like a character in one of his stories he feels he
has taken Fate's goodwill for granted and been inevitably punished for
doing so. (There are, of course, characters in the stories, like Ameera in
"Without Benefit of Clergy" from *Life's Handicap,* who do not take Fate
for granted at all and still get punished.)

It is after Kipling's return to England and the brief reference to
John's birth that the preoccupation with the two-sidedness of Fate shifts
from the personal level to the national. What has happened to the individual can just as easily happen to the nation (and, perhaps Kipling is suggesting in *Something of Myself,* has happened). If the nation takes its good
fortune as its due, then it too will be punished, unless it is made to realise
what it is doing in time. The point at which Kipling clearly marks the transition from personal to national level is appropriately in his account of
how "Recessional" came to be written. He was, he says, worried about
events in South Africa and

> into the middle of it all came the Great Queen's Diamond Jubilee, and a
> certain optimism that scared me. The outcome, as far as I was con-
> cerned, took the shape of a set of verses called "Recessional," which
> were published in *The Times* in '97 at the end of the Jubilee celebrations.
> It was more in the nature of a *nuzzur-wattu* (an averter of the Evil Eye),
> and—with the conservatism of the English—was used in choirs and
> places where they sing long after our Navy and Army alike had in the
> name of "peace" been rendered innocuous. (173)

Read carefully, this passage suggests a good deal not only about Kipling's
conception of Fate, but also about his conception of poetry, and the dangers of English "conservatism" (cf also Section III). A sense of humility
and national responsibility, that would have been the appropriate response during the Jubilee celebrations, not "a certain optimism." Kipling
casts himself here, as he often did, in the role of the singer of the tribe
who is, simultaneously, the mouthpiece of its conscious and unconscious
aspirations, and the medicine man who tries to avert the anger of the
gods. Kipling's deepest intuitions about poetry tend to centre in its ori-

gins in tribal magic and ritual, and his belief that it can still be used for the benefit of the tribe, even if that tribe is now so large that it has become a nation controlling an Empire. From the sarcastic tone with which he goes on to describe the subsequent history of "Recessional," it seems clear that as far as he is concerned it has failed as a "*nuzzur-wattu.*" The way in which it has been effortlessly absorbed into English institutional life (and therefore neutralised) is symptomatic of precisely the process that it was originally intended as a warning against.

England's disarmament policy (for Kipling, a prominent feature of this process) is also ironically alluded to here as among the more dangerous consequences of this hubristic optimism, and this requires more detailed discussion. Why does Kipling consider disarmament so dangerous? Because he sees it as a product of "liberal 'principle'" and "liberal 'principle,'" as he says in one of his withering asides in chapter 3, "so far as I have observed ends not seldom in bloodshed" (93). Kipling's domino-theory goes like this: "liberal 'principle'" creates a political climate in which radicals can exist; radicals never have the national interest at heart and promote disarmament; disarmament means that England will not be able to defend the Empire, nor in the end herself; defencelessness, like pride, tempts Fate. (Kipling had been predicting the First World War from the mid 1890s and clearly anticipated the Second which he very nearly lived to see.) He expounds most of these fears in chapter 4 in an extended reminiscence about the "progressives" whom he met after returning to England in 1889. The passage is too long to give in full (it contains some of his best political invective), but its main thrust is that these individuals, who are social parasites in league with "liberals," understand nothing about the Empire and spend their time preparing to snatch away "England's arms when she isn't looking . . . so that when she wants to fight she'll find she can't" (127). (Kipling's anti-liberal, anti-radical views as he spells them out here are incidentally identical to those he had expressed thirty years earlier in his political parable, "The Mother Hive" from *Actions and Reactions*.) Writing *Something of Myself* in the mid 1930s, with England still pursuing a policy of disarmament, Kipling is looking back and showing how he thinks the present situation developed from a wrongheaded optimism which allowed the radicals and "liberals," the enemies within, to gain power. If *Something of Myself* has one principal concern apart from giving some account of Kipling's life, it is to bombard the reader with warnings that unless England stops indulging in a self-destructive national pride, it is heading for disaster.

III

The third layer which I intend to consider leads on naturally from what I have just been saying about Kipling's conception of Fate and England. One might call this layer "What do they know of England who only

England know?" since it is primarily concerned with Kipling's very mixed feelings about England and what it is to be English. He himself seems always to have felt a foreigner in England. If *Something of Myself*, unlike many autobiographies, is deliberately not a search for the Self, it is very much a search for a Home. It is the autobiography of an "orphan" looking for somewhere to belong to, somewhere to put down roots. Kipling emphasises how many "worlds" opened up to him as a writer, but the interesting thing is that as a man each new "world" either abandoned him or had in its turn to be abandoned: India, Southsea, Westward Ho!, India again, London, America, England and South Africa, until finally he found "The Very-Own House" in Sussex. Describing his return to his parents in India in 1882, he says: "my English years fell away, nor ever, I think, came back in full strength" (85). On his last visit to India in 1891, just before his parents came "Home" for good, he says: "this was my last look round the only real home I had yet known" (138). The Anglo-Indians' natural confusion (which Kipling is deliberately bringing out here) about whether "Home" was England, or India where they spent most of their adult lives, could never in his own case be finally resolved. England was always to remain "Home" for him, and yet a foreign country, and even English to be in a sense a foreign language. He recounts how he and his sister as small children would be sent in by their Indian servants to see their parents

> with the caution "Speak English now to Papa and Mama." So one spoke "English," haltingly translated out of the vernacular idiom that one thought and dreamed in. (56)

In 1882 he finds himself back in Bombay "where I was born, moving among sights and smells that made me deliver in the vernacular sentences whose meaning I knew not" (85). Describing his very first visit to England (or it may be his second, since he seems to conflate the two) he says:

> There was next a dark land, and a darker room full of cold, in one wall of which a white woman made naked fire, and I cried aloud with dread, for I had never before seen a grate. (58)

This passage not only implies the "sahib consciousness" with which Kipling was naturally brought up and maintained all his life ("white" women doing servants' work), but also just how strange and foreign England (that "dark land") was always to remain to him. After the unsuccessful attempt to settle in Vermont, Kipling returns to England in search of a Home. Finally he buys Bateman's, "The Very-Own House" as he emphatically calls it, although for years after this he and his family continued to spend six months of every year in South Africa. Bateman's and the surrounding area of Sussex were for Kipling the nearest he ever came to a Home after India, but he retained to the very end of his life a sense of the English as foreigners. As he says of them in one of his strategic parentheses: "(The inhabitants of that country never look further than their annual seaside resorts)" (173).

Kipling, it seems from *Something of Myself*, had been aware from very early on that this enforced detachment put him in a unique position to comment on England and the English. He recounts, after his return in 1889, how

> I had been at work on the rough of a set of verses called later "The English Flag" and had boggled at a line which had to be a key-line but persisted in going "soft." As was the custom between us, I asked into the air: "What am I trying to get *at*?" Instantly the Mother, with her quick flutter of the hands: "You're *trying* to say: 'What do they know of England who only England know?'" The father confirmed. (126)

"What do they know of England who only England know?" is a perspective constantly offered to the reader throughout the autobiography. It is true that there are sides to the English character (English humour, for instance) for which Kipling shows an uncontrolled delight:

> There is no race so dowered as the English with the gift of talking real, rich, allusive, cut-in-and-out "skittles." Americans are too much anecdotards; the French too much orators for this light-handed game, and neither race delivers itself so unreservedly to mirth as we do. (171)

At the same time, other aspects fill him with frustrated amazement. How England can control so vast an Empire and yet its inhabitants remain so complacently insular in their interests and outlook is a subject to which he returns on several occasions. This insularity he finds as rampant in London literary circles ("London is a parish," he warns the young would-be writer in chapter 8), as it is among the bourgeoisie or the village community. The blinkered bourgeoisie are firmly nailed in place in the passage following his account of watching the man cut his throat in Villiers Street. He recalls how

> through all this shifting, shouting brotheldom the pious British householder and his family bored their way back from the theatres, eyes-front and fixed, as though not seeing. (124)

In this picture of the English who refuse to see what is all around them, we have a perfect example of how Kipling uses the "attributes of words in relation to other words" (112), since the whole tone here is set by the ironic proximity of the words "brotheldom" and "pious." For Kipling, the enemy within is not only to be found among "liberals" and radicals, but also in the so-called English virtues or in the kind of provincial small-mindedness that he attacks so often in the stories and poems, in the refusal to think internationally, to imagine a world beyond the English Channel. This complacency is merely another way of tempting Fate.

It would be inappropriate, however, to finish this section on so pessimistic a note, since Kipling himself carefully places an expression of his belief in the English character at the very end of the chronological account of his life (the end of chapter 7). That he was particularly preoccupied at this time both with the dangers that he saw besetting England and with England's ability to survive them can be seen from the conclusion to the speech which he delivered to the Royal Society of St George on 6 May 1935, a transcript of which is reproduced in Lord Birkenhead's biography. In the main body of the speech he sums up what he feels has been happening to England since the First World War, reiterating several of the warnings with which I am concerned in this article, particularly those against disarmament. After admitting that England's post-War policy of "State-defended defencelessness" seems to have been reversed in the last year, and hoping that it is not too late, Kipling finishes with this deeply-felt eulogy to the English spirit:

> And yet, the genius of our race fights for us in the teeth of doctrine! The abiding springs of the English spirit are not of yesterday or the day before. They draw from an immemorial continuity of the Nation's life under its own Sovereigns. They are fed by a human relationship more intimate and more far-reaching than the world has ever known. They make part of a mystery as unpurchasable as it is incommunicable.[5]

To suggest that "The Swedish Lady's Tale" (as I shall call it) at the end of chapter 7 of *Something of Myself* is a similar expression of Kipling's faith in "the abiding springs of the English spirit" may perhaps seem absurd. And so it is, unless one is sufficiently attuned to Kipling's late manner and his fondness for the "parable-anecdote." (Briefly, I would define the "parable-anecdote" as an apparently quite trivial, even ludicrous, story which by virtue of its placing and the use of "pointers" shows itself to be simultaneously about something quite different. The device is not uncommon in the later stories, and I shall be discussing two further instances of it in *Something of Myself* in Section IV.) "The Swedish Lady's Tale" begins:

> At that epoch staid women attached to the public wash-houses washed in a glorious lather of soap, worked up with big bunches of finest pine-shavings (when you think of it, a sponge is almost as dirty a tool as the permanent tooth-brush of the European), men desirous of the most luxurious bath known to civilisation. But foreigners did not always catch the idea. Hence this tale told to me at a winter resort in the deep, creamy contralto of the North by a Swedish lady who took, and pronounced, her English rather biblically. The introit you can imagine for yourself. (218–19)

The finale then tells how one of these "staid women" comes to wash an Englishman. He retreats deep into the water and shouts at her to go away. She refuses, saying that she has come to wash him. He turns over on his face and waves his legs in the air, telling her to "Go a-dam-way away!" So she complains to the Direktor that there is a "mads" in her bath who will not let her wash him. To which the Direktor replies: "Oh, that are not a mads. That are an Englishman. He will himself—he will wash himself" (219).

On the face of it this is just a bit of farce in a Swedish bath-house; smug, insular, piously bourgeois, on the edge of disaster, the English may be, but for Kipling there is no race that can match their incorrigible and inimitable gift for sheer "lunacy." Certainly, he valued what he saw as this peculiarly English gift very highly, but that in itself hardly seems to warrant or explain the placing of the anecdote at the conclusion of the chronological account of his life, nor does it rescue the anecdote itself from the charge of being really rather silly and extraneous. What does rescue it and reaffirms Kipling's belief in the English spirit are two puns, puns which are only made possible by Kipling's deliberate use (which he carefully draws attention to) of the Swedish lady's Biblical English and phrasing. The puns are both contained in the very last sentence: "He *will* himself—he will *wash* himself" (my emphasis). In that "He *will* himself" is a concentrated expression of Kipling's belief that what is uniquely distinctive about the English will survive, because they can and do "will" themselves; that is, both individually and collectively they create their own destiny. (This contrasts interestingly with Kipling's own sense, in his working life at least, of not having "willed" himself.) And "he will wash himself" asserts Kipling's belief in the Englishman's ability to purify and renew himself; thus (somehow) surviving all the dangers against which he is so busily being warned.

IV

One of the most persistent dangers which Kipling is warning against is America. Kipling seems to have been initially very attracted to the United States (although one would never guess this from the autobiography), but the experience of living there radically changed his attitude. In a striking passage in chapter 5, he remarks that

> Every nation, like every individual, walks in a vain show—else it could not live with itself—but I never got over the wonder of a people who, having extirpated the aboriginals of their continent more completely than any modern race had ever done, honestly believed that they were a godly little New England community, setting examples to brutal mankind. This wonder I used to explain to Theodore Roosevelt, who made the glass cases of Indian relics shake with his rebuttals. (153)

As I said in Section I, Kipling continually criticises the United States's lack of any conception of "law-abidingness"; he is equally scathing about its desire to gain an Empire for itself, and to tell countries like England how to run theirs. Here in chapter 5 he wryly goes on to recall how

> The next time I met him [Theodore Roosevelt] was in England, not long
> after his country had acquired the Philippines, and he—like an elderly
> lady with one babe—yearned to advise England on colonial administra-
> tion. His views were sound enough, for his subject was Egypt as it was be-
> ginning to be then, and his text "Govern or get out." He consulted
> several people as to how far he could go. I assured him that the English
> would take anything from him, but were racially immune to advice.
> (154)

Kipling neatly manages to fuse together a warning to England, a delighted joke about the English character, and a further example of the
United States's addiction to minding other countries' business. He was
quick to appreciate why they needed to cultivate and manipulate internal hatred against England, so that it became "the hoop round the forty-
four (as they were then)" (151), but their "lawlessness" he could never
forgive and their pretensions to Empire-building he could only view with
a mixture of headshaking bewilderment and alarm. In chapter 5, the first
half of which is principally concerned with America, Kipling suggests
some of his other reservations: the gross materialism, for instance, and
the debilitating effect of the death of so many "autochthonous 'Americans'" (157) in the Civil War—a point he had made years before through
Mrs Burton, a character in "The Edge of the Evening" (*A Diversity of
Creatures*). It is, however, 'lawlessness' and Empire-building which, I
think, form the basis of his deeply distrustful attitude towards that country. In fact, so important are these two particular reservations, that he re-
states them again towards the end of chapter 7, albeit in a characteristically oblique way.

First, there is America's lack of "law-abidingness." He has been describing the kindness and goodwill which he and his wife experienced
during their trip across Canada in 1906. But, he says, there was

> always the marvel—to which the Canadians seemed insensible—
> . . . that on one side of an imaginary line should be Safety, Law, Honour,
> and Obedience, and on the other frank, brutal, decivilisation; and that,
> despite this, Canada should be impressed by any aspect whatever of the
> United States. (216)

With this firmly in the forefront of our minds, he moves on to American
Colonialism. His reservations about this are here typically concealed
under what seems to be nothing more than an unconnected and apparently quite trivial anecdote told to him by William, the black Pullman
porter who supervised their trip. "William's Tale" is, in fact, like "The
Swedish Lady's Tale," a "parable-anecdote." (The other main "parable-
anecdote" in *Something of Myself* occurs in chapter 6 where Kipling and
his friend Jameson watch the lawn-mower pony trying unsuccessfully to
imitate the way the zebras get under the fence. The only difference is that
in that case Kipling spells out the moral—that the pony is the British, the

zebras the Boers. In "William's Tale" and "The Swedish Lady's Tale" we have to work it out for ourselves.) "William's Tale" begins:

> Before we parted, William told us a tale of a friend of his who was consumed with desire to be a Pullman porter "bekase he had watched me doin' it, an' thought he could do it—jest by watchin' me." (This was the burden of his parable, like a deep-toned locomotive bell.) (216)

In the end William does arrange a job for his friend as a Pullman porter in the car next to his own. Knowing that his friend will soon be needing his help, William puts all his "folks" to bed early and, sure enough, all his friend's "folks" want to be put to bed at the same time. He, of course, cannot manage, despite the fact that he has watched how William does it. William eventually finds him in the broom-closet with all his "folks" banging on the door. So William puts them all to bed in a trice, explaining about his friend, at which they all laugh "heaps an' heaps." "But," ends William, "he thought he could do it havin' watched me do it" (217). Kipling adds another layer to William's story about his friend who thought he could be a Pullman porter just by watching him, and neatly turns it into a story about American Empire-building. He does this partly by the anti-American context into which he places the anecdote and partly by the use of another of his parenthetical "pointers": "(This was the burden of his parable)." William's "parable" is self-explanatory; Kipling's is that America cannot run an Empire just by watching how England does it. It is pleasing to notice that for the purposes of his parable Kipling is quite happy to have a black Pullman porter stand for England.

V

According to Carrington, Mrs Kipling said that *Something of Myself* was to "deal with his life from the point of view of his work,"[6] and in this article I have been trying to show how this remark is true in the double sense that it not only focuses on the work, but is written in the point of view of the work, particularly in the point of view of the late manner. This is especially important if we are to understand the relationship of "Working-tools," the last chapter, to the rest of the autobiography. As far as the surface layer of *Something of Myself* is concerned, the relationship is clear. After seven chapters in which he presents a more or less chronological account of his life up to the time he received the Nobel Prize, Kipling abandons chronology and concludes with a chapter in which he ruminates about his craft. Here he plays the part of the old professional passing on a few do's and don'ts of the trade to the young apprentice, or that of the much-loved author allowing his curious readers a peep into his "mould-loft" (240). Read in this way, it is engaging and not uninformative (for instance, about how crucial a role his parents and the Club played as early audience and critics of his work, or what influence his training as a journalist had on his technique as a short-story writer), but, as with so much of *Something of Myself,* he always seems to stop just when he is getting really interesting. If, however, we read the chapter as I have been suggesting that we should read the rest of the autobiography—that is, alert to the possibility of submerged layers—then it has a rather different and far more vital connection to the earlier chapters.

From this point of view, what is most distinctive about "Working-tools" is that it is full of warnings; it is, in fact, made up of one warning after another. These are not, of course, all warnings of the same kind (some are warnings about England, some about writing, some about the Jews, some about "psychical experiences," etc.), but the result of the accumulated weight of all these warnings is to create a highly charged atmosphere of imminent danger. To the psychoanalyst this may suggest that Kipling knows (subconsciously, if not consciously) that he is about to die; for my purposes it is interesting for other reasons. "Working-tools" is full of warnings, because that is what on one level the autobiography itself has been about. I have been trying to show how *Something of Myself* is made up of a number of layers below the surface layer, and I said at the outset that all these layers were interrelated, and so they are. They are interrelated, because they are worked together in the telling of the story of his life, and also because they all essentially share the same preoccupation—with England. England in Kipling's youth and early middle age, England at the time of writing, England in the immediate future, Kipling warning England that she is getting closer and closer to catastrophe; that is the subtext of his autobiography. If one were trying to choose a subtitle for "Working-tools" (perhaps even for *Something of Myself*), that subtitle might appropriately be the motto which Kipling carved on the sundial at Bateman's: "Later than you think." In the last chapter Kipling is reinforcing by a sustained salvo of warnings his conviction that for England (and the contemporary English readers) it is "later than they think." He cues us into this layer by repeated emphasis on the idea of warning, by the placing of abrupt and deliberately enigmatical sentences, such as "Which things are a portent," "That simple explanation may stand as a warning," and by the use of parenthetical "pointers"—"('And which it may subsequently transpire')." There are also more overt clues. Discussing the reception of "The Islanders," Kipling recalls how he was accused of saying

> that "a year of compulsory service" would be "effortless, ordered," etc. etc.—with the rider that I didn't know much about it. This perversion was perversified by a man who ought to have known better; and I suppose I should have known that it was part of the "effortless, ordered" drift towards Armageddon. You ask: "Why inflict on us legends of your Middle Ages?" Because in life as in literature, its sole enduring record, is no age. Men and Things come round again, eternal as the seasons. (235)

Here he clearly seems to be returning to his previous warnings about the dangers of disarmament. He is also, I think, giving his justification for the spate of warnings in this last chapter and indeed throughout *Something of Myself* as a whole.

In general, *Something of Myself* is precisely the kind of autobiography one should expect from Kipling: vivid, ironic, apparently nonchalant, cryptic and above all layered. It is misleading to read it as if it were separate from the other later work; it is an integral part of that work, adopting the same technical devices and sharing many of the same preoccupations—with Fate, pride, complacency, disarmament, American Colonialism, and the English character. Considered exclusively as autobiography, it cannot be claimed as one of the great autobiographies (and even in terms of Kipling's own work it is less successful than the best of the short stories where the submerged layers blend more unobtrusively), but attentively read it is far more complex and interesting, and even in its oblique disclosures more informative than it has ever been given credit for. What stands out, apart from its tone which is persistently more ironic than it appears, is a sense of division, and it is this paradoxically which gives *Something of Myself* a kind of unity. This sense of division is clearly present in several of the quotations I have given: in the anecdote about the man cutting his throat, where the window shifts from being a mirror which "I" looks into to a window through which he looks out; in the patronising Canadian students who in one sentence are playing the fool with Kipling and are in the trenches the next; in the England that is "Home" and a foreign country; and in the continual contrasts between black and white, dark and light, upper and lower. And this is the note on which *Something of Myself* closes, as Kipling with characteristic originality and nerve changes in the last two pages to the posthumous tense and ends where all autobiographies should logically end—with the words "my death":

> Left and right of the table were two big globes, on one of which a great airman had once outlined in white paint those air-routes to the East and Australia which were well in use before my death. (242)

Notes

1. C.A. Bodelsen, *Aspects of Kipling's Art* (Manchester: Manchester U.P., 1964), pp. 100, 88.

2. *Something of Myself, The Sussex Edition of the Complete Works in Prose and Verse of Rudyard Kipling* (London: Macmillan, 1937–9), XXXI, 208. All subsequent references to this work refer to the above edition and will be inserted parenthetically in the text. In the absence of a definitive edition of Kipling's work, I have used the Sussex edition since this was the one which Kipling himself was helping to prepare when he died.

3. J.M.S. Tompkins, *The Art of Rudyard Kipling* (London: Methuen, 1959), p. 230.

4. Rudyard Kipling, *Uncollected Prose I, The Sussex Edition* (London: Macmillan, 1937–9), **XXIX**, p. 294.

5. Lord Birkenhead, *Rudyard Kipling* (London: Weidenfeld and Nicolson, 1978), p. 351.

6. Charles Carrington, *Rudyard Kipling: His Life and Work* (London: Macmillan, 1955), p. 501.

The Kipling Controversy

Rudyard Kipling and the Establishment: A Humanistic Dilemma

Rudyard Kipling's history as a writer illustrates one of the most serious problems in modern criticism, the relationship between members of the Establishment (in both England and the United States) and writers who, for one reason or another, do not seem to satisfy the Establishment's expectations of what they *should* be saying and writing.

If, in part, my review of the problem is anecdotal, it derives from my strong sense that Kipling led a fascinating life. In recent years I have been reading, collecting, and annotating a large number of interviews with, and recollections of, Kipling by people who knew him. There is no better way to learn about the personality of a writer than to go through the steps involved in the compilation of such an anthology. From the hundreds, and perhaps thousands, of anecdotes that have been recorded, I would like to cite three to illustrate the vivid qualities of Kipling's personality.

First, however, may I note the divisions in Kipling's life. There is no consensus as to which years form a particular phase of development, and I should like to make clear at least my own point of view, to help the reader follow some later statements.

The first twelve years of Kipling's life, from 1865 to 1877, form a distinct unit. Joseph Rudyard Kipling was born in Bombay to John Lockwood Kipling, an artist of Yorkshire stock, who was serving as the curator of the Lahore Museum. His mother, Alice Macdonald of Birmingham, came from an artistic family; one sister married Edward Burne-Jones, another Edward Poynter, distinguished artists in their own right. Between 1871 and 1877 Kipling lived in Southsea, England, and received an education while living, as an unhappy and very lonely child, among people he did not like.

The second period extends from 1878 to 1882, the span of years during which he attended the United Services College, or Westward Ho!, in North Devon, and became friends with a number of boys who were

* Reprinted from the *South Atlantic Quarterly* 81, no. 2 (Spring 1982): 162–77, by permission of the publisher. © 1982 by Duke University Press.

213

later to earn honors and fame as generals and admirals in the armed services.

The third period stretches from 1882 to 1889, when Kipling, having returned to India, became a reporter, editor, and factotum for the widely read and influential *Civil and Military Gazette* in Lahore, and for the *Pioneer* in Allahabad. His notoriety began in these years with the publication of the flashy, satirical *Departmental Ditties* (he became known as a smart alec, and the reputation later proved difficult to live down) and of *Plain Tales from the Hills*, a series of 2,000-word stories originally printed as newspaper columns in the *Civil and Military Gazette*.

The next period—which runs between 1890 and 1910—can only be described as the middle years. They consist of confused alternations between England, where he became a literary lion and published a stream of successful books (*Soldiers Three, Wee Willie Winkie*, and *The Light That Failed*); the United States, where he lived for several years; and South Africa, where he enjoyed the friendship of Cecil Rhodes. It was an enormously productive period, and saw the publication of *Barrack-Room Ballads, The Jungle Book, The Seven Seas, Captains Courageous, Stalky & Co.* (his thinly disguised account of life at Westward Ho!), *Kim*, and a dozen other books. In 1907 he won the Nobel Prize for Literature, the first time it was awarded to an Englishman.

The final years of Rudyard Kipling, from 1910 to 1936, are somber, rapidly darkening years. In 1915 he lost his son John during the Battle of Loos, but did not abandon—for a full two years—his hope that the "missing in action" classification might be cleared up by John's return. His stories became more complex, more heavily symbolic. Illness and death were more prominent subjects in his fiction; cancer seemed to be the controlling metaphor. He was disheartened by the deaths of many of his friends, by critical attacks made on his political ideas (many of which were misrepresented—but of this more later), and by his general sense that England was abandoning its responsibilities as an imperial power in the postwar years. Perhaps it did not take any great clairvoyance in the late 1920's and early 1930's to see the probability of a second world war. But Kipling's consciousness of the close relationship between the failure of the national will to protect its vital interests and the startling, swift rise of fascism and Nazism on the continent of Europe is worth remembering even at this late date.

The first glimpse of Kipling I want to share with you is of a jack-of-all-trades in the pressroom in the *Civil and Military Gazette*. Because the type for the paper was set by Indians ignorant of the English language, proofreading was "a trial to the soul." Kipling had his troubles in the printing office, too, for his poems and articles had to be cut to fit the available space. The foreman used to say to him, "Your po'try, good sir, just coming proper length to-day."

During Kipling's seven years' hard in India, he endured—is there a better word?—his apprenticeship. Imagine, if you can, the Indian press-room on a hot night. It is lighted by flickering dips, with a hurricane lantern here and there. Half-naked men turn the presses. They look picturesque in the uncertain light as they loll against the walls and wait for their call. The presses loom as mysterious and ghastly, and from the far end comes the tick-tick of the type being set up by yawners in white sheets. They carry candles. Often the grease sputters on to the type. Little naked boys, who have no known business in the world there, have curled up on one of the big tables and gone to sleep.

E. Kay Robinson, assistant editor of the *Civil and Military Gazette* of Lahore, has left us a vivid picture of Kipling in these surroundings, and a half-amused, half-annoyed comment on the amount of ink Kipling used to throw about. "In the heat of summer white cotton trousers and thin vest constituted his office attire," Robinson reminisced for *McClure's Magazine* in July, 1896, "and by the day's end he was spotted all over like a Dalmatian dog. He had a habit of dipping his pen frequently and deep into the ink-pot, and as all his movements were abrupt, almost jerky, the ink used to fly. When he darted into my room, as he used to do about one thing or another in connection with the contents of a paper a dozen times in the morning I had to shout to him to "stand off;" otherwise, as I knew by experience, the abrupt halt he would make, and the flourish with which he placed the proof in his hand before me, would send the penful of ink—he always had a *full* pen in his hand—flying over me. Driving or sometimes walking home to breakfast in his light attire plentifully besprinkled with ink, his spectacled face peeping out under an enormous, mushroom-shaped pith hat, Kipling was a quaint-looking object. This was in the hot weather, when Lahore lay blistering month after month under the sun, and every white woman and half of the white men had fled to cooler altitudes in the Himalayas, and only those men were left who, like Kipling and myself, had to stay. So it mattered little in what costume we went to and from the office. In the winter, when "society" had returned to Lahore, Kipling was rather scrupulous in the matter of dress, but his lavishness in the matter of ink changed not with the seasons." (Christopher Plummer, in the first ten minutes of John Huston's splendid film version of *The Man Who Would Be King*, provides a wonderfully faithful image of Kipling in a white suit generously besprinkled with ink spots).

The second glimpse of Kipling is a poignant moment in March, 1899. He fell ill in New York, with one lung seriously inflamed, at the same time that his daughter, Josephine, suffered from pneumonia. When the inflammation spread to the other lung, newspapers all over the world carried the news on their front pages. As the medical bulletins changed from "serious" condition to "alarmingly difficult" respiration to the ominous note, "greatest apprehension for the outcome," a worldwide demonstration of affection and sympathy for Kipling, such as no other writer had ever experienced, took place. But when the crisis passed—when, after passing out of danger and still desperately weak, he lay in his hospital bed—Josephine, who lacked her father's reserve of strength, sent her love to "Daddy and all"—and died the next morning. By order of the physicians, the news of Josephine's condition was kept from her father. Kipling knew nothing of her death until after her burial. When the time came to tell him, Frank Doubleday, the publisher, was chosen to speak the words. "It was the hardest task I ever undertook," said Doubleday, who had been in almost hourly attendance upon the sick man, "but it had to be done. I took a seat beside him and told the story in as few words as I could. He listened in silence till I had finished, then turned his face to the wall."

The third story about Kipling worth recounting at this point—and there are many more, for nobody who met Kipling could forget him, and the literature on Kipling's personality is enormous—has to do with his love of Sussex, to which he moved in 1902. There he lived in a stone Jacobean house called "Bateman's," and there he fell in love with the people and the land. Above all, he admired the changelessness of Sussex. Behind his outward championship of modern progress (I am quoting Fletcher Allen's beautifully written essay in the *New York Times Magazine* of April 27, 1924)

> he loves the unalterable, untouched something in the Sussex people. He has been careful to safeguard Sussex mediaevalism by refusing to install the telephone at Bateman's, and where it has been possible has preserved the ancient customs and traditions on the farm. To this day, therefore, all the gates at Bateman's are "heave-hatches," just as they were in Saxon times—simple bits of rail fence, which may be taken out of their mortises and put in again. True, he has an American motor plow, but it is held in disrepute by the natives, and Kipling rejoices in himself when his bailiff gives expression to his disgust: "This ol' motor plow," says the bailiff, "may be all right in Ameriky, but it don't turn the earth not a spit deep—taint no good for the honor of the land."
>
> The honor of the land indeed. One remembers Kipling's almost feverish insistence for that honor, that it shall be known and recognized. Round about him are the oak, the hawthorn and the ash. It is Burwash timber that he means in:
>
> > Of all the trees that grow so fair,
> > Old England to adorn,
> > Greater are none beneath the sun
> > Than Oak and Ash and Thorn.

Such anecdotes reveal the human side of Kipling, of the real man behind the legend and the reputation.

Currently Kipling's books are selling at the rate of approximately 250,000 copies a year, more in the United Kingdom than in the United States, of course, but the record of sales—taken altogether—is fairly creditable for an author now almost half a century dead and buried. Even those who do not customarily care about reading have—whether consciously or not—adopted attitudes and quoted lines from Kipling's writings as if he were "the Great Anon." Once Kipling's son John praised "a piece of poetry" that he had found in a book, and was surprised to learn that his father had written it. By that year—1914—Rudyard Kipling's novels and short stories had sold millions of copies, and his poems had become the currency of all English-speaking nations; his opinions on anything and everything were more widely disseminated than those of George Bernard Shaw, Arnold Bennett, and H. G. Wells combined. More than one military historian has noted that British soldiers may have learned to talk like Tommy Atkins *after* reading *Barrack-Room Ballads, Departmental Ditties, Plain Tales from the Hills,* and *Soldiers Three.* Baden-Powell's "wolf-cub" organization, the Boy Scouts, was based directly on the *Jungle Books.* Practically all inscriptions used by the War Graves Commission to commemorate the fallen dead of England— including the famous phrase, "Their name liveth for evermore"—were written by Kipling. He coined catch-phrases like "the white man's burden" and "the bear that walks like a man." In the preface to his *Dictionary,* Dr. Samuel Johnson remarked that every quotation contributes something to the stability or enlargement of the language. To be occasionally quoted, as Alexander Smith once said, is the only fame some writers care for. But Kipling was and is quoted more than "occasionally": for example, the third edition of *The Oxford Dictionary of Quotations* (1979) lists more than two hundred Kiplingisms. He illustrates marvelously well the process whereby one man's wit becomes all men's wisdom.

Many of us recall Kipling's vivid verses on the Fuzzy-Wuzzy as "a pore benighted 'eathen but a first-class fightin' man," as well as those on Gunga Din:

> "Though I've belted you and flayed you,
> By the livin' Gawd that made you,
> You're a better man than I am, Gunga Din!"

We have heard singers mangle the ballad,

> On the road to Mandalay,
> Where the flyin-fishes play,
> An' the dawn comes up like thunder outer China 'crost the Bay!

We grew up with the exhortations of "If," that poem so often immortalized in needlework: "If you can talk with crowds and keep your virtue, / Or walk with Kings—nor lose the common touch. . . ." And, though many would have difficulty in naming "Tommy" as the poem in which the phrase "thin red line of 'eroes" was first recorded, we can greet as an old friend the lines which read:

> "For It's Tommy this, an' Tommy that, an' 'Chuck 'im out, the brute!'
> But it's 'Saviour of 'is country,' when the guns begin to shoot."

With Kipling it is as if we are dealing with a bottomless well. The recent Russian invasion of Afghanistan drew up from that well a quotation (from "The Young British Soldier") that has since been widely publicized:

When you're wounded and left on Afghanistan's plains,
And the women come out to cut up what remains,
Jest roll to your rifle and blow out your brains
    An' go to your Gawd like a soldier.

But so much of Kipling is uncredited, let me pause for a moment to remind us all that he first formulated the phrases "hot and bothered," "I've taken my fun where I've found it," "An' I learned about women from 'er," and "The female of the species is more deadly than the male." Perhaps many of us would like to forget forever the male chauvinist remark, "A woman is only a woman, but a good cigar is a smoke"—yet in its time it was the same as a proverb. It was Kipling who, in a poem on public waste, denounced "Little Tin Gods on Wheels." After the Boer War, he wrote, "We have had a jolly good lesson, and it serves us jolly well right!" And he added, "We have forty million reasons for failure, but not a single excuse." The very phrase "east of Suez" is Kipling's; there "the best is like the worst," for there "aren't no Ten Commandments, an' a man can raise a thirst." He told us first that "the Colonel's Lady an' Judy O'Grady / Are sisters under their skins!" He put into words what soldiers all over the world have suspected instinctively: "The backbone of the Army is the Non-commissioned Man!" And if I quoted only the first line of the famous couplet in "The Winners," "Down to Gehenna or up to the Throne," you can complete it without thinking twice: "He travels the fastest who travels alone." We have a vulgarized version in American slang about hitting a mule with a two-by-four to get his attention; but see how much better Kipling said it: "If you hit a pony over the nose at the outset of your acquaintance, he may not love you, but he will take a deep interest in your movements ever afterwards." How often Kipling said it once and for all, for all of us, as in the famous exchange in *The Light That Failed*: "What did the Governor of North Carolina say to the Governor of South Carolina?"—"Excellent notion. It *is* a long time between drinks." He asked us first the question, "It's pretty, but is it Art?" One of the finest after-dinner toasts I know is Kipling's famous conclusion to the St. George's Day Dinner of 1920: "For what there is of it—for such as it is—and for what it may be worth—will you drink to England and the English?"

We all want to reclaim from the bottomless depths of our readings over a lifetime that which has been said with special felicity, with an energy that attracts and sustains attention, with conviction, and with memorable brevity. A quotable line need not be beautiful; it does not necessarily testify to the joy of living; it may be cheaply sentimental; it is seldom true in any absolute, widely agreeable, or final sense. Nevertheless, how many of Kipling's formulations are we unwilling to forget! They are now part of the folk consciousness. Arthur O'Shaughnessy's "Ode" anticipated Kipling's popularity as one of the great "Music-makers" of world literature:

> With wonderful deathless ditties
> We build up the world's great cities,
>   And out of a fabulous story
>   We fashion an empire's glory. . . .

Why, then, is it possible to write—as E. L. Gilbert wrote in 1965 when editing a collection of critical reviews about Kipling—that "it would be difficult to think of another artist, dead thirty years, who continues to be at once so popular and so cordially hated as Rudyard Kipling is today"? *Hated*? That is a strong word even for a living writer who helps to change public opinion on controversial issues, perhaps in the form of newspaper columns. But columnists like George Will and James Reston do not pretend to be novelists, or writers of short stories and poems. Kipling, once he left India in 1889, was not a newspaper columnist, but a serious and dedicated man of letters. We are confronted here by a genuine problem: the hostility of generations of critics, many of them men of good will, toward Kipling both as man and as artist. This continuing distortion of what Kipling actually wrote obviously goes beyond the back-handed compliment of T. S. Eliot, "We have to defend Kipling against the charge of excessive lucidity. . . ." There was abrasiveness from the beginning, and it stimulated a counterreaction: too much had been claimed. Oscar Wilde spoke for many when he sneered at the remarkable things that Kipling had seen through keyholes. Andrew Lang noted as early as 1891 that Kipling's "false air of hardness" contradicted the "sentiment in his tales of childish life." Henry James resented Kipling's unearned reputation for wisdom, and described the young Englishman, but recently returned from India, as "a strangely clever youth who has stolen the formidable mask of maturity and rushes about making people jump with the deep sounds, the sportive exaggerations of tone, that issue from its painted lips."

Even today, it is easy enough to compile a damning bill of indictment: that Kipling is insincere ("a mixture of Isaiah and Mr. 'Enry 'Awkins"), brutal, obsessed with death, perpetually out of date (he was never a democrat, he detested female suffragism, he despised the very concept of mass education), "knowing" about sham-technical details, grossly unfair to the quality of education and the civility of the soldiers and sailors who became his special province of authority, and perpetually arrested at the sixth-form level of humor (elaborate practical jokes in *Stalky & Co.*, the faking of a complete medieval manuscript in "Dayspring Mishandled," and so on).

Something can be said to counter each of these charges. Indeed, Hilton Brown, trying to defend Kipling, wrote a lively book back in 1945 that some critics thought might herald a "revival," though the revival did not come, at least not among the serious liberal critics who, in both England and the United States, constitute an Establishment.

The problem in Kipling's case is a humanistic dilemma, and a truly extraordinary one. Kipling—as E. L. Gilbert noted in his review of the development of Kipling criticism—is wholly unlike other writers whose lasting reputation has been made by "the long-term respect of serious readers and responsible critics." Kipling is an extremely popular writer (I really ought to mention the enormous sales of his works in the Soviet Union). But "the political views with which his name is commonly associated are considered old-fashioned, if not actually dangerous." Moreover, he has no "serious critical reputation" except among a very few members of his audience. Some five years ago Malcolm Cowley wrote to me on the question of the commercial viability of a *Viking Portable Library Kipling*. He said, with considerable distaste (since he did not care much for Kipling personally), that Kipling's reputation had declined so seriously that it would not come back again during his lifetime or mine. He added that he was as sure of his prophecy as he could be about any event in the future.

In Rudyard Kipling we have a writer whose reputation is not so much in decline—on this point I would disagree with Cowley—as it is unclear, unfixed. It is easy enough to attribute the problem of Kipling's reputation to the way in which Kipling is seen as a political animal by those who dislike him, and as an artist by those who do. But are the political issues with which Kipling dealt obsolete, no longer of interest to us in the 1980's? Has the heat of the battles in which he fought died down?

Before I answer this, here are a few more of the adverse judgments rendered, over the years, on Kipling's work. In 1900 Robert Buchanan, a Scottish author-critic of some standing in the late Victorian era, denounced Kipling as a "hooligan," a man who rode the crest of "a great back-wave" which was irresistibly sweeping civilization "in the direction of absolute barbarism." Buchanan characterized Kipling as one who, with his brutish jingoism and his cockney vulgarity, adumbrated in his single person "all that is most deplorable, all that is most retrograde and savage, in the restless and uninstructed Hooliganism of the time."

Max Beerbohm hated Kipling. Over a period of thirty years he produced at least nine savage caricatures of the writer and two critical articles. Reading these attacks, one would never guess that Beerbohm had acquired a reputation for self-control, for delicacy in his irony. In a parody written for *A Christmas Garland*, Beerbohm took on the manner of the poet he hated, in six lines "borrowed" from what he called "Police Station Ditties":

> Then it's collar 'im tight,
>   In the name o' the Lawd!

'Ustle 'im, shake 'im till 'e's sick!
Wot, 'e *would*, would 'e? Well,
Then yer've got ter give 'im 'Ell
An' it's trunch, trunch, truncheon does the trick!

In 1942, George Orwell wrote in a self-assured manner, not expecting contradiction, that for five literary generations

every enlightened person has despised him. . . . It is no use pretending that Kipling's view of life, as a whole, can be accepted or even forgiven by any civilised person. It is no use claiming, for instance, that when Kipling describes a British soldier beating a "nigger" with a cleaning rod in order to get money out of him, he is acting merely as a reporter and does not necessarily approve what he describes. There is not the slightest sign anywhere in Kipling's work that he disapproves of that kind of conduct—on the contrary, there is a definite strain of sadism in him, over and above the brutality which a writer of that type has to have. Kipling *is* a jingo imperialist, he *is* morally insensitive and aesthetically disgusting. It is better to start by admitting that. . . .

Lionel Trilling wanted to say something on behalf of the Kipling he had read and loved while he was growing up. But he found it difficult, perhaps impossible, to stomach Kipling's politics, and he separated Kipling's conservatism from that of Dr. Johnson, Edmund Burke, and Walter Scott. He went on in a language so withering I think it a wonder that anything remains of Kipling's reputation:

Kipling is not like these men; he is not generous, and, although he makes much to-do about manliness, he is not manly; and he has none of the *mind* of the few great Tories. His Toryism often had in it a lower-middle-class snarl of defeated gentility, and it is this, rather than his love of authority and force, that might suggest an affinity with Fascism. His imperialism is reprehensible not because it *is* imperialism, but because it is a puny and mindless imperialism. In short, Kipling is unloved and unlovable not by reason of his beliefs but by reason of the temperament that gave them literary expression. [And there is more, much more, in this vein:] I have said that the old antagonism between liberalism and Kipling is now abated by time and events, yet it is still worth saying, and it is not extravagant to say, that Kipling was one of liberalism's major intellectual misfortunes. . . . We must make no mistake about it—Kipling was an honest man and he loved the national virtues. But I suppose no man ever did more harm to the national virtues than Kipling did. He mixed them up with a swagger and swank, with bullying, ruthlessness, and self-righteousness, and he set them up as necessarily antagonistic to intellect. He made them stink in the nostrils of youth. . . .

That doesn't sound as if the political issues with which Kipling dealt are moribund; the heat of the battles in which he fought has not cooled down. It will do no good to repeat the "triumphantly know-nothing defenses" of imperialism which were made by many readers who admired

Kipling. These defenses all too often sought to protect Kipling's writings against the charge of jingoism by conveniently redefining the "jingo" as the protector of national virtues and various colonial populations. Moreover, politicians and retired army officers, many of them with Indian connections, believed passionately that they knew more about the subjects Kipling treated than mere literary critics did, or could, and the brutality with which they responded to unfriendly comments on their hero was not only arrogant and unforgiving, but guaranteed the continuing, and the deepening, of further controversy. For example, when Oscar Wilde characterized *Plain Tales from the Hills* as a book that made a reader feel as if he "were seated under a palm tree, reading life by superb flashes of vulgarity," an angry correspondent wrote to the *Times* protesting against Wilde's attack on vulgar Anglo-Indians. Wilde had to explain that neither he nor Kipling meant to imply that every Englishman in India was vulgar. It is not unusual, when one reviews the history of Kipling criticism, to come across a proposal that Kipling's works should be banned for the duration of World War II, or to a comparison (made by H. E. Bates) between Rudyard Kipling and Adolf Hitler, since both men liked swastikas!—or, to the anger of Kipling's official biographer, C. E. Carrington, against the statement made in a new history of English literature by "one of our abler young men," that *Kim* was "a typical defence of the policy of British expansion." Carrington exploded, "How can respectable writers demean themselves by such impudence? One might as well say that *Jane Eyre* is a defence of polygamy."

It may be amusing, and it is certainly instructive, to look back over a long list of such comments. But the liberals who detested Kipling's political views have no right to feel complacent about their moral rectitude. The record shows that all too often they substituted political for literary judgments. On the basis of hindsight we can see that Kipling's political judgments were astonishingly prophetic, and more often right than wrong. As early as World War I, one could document a case—as Katharine Fullerton Gerould did in the *Atlantic Monthly* in January, 1919—"that . . . Kipling was right about preparedness, right about the Colonies, right about Germany, right about Russia, right about the Boers, right about Kitchener, right about demagogues and 'labor,' right about the elderly politicians, right about the decent British code, right about patriotism and the human heart—right above love." Frequently the critics ignored changes in Kipling's ideas. They treated his opinions of the period following the Great War as if they had neither developed nor matured since the late 1880's; but if we know anything about Kipling, it is that he became a wiser and sadder human being as personal tragedies beat him over the head, and as the world changed. For example, Kipling believed in war as a panacea for only two or three years in the early 1890's; yet he has been repeatedly accused of glorifying war all his life as a permanent social solution. The liberals have confused the political opinions of fictional characters, or of the persona used in a given poem, as those of Kipling; and since Kipling drew realistic portraits of an astonishingly large number of different, and often unattractive, men and women, he has been blamed for holding opinions that he personally may have detested. To be sure, critics whose political convictions extend over a very wide spectrum often fail to differentiate between the art and the artist. Nevertheless, the failing in sensibility seems more gross, and more unforgivable, when it is exhibited by critics of a liberal persuasion, who stand as sentinels at the gate and who like to think of themselves as the defenders of humane and civilized values, as the champions of toleration. In Kipling's case they have failed to be true to their own standards of fair play. To understand why, we must look more closely at what Kipling, in fact, believed about imperialism.

A new basis for judging Kipling's achievement must replace the old, if only because the wreckage of empire has led, in the last two decades, to the writing, by revisionist historians, of a series of studies that document the fragility of the world Kipling knew. The imperialists of the Queen's reign, we are now told, were champions of a lost cause from the very beginning. As Horatio observed to Hamlet,

> There needs no ghost, my lord, come from the grave
> To tell us this,

and it may well be that everyone understands why the British Empire collapsed. Yet the point of George Bernard Shaw's remark—Kipling never grew up; he began by being behind the times—has been blunted by our growing awareness that in 1897, the year of the Diamond Jubilee, millions of people (not merely Kipling) believed, on the basis of incomplete information, that having the world's largest empire was "a good thing." They did not want to be told of the crushing economic costs of maintaining such an empire and of keeping their armed forces large enough, and in sufficient readiness, to repel threats to the British flag anywhere they might materialize. It was difficult to calculate those costs anyway because there were so many ways of disguising them in the budget. In the words of Max Beloff, the ambiguity of the word "commonwealth" always disguised reality: "the British were not an imperially minded people; they lacked both a theory of empire and the will to engender and implement one."

Kipling's views on imperialism must not be oversimplified for the sake of an early dismissal. More often than most of his contemporaries who enthusiastically supported empire building, Kipling had personally visited the outposts of empire. All his life he disliked evangelical cant about the morality of ruling over lesser breeds without the Law. He praised the strong men of any race, as in "The Ballad of East and West," and had little that was favorable to say about the economic royalists who were exploiting the resources of entire continents. And it was Kipling who, in "Recessional," wrote the most extraordinary single warning of the Jubilee Year:

> Far-called, our navies melt away;
>   On dune and headland sinks the fire:
> Lo, all our pomp of yesterday
>   Is one with Nineveh and Tyre!

Kipling saw clearly, long before the coming of the Great War, the dangers inherent in a blind expansionism that failed to assume the full responsibilities of the governor toward the governed. Moreover, he delivered his warning early, as a responsible citizen; he is not to be blamed today because the Great Wall fell.

Much of Kipling's political philosophy centered on two concepts, the Law and the Game. The Law of the Jungle, recorded in *The Second Jungle Book,* is a paradigm of the Greater Law. Kipling reminded his reader that he could render only a series of "specimens of the simpler rulings," and that several hundred more laws were in existence. Animals who keep together survive: "For the strength of the pack is the wolf, and the strength of the wolf is the pack." To each season of life due homage must be paid. The lords of the jungle must be respected. The home is sacred. One may kill only for food essential to survival, and never for pleasure. Each member of the pack has his rights ("pack-right," "cub-right," "lair-right," etc.), and these may not be violated. If the Law is not explicit, the word of the head wolf is Law.

The significance of the Game is more subtle. One must learn, through practice, "many times over," how to play the Game perfectly; only then will approval be granted. What, after all, does the Game amount to? It is more than the game of espionage dramatized in *Kim,* much more than an exercise of memory, or practice in the arts of make-up and disguise, or an ability to keep secrets, or a willingness to learn. The Game teaches Kim how to improve his all-too-human *judgment.* Lurgan Sahib has promised Kim that a reward will follow obedience: an improved sense of the interrelationships of human beings. The passage in which Kim learns that he can never free himself from the Wheel of Things is worth quoting because Kipling appreciated the value of mysticism and private meditation, and at one time had seriously been tempted by the Eastern way of life:

> He did not want to cry,—had never felt less like crying in his life,— but of a sudden easy, stupid tears trickled down his nose, and with an almost audible click he felt the wheels of his being lock up anew on the world without. Things that rode meaningless on the eyeball an instant before slid into proper proportion. Roads were meant to be walked upon, houses to be lived in, cattle to be driven, fields to be tilled, and men and women to be talked to. They were all real and true—solidly

planted upon the feet—perfectly comprehensible—clay of his clay, neither more nor less.

Kim thus puts away the temptation to retreat from the nettling and frustrating concerns of India, that microcosm of the greater world. Like Kipling, he goes forth to meet that world, to grapple with it; in E. M. Forster's classic phrase, *to connect*.

We need to reconsider a currently fashionable view of Kipling's philosophy. Where there is no vision, an artist, however gifted, will perish no less than a people. An attempt to discover and define Kipling's vision has concentrated, in recent years, on his concept of man's relationship to the greater powers of the universe. The argument runs like this: much of what gives offense in Kipling's art is related to the unwillingness of many readers to accept as true for themselves what Kipling, as a young man, pretended (and what he, as an older man, believed) to be the universal condition.

In *Puck of Pook's Hill* the Great Wall of England is substantially the same metaphor as the North-West Frontier of India in Kipling's earlier fiction. From the 1880's on, that metaphor was important to Kipling, whose attitude toward history began, and remained, bleak during a lifetime of ripening insights. Andrew Rutherford has put it thus: "the defence of civilisation against savagery by men whose chosen duty it is to spend themselves in such a cause" is "one of the major themes that fired his imagination." Others go further, and claim that failure, or at best a limited and temporary success, was Kipling's only theme. An enormous fraction of Kipling's creative output treats the irrationality of human existence. "Without Benefit of Clergy," a famous early story, speaks of a sick land suffering from drought: "The children of immature fathers and undeveloped mothers made no resistance. They were cowed and sat still, waiting till the sword should be sheathed in November if it were so willed." Not even ritual can save the lovers Holden and Ameera from the doom that must come. In India, death, the red audit, is everywhere; the cheapness of life is casually mentioned; it hardly seems worth mentioning at all. Long after India had ceased to interest Kipling as a locale for his stories, pain, grief at the loss of loved ones, and shock at the horrors of the Great War are reflected in his art. "Abyss" becomes an important word for him, and he never wanders far from the darkness of an unknowable, even absurdist universe. In "Mrs. Bathurst" the unconnected, terrifying flashes of an inscrutable reality in one of England's first newsreels—the word "blindishly" has resonances—are central to the meaning of that story.

However plausible this interpretation of Kipling, however elaborately worked out, there is something disquieting about it. Very few contemporaries of Kipling would have recognized its truth, and admirers of Kipling today may react strongly against the notion that his art is cheerless. The popular view of Kipling as a Stoic who affirms the possibility of "new growth" is, I believe, more solidly based. Yet the value of this new interpretation of Kipling lies in the fact that it demonstrates how a serious, and consistent, case for Kipling as a thinker can be built up, if only we pay attention to the things that he really was saying *in propria persona.*

Kipling's continuing importance to serious readers, if I may sum up at this point, lies not in his assessments of political trends or even in the authenticity (occasionally denied) of his portraits of societies operating outside England. It rests firmly on a body of work that for consistency and quality, and for its capacity to surprise with delight, is worth reconsidering.

Much more often than is generally understood, Kipling supplies the data for a reader's judgment. He does so by creating points of view behind which he can and does hide his own committed feelings. The resolutions of these tales are often startlingly and unexpectedly open-ended. More questions are raised than settled. If we believe that we know what Kipling thinks on the basis of what his characters think and do, we are not reading the stories carefully enough for their shadings, ambiguities, and reserved responses to strongly emotional situations. Kipling indeed is a relatively remote and mysterious figure behind all the fictions. W. W. Robson has even gone so far as to claim that Kipling "never wrote a line of prose or verse for the purpose of 'expressing his personality,'" that he "maintained a reticence about his private thought and feelings which modern readers may think old-fashioned, and in his personal life he clung to privacy with all the determination of Tennyson." Modern art, which values impersonality as a means of escaping from Romantic attitudinizing, may well want to take another, closer look at Kipling.

For Kipling's dedication to literature has never been in question. The body of work that he left behind maintained the highest standards of craftsmanship. Randall Jarrell, even in the process of noting that "Kipling's account is still unsettled," felt compelled to record a final personal judgment: "The stories themselves are literature. While their taste is on my tongue, I can't help feeling that virtue is its own reward, that good writing will take care of itself. . . . The man Kipling, the myth Kipling is over; but the stories themselves—Kipling—have all the time in the world. The stories—some of them—can say to us with the calm of anything that has completely realized its own nature: 'Worry about yourselves, not us. We're all right.'"

A number of writers and critics have compared Kipling with Shakespeare. There is, indeed, a *bigness* about Kipling's sense of life, a range of sympathies, an energy, an enthusiasm, and a matching creative skill, that often seem Shakespearean. The evidence, at any rate, is available for judging. It is time for responsible critics of our new decade to reexamine his artistic achievement; to do so without political bias; to recognize the importance of changes in his career and in his ideas; and to distinguish between Kipling's fictional characters and Kipling himself.

One of Kipling's greatest admirers, Mark Twain, believed that the public is the only critic whose opinion is worth anything at all. The public can be wrong, and often is, spectacularly; but *vox populi* in the case of Rudyard Kipling has been consistent to a degree, and over a sufficiently long period of time, that a serious question must be raised about the relationship between the kind of criticism Kipling has received—more precisely speaking, been subjected to—and the kind of criticism he, as a serious artist, was entitled to from the very beginning. There is an old saying that a critic is a legless man who teaches running; the formulation is a wittier way of saying that critics are failed poets. As Oliver Wendell Holmes put it, in *The Professor at the Breakfast-Table* (1859), "What a blessed thing it is that Nature, when she invented, manufactured, and patented her authors, contrived to make critics out of the chips that were left!" The implication of this argument may be no more than a creative writer's attempt to strike back at the critic, who, from a superior and well-protected position, hurls thunderbolts at things he doesn't like. Moreover, the facile distinction between a critic and a creative artist in such a formulation is untrustworthy: the luminous examples of Dryden, Coleridge, and Arnold are only the most notable of a long line of artist-critics who, coming down in our time to T. S. Eliot and E. M. Forster, destroy the stereotype that critics are men who cannot succeed in literature and art.

Nevertheless, a humanistic dilemma occurs when, for reasons arising from passionate involvement with topical issues, a majority of critics desert their long-standing obligations to the art of literature and treat a writer as primarily a propagandist for a cause. The seriousness of the problem is not directly related to whether the cause is a good one or whether it is suspect. We have seen in the quite recent history of American literature any number of writers who abused their God-given talents to manipulate fictional characters and move toward predetermined conclusions in their art: John Dos Passos, Edna St. Vincent Millay, Richard Wright, Robert Sherwood. In British literature comparable cases may be cited, writers like W. H. Auden, Evelyn Waugh, Graham Greene, and C. P. Snow, whose works are praised up or voted down according to political biases. But Kipling's case has been very special, perhaps unique, in that the animus of those who despise what they think Kipling wrote—and what, in fact, Kipling neither wrote nor intended to say—has outlasted Kipling's life by fully half a century.

All critics of the liberal persuasion (or any other, for that matter) should recognize the transitory nature of any given political or social situation; they should understand that the rights and wrongs of issues competing for newspaper-headline treatment change almost daily. It may be that "the absence of humility in critics is something wonderful." We would all be better off if we asked ourselves—as Thomas Jefferson asked himself in 1816—whether a work of literature gives us pleasure; whether it is animating, interesting, attaching; whether, indeed, it tells us more about humanity and human issues than we already know. If it makes us more intensely aware of what it is to be human, it has genuine merit. If it does not, the approbation of a critic who is politically motivated will not affect, ultimately, the verdict of a reading public. That verdict, I venture to say, is now in, so far as Rudyard Kipling is concerned. Sooner, rather than later, the Establishment critics must, and will, make their peace with him, and with his millions of readers throughout the world.

INDEX